Praise for
THE SEA HUNTERS

"Compelling. . . . A fast-paced, riveting read, great fun for salts and landlubbers alike."

—*Flint Journal* (MI)

"Cussler entertains and enlightens at the same time. . . . His infectious enthusiasm will have more than one reader wondering if there's any way he can hook up with him on his next adventure."

—*The Denver Post*

"In *The Sea Hunters,* truth appears at least as fun as, and sometimes stranger than, fiction."

—*Men's Journal*

"Readers who have enjoyed Cussler's fictional derring-do will likely enjoy these true stories, which are told with easy charm, humor, and no bombast whatever."

—*Chicago Tribune*

"Fascinating reading. . . . Cussler is a true adventurer."

—*Birmingham News* (AL)

"Cussler proves himself as gifted at nonfiction as he is at fiction."

—*The Fresno Bee* (CA)

"Cussler can keep anyone on the edge of their chair with his gripping descriptions of action."

—*United Press International*

CLIVE CUSSLER

& CRAIG DIRGO

THE SEA HUNTERS

TRUE ADVENTURES WITH FAMOUS SHIPWRECKS

POCKET BOOKS

New York   London   Toronto   Sydney

Pocket Books
A Division of Simon & Schuster, Inc.
1230 Avenue of the Americas
New York, NY 10020

This Pocket Books trade paper edition June 2011

DIRK PITT is a registered trademark of Clive Cussler.

POCKET and colophon are registered trademarks of Simon & Schuster, Inc.

For information about special discounts for bulk purchases, please contact Simon & Schuster Special Sales at 1-866-506-1949 or business@simonandschuster.com.

The Simon & Schuster Speakers Bureau can bring authors to your live event. For more information or to book an event contact the Simon & Schuster Speakers Bureau at 1-866-248-3049 or visit our website at www.simonspeakers.com.

Manufactured in the United States of America

10 9 8 7 6 5 4 3 2 1

ISBN 978-1-4516-4776-1

Acknowledgments

The authors are indebted to Joaquin Saunders, author of *The Night Before Christmas;* Ray Roberts, author of *Survivors of the* Léopoldville *Disaster;* and those men of the 66th Panther Division who survived the terrible tragedy off Cherbourg, France, on the evening of December 24, 1944, for their stories of horror and heroism. It is truly an event that should not be swept away into the mist of time.

To the men and women who have supported the National Underwater & Marine Agency from its inception. Through the tough times and the fun times, their loyalty has remained solid and enduring. This is merely a partial record of their remarkable achievements. Without their efforts, over sixty shipwrecks of historic significance might still lie on the bottoms of the seas and rivers, ignored and forgotten for all time. Some ships are gone, dredged out of existence or buried under modern construction. Some are still intact. Now that the way has been shown, we leave it to future generations to recover the knowledge and artifacts that remain of our maritime heritage.

And to my wife, Barbara, for her enduring patience,
and my children, Teri, Dirk, and Dana,
who grew up with a father who never grew up.

Contents

CONTENTS

PART 8
H.M.S. *Pathfinder, U-21,* and *U-20*

PART 9
The Troop Transport *Léopoldville*

PART 10
They Can't Be Found if You Don't Look

Introduction

It's said that Jules Verne wrote *Around the World in Eighty Days* without ever leaving Paris. He seldom stepped out of the room where he created the most imaginative novels the world has enjoyed. Most fiction authors, when I ask them what interests they have besides writing, look at me like my head is lopsided. They can't believe there are other pursuits in life beyond creating plots and characters, promoting their books, arguing with editors, or demanding better deals from their literary agents. Their lives are entwined around what comes out of their word processors.

A reporter who interviewed me several years ago wrote that I "follow the beat of a drummer playing with a marching band in a field on the other side of town." I suppose that's true. Feeding my readers adventure tales based on a devil-may-care character by the name Dirk Pitt is only one chapter of my existence. I'm addicted to the challenge of the search, whether it's for lost shipwrecks, airplanes, steam locomotives, or people. I also collect and restore classic and vintage automobiles. If it's old, I'm into it.

There is a piece of me in Dirk Pitt and a slice of him in me. We're both about six feet three. His eyes are greener than mine, and he certainly enthralls the ladies more than I ever did. We have the same taste for adventure, although his escapades are far more extreme than mine. I never raised the *Titanic,* for example. Nor have I saved the life of the President or found a great hoard of Inca gold at the end of an underground river.

I have, however, attempted some crazy things besides tramping through humid backcountry looking for old cannons or being tossed around a small boat during a Force 8 storm while searching for a sunken submarine. Like riding a bicycle over the Rocky Mountains and through the deserts to California when I turned fifty, taking the stick of a glider at fifty-five, and bungee jumping at sixty. I'm thinking of skydiving on my sixty-fifth.

How did this attempt to mirror fantasy with life begin?

Perhaps you remember me. I was the kid in your high school algebra class who stared out the window while the teacher lectured on fractions. I was lost in another time, a million miles away, manning a cannon on John Paul Jones's ship, the *Bonhomme Richard,* charging up Cemetery Ridge with Pickett's division, or reversing the tide at the Little Big Horn and saving Custer and his 7th Cavalry. When called upon to recite, I could only stare at the floor like an amnesiac and mutter an answer so utterly out of context that the teacher thought I had wandered into her class by mistake.

I was lucky growing up when and where I did. Within four blocks of my family's middle-class, 1940s home in Southern California, there were five neighborhood boys my own age who had imaginations as varied as mine. Together, we built tree houses and clubhouses, dug caves, constructed a ship out of scrap wood in a vacant lot, constructed miniature streets and buildings out of mud and wooden molds, and devised ghostly scenes in my father's garage on Halloween. The Little Rascals had nothing on us. Only when five o'clock rolled around did we dash home to turn on the radio and listen to the adventures of Jack Armstrong, the

All-American Boy, picturing ourselves slogging through the Congo jungles at his side.

Sea stories had a particular allure to my wandering mind. I was always immersed in books describing ship-to-ship battles, which included the ironclads of the Civil War, the fights of famous American frigates against the British in the War of 1812, and the Napoleonic sea wars of Nelson, especially the fictional accounts of Horatio Hornblower by C. S. Forester.

Since I'm a Cancer, I've always had an affinity for water. The first time I looked upon the Pacific Ocean I was six years old. I ran directly into the surf, only to be promptly deposited back on the beach by a breaker. Undaunted, I ran back in over my head. Not a bright move because I had no idea that you were supposed to know how to swim. I recall opening my eyes and marveling at the blurred world beneath the surface. I even saw a small fish before it dawned on me that I couldn't breathe. My father, since it was the only decent thing to do, frantically groped around in the depths until he found me and pulled me back into the atmosphere. My mother, fearing a repeat of my underwater ballet, quickly signed me up at the nearest public pool for swimming lessons.

Because I was an only child, I made up games to play. One was with poker chips stacked in the shape of warships. Some hulls had a row of single chips, others two and three rows. The size of the cannon was dictated by the strength of rubber bands. Naturally, the rubber slings of my fleet always blew the chips of the enemy fleet all over the linoleum floor of my mother's kitchen and dining areas. The same basic concept was used in the bathtub, where I floated ships folded from newspaper and then dive-bombed them with marbles until they either soggily disintegrated or sank under the weight of the shooters and aggies that failed to penetrate their thin decks.

I did all the crazy things kids did in the leisurely days before television, like riding my bicycle down a hill and off a small cliff into the tree branches below, jumping off the roof of a house under construction into a sandpile, or building a makeshift raft and sailing down a rushing stream during a rainstorm. There must be guardian angels somewhere up there who watch over crazy, daredevil boys. Amazingly, I never broke a bone until I passed the age of fifty. Since then, I've suffered one fractured ankle while jogging; two cracked vertebrae, when thrown out of a jeep careering over a beach while I held a metal detector, looking for a buried shipwreck; and six cracked ribs, two of them surfing and one on a mountain bike. The others came from stupid accidents.

One thing I learned early is that adventure can come cheap. In college, a close friend, Felix Dupuy, and I loaded up his 1939 Ford convertible and set out one summer on a drive around the country. In three months we covered over thirteen thousand miles and thirty-six states. We slept in bandstands in Vermont, railroad boxcars in Texas, and in the bushes beside the nation's Capitol in Washington, D.C. The entire trip cost me only $350. We returned home just in time to enlist in the Air Force after the outbreak of the "police action" in Korea, more out of boredom with school than any great patriotic fervor.

I have never forgotten Felix, Jack Hawkins, and me, sitting in the recruiting office looking at each other and repeating over and over, "I'll go if you go," or "If you join, I'll join." I can't recall who raised his hand first and took the oath to defend the country from foreign invaders, but I have never forgiven him.

Despite my applying for aerial photography or the intelligence department, some sneaky sergeant in the Training Command found out I was a California hot-rodder and sent me to aircraft engine school. After my graduation, the Air Force demanded I be attached to Hickam Field, Hawaii, to work on mammoth twenty-eight-cylinder radial engines mounted on C-97 Boeing Stratocruisers. These were large propeller-driven aircraft the Air Force used as transports to fly critical personnel and supplies to Korea before airlifting the wounded back to hospitals in the States.

During the three years I was stationed on Oahu, my buddies Dave Anderson and Al Giordano, a gritty and witty Italian who was the model for Al Giordino in my books, and I explored the inner jungles of the island, searching for lost aircraft, ancient Hawaiian burial caves, and missing people. I recall finding none.

We also became early diving fanatics. This was in late 1951 and there was little in the way of underwater equipment. We made our own camera cases, spearguns, and floats. My first mask was a weird affair made in France that covered the entire face, with two snorkels that contained Ping-Pong balls to halt incoming water. As I recall, it was made of gum rubber. The early commercially produced dive fins fit your feet like bedroom slippers with flaps.

We hit the water every chance we had, exploring the bays and coves around Oahu. I also took my gear and dove around Midway and Wake islands during refueling stops on flights to Tokyo. Those were the days when you seldom ran across another diver.

Wanting to go deeper, my buddies and I ordered what we were told was the first tank and regulator to be shipped to Honolulu. After picking it up in a crate from the sporting-goods store, we rushed back to an aircraft maintenance hangar, where we pumped two hundred pounds of stale air from a compressor into the tank. Then we took turns diving off a reef in twenty feet of water. Those were the days before scuba certification by qualified instructors, and it was a wonder we didn't suffer any number of diving maladies. Air embolisms and decompression times were vague terms and were not considered by most sport divers in 1951.

Upon returning to civilian life, I tried college again, but found that nothing had changed. The same musty classroom smell still nauseated me and, besides that, I had no thought of what I wanted to be when I grew up. Drawn back to the smell of oil and gasoline, my old school chum, Dick Klein, and I bought a gas station just off the San Bernardino Freeway six miles outside Los Angeles, and we operated it for almost four years.

On weekends, Dick and I used to travel around the deserts of Southern California in an old 1948 Mercury convertible that we stripped before installing oversized truck tires on the wheels. A shame. In pristine condition today that car would be worth the price of a new one. We searched for lost gold mines, lost ghost towns, and any sign of an artifact that looked as if it had been forgotten by old prospectors or the early Spanish explorers. Success usually eluded us, but we did have a great time shooting antique rifles at rocks in the distance.

I finally became a certified diver after quitting a high-falutin advertising job in Hollywood to work as a clerk with a small chain of dive shops in Orange County. There was a method to my madness, however, as I had decided to write sea stories, and what better place to launch my career as a writer than from behind the counter of a dive shop? Don Spencer, Ron Merker, and Omar Wood, legendary divers and owners of the Aquatic Center dive stores, wondered which part of the moon I'd dropped from when I applied for a job that paid $400 a month after making $2,000 a month as creative director for a national advertising agency. But shrewd and canny guys that they were—Spencer has since passed on—they put aside their doubts and hired me. They became good friends and I've always owed them all a great debt of gratitude. I fondly recall when Merker certified me with a Los Angeles County card. He wasn't awfully impressed with my diving abilities even after I reminded him that the Red Baron, Manfred Von Richthofen, who shot down eighty Allied planes in World War I, had nearly flunked out of flight school.

With great trepidation, he sent me to Catalina as divemaster on a chartered boat with twenty other divers. Staring up at the kelp from the seafloor as it spirals toward the surface is a sight you'll always remember. I know I'll never forget how the sport divers attacked the food spread on the deck like a school of malnourished barracuda.

Using my devious talents for promotion, I pulled off all types of crazy stunts to increase business, endeavors that doubled sales inside six months. Besides standing a bikini-clad mannequin out on the curb in front of the store, painting an aircraft belly tank fluorescent orange and installing it on the roof after filling it with more bikini-clad mannequins, I began phrasing strange witticisms on a theater marquee in the parking lot. One traffic stopper, as I remember, read, KEEP AMERICA GREEN, BAN LOBSTERS FROM THE HIGHWAYS. I always felt smug about the fact that we far outsold Mel Fisher's dive shop in Manhattan Beach. Of course, Fisher got the last laugh after he found the treasure-laden Spanish galleon *Atocha.*

I also became a legend of sorts when I took over the recorded dive report that divers phoned for water conditions before heading into the deep. Instead of the old austere "This is the Aquatic Center dive report," in a droning voice that murmured, "The surf is three to four feet, the water temperature is seventy-six degrees, and the visibility is ten feet," I came on and said, "Hi, ho, divers, this is your daredevil darling of the dismal depths, Horace P. Quagmire, once again with the latest report on diving conditions." I even threw in recipes for abalone. And, not one to let an opportunity pass, I ended the report by mentioning several items of merchandise that happened to be on sale. Don't ask me why, but they loved it. California divers still ask me to autograph their books with Horace P. Quagmire.

When business slowed in midafternoon, I sat at a card table in the back of the store and wrote a book called *The Mediterranean Caper* on a portable typewriter. After making up my mind that I had at last found my niche in life, and signing with New York literary agent Peter Lampack, I sadly left the Aquatic Center dive shops to pursue my new career as a writer. Spencer, Merker, Wood, and I shook hands all around, and they were kind enough to present me with an orange-dial Doxa dive watch that I've treasured for over twenty years. I wrote all three of them in as characters in *Raise the* Titanic*!,* which became a best-seller and a terrible movie.

Suddenly, and quite unexpectedly, with the success of *Raise the* Titanic*!,* I now had the time and funds to search for lost shipwrecks.

In December of 1977, I read in one of the books written by Peter Throckmorton, dean of American marine archaeology, that a gentleman in England, Sidney Wignall, was following up leads to John Paul Jones's famous Revolutionary

War ship, the *Bonhomme Richard,* which sank after an epic battle off Flamborough Head in the North Sea. Having studied the famous fight where the underdog shouted, "I have not yet begun to fight," when his ship was shot to shreds, I bit the hook when I learned that Wignall was casting about for money to launch a search.

My British publishers tracked down Wignall, and I called him. A peppery Welshman, he assumed that I was some kind of deranged con man when out of the blue I offered to fund an expedition to locate the *Richard.* Reasonably satisfied that I didn't wear a Napoleon hat and a straitjacket, we arranged for a meeting to discuss the basics for organizing a search expedition, not the least of which was the budget. In this case a cool $60,000.

The final cost was $80,000.

Sidney had discovered a Spanish Armada galleon and searched for Sir Francis Drake's lead coffin off Portobelo in Panama. He was a top-notch historian, but organizational know-how was an enigma to him. I should have been a bit more cautious of striking off into the unknown, but with shipwreck fever mounting to a heated pitch, I plunged in up to my ears. I now know where the term "babe in the woods" comes from.

The expedition later veered two degrees beyond a fiasco. Tons of unnecessary equipment, including a decompression chamber, were loaded aboard an old World War II British minesweeper used for geological survey by an outfit I suspected of operating as the Shagnasty Barn Door and Oil Company. The Flying Dutchman sailed in a better ship than this one. Its geriatric diesel engine broke down with agonizing regularity three times a day. The ship's crew would have made a saloon full of heavy-metal bikers hold their noses and run for the exits. These guys thought *bath* was a city in England. There was one crewman who for some inexplicable reason has never left my mind. His name was Gonzo. I recall the name because it was tattooed on his forehead. The boat was called the *Keltic Lord.* Being a dumb American, I always thought Keltic was spelled with a C.

Everyone assembled in Bridlington, England, a blue-collar Las Vegas, during August of 1978. Several divers from the University of Wales showed up to participate. My son-in-law and daughter, Bob and Teri Toft, had arrived early to work with Sidney Wignall assembling the gear and gluing together an old boat that was to be used to ferry the search team and supplies between the *Keltic Lord* and shore.

The devil-may-care Gary Kozak showed up to operate the side scan sonar, an electronic instrument that records acoustic imagery of the sea bottom. The image the sonar signal reflects looks much like a photograph that has been copied three or four times.

Marty Klein, the little giant and CEO of Klein Associates, Inc., the builder of the sonar unit, also came along on the hunt for the *Bonhomme Richard*. On thinking back, I realize the sonar was the only unit, man-made or otherwise, that performed flawlessly. I was also introduced to Colonel Walter Schob, who had come off the *Mary Rose* project and volunteered to dive when and if we found the remains of John Paul Jones's ship. If nothing else came out of my amateurish inauguration at mounting a shipwreck expedition, Gary, Marty, and Walt became my good pals and have remained so for nearly two decades.

My wife, Barbara; younger daughter, Dana; and son, Dirk, also joined the expedition. I found it comforting to have friendly shoulders to cry on as the project began to unravel. We all stayed at a hotel on the beach, called the Excelsior, which I was told was a Latin form of "high excellence." An interesting place. I doubt if it's been remodeled since the Romans left for home. My wife's perfume turned up missing, as did Teri's camera. Noticing that the bedding was unusually rumpled one evening, I asked the chambermaid if she had changed the sheets that day.

She looked at me queerly and asked, "Did you want your sheets changed?"

Ah, yes, innocents abroad. But we evened the score down in the dining room. At most English seaside hotels, you are given a particular table to eat your meals. Even single people chat across the room while sitting alone at their respective tables.

I was usually the first one up in the mornings and read the paper over breakfast. When Gary and Marty walked into the room, I'd invite them to sit with me. Then Dana and Dirk would go over and sit with Teri and Bob. This threw the dining-room staff into a frenzy.

"Sorry, but you are not supposed to seat other guests at your table," the maître d' admonished me, face red with stress. "Each guest is assigned their own table."

"Is it a privilege or a penalty?" I asked innocently.

The humor escaped him. "These people cannot sit with you. They must dine at their required table."

I looked at Marty and Gary, who held their silverware in a death grip. "I believe these gentlemen are happy right where they are and would like a menu."

"This is not the way we manage things here," the maître d' hissed in total exasperation.

"Then it's either my way, or I'll complain to the health commission about the sea gull droppings on the balcony outside my room."

It was a small battle, but I was happy to win it.

Dinner involved creative ways to eat boiled potatoes with catchup and Worcestershire sauce. Once I asked the hotel bartender for a martini straight up. I got exactly that, Martini-brand vermouth straight up. Teri was about eighteen at the time. Bless her heart. She took it upon herself to set the bartender straight and instruct him on how to make bloody Marys and screwdrivers.

The opening day of the search didn't get under way until almost eleven o'clock in the morning. The sea was fairly rough and the boat ride from the dock to the *Keltic Lord* was an adventure in itself. When we came alongside, Gonzo and another crew member helped everyone climb aboard the ship but me. I was left ignored and forgotten on the leaky ferryboat in a rainstorm, knocked up and down against the hull by aggressive wave action, while clutching a briefcase containing my research material, charts of the search area, and a sack of cookies pressed on me by my wife.

My faithful ship's crew, my loyal team of technicians, had all rushed into the galley for a cup of coffee.

Struggling over the railing with my load, I reached the galley soaked through to my undershorts. No one gave me so much as a glance. Sid Wignall acted as though I didn't exist. It was then I introduced my *hand routine,* which became beneficial over the years in dealing with mutinous boat crews and dive teams.

I raised my right hand into the air and inquired in a loud voice, "Does everyone see this hand?"

They all stared indifferently and nodded silently.

"Whatever happens," I continued, "a fire aboard ship, we strike an iceberg, or we're torpedoed by the crew of a U-boat who forgot to surrender, you save this hand."

Good old Gonzo sailed into the net. "Why should we bust our arse to save that hand, mate?"

I had the power, the Force was mine. I looked him square in the eye and said, "Because *this* is the hand that writes the checks."

It was amazing how I went from Rodney Dangerfield to Arnold Schwarzenegger in the space of thirty seconds. Now *I* was the first one helped on board the ship. Gonzo became my pal and always kept my coffee cup full. Even the captain began calling me "sir." I knew then that searching for shipwrecks was in my blood.

Because of the late start during the first days into the search, by the time we began running our lanes in the search grid, which meant towing the side scan sensor back and forth as though we were mowing a lawn, half the day was gone and we had to return to Bridlington before dark. When I discussed this problem with Sidney, he came up with a brilliant solution: "Tomorrow we'll pull up the anchor and head to the search area promptly at six o'clock in the morning." There was groaning in the ranks, but they all agreed that if we were to accomplish anything we had to get off the mark early.

The shore team showed up at the dock promptly at 5:30. Solid Walt Schob was already there with the boat, standing by to ferry us to the *Keltic Lord.* Poor Marty Klein looked as miserable as a lobster in the desert. Gary Kozak had one of the worst hangovers I'd ever seen. It was not a pretty sight.

When we reached the boat, after groping our way through a thick fog, we boarded and found the decks devoid of life. The crew, the British dive team, and Sidney Wignall were all sound asleep, no doubt with visions of Yorkshire pudding dancing in their heads.

Eyes brimming with malice and undisguised contempt for those who hadn't suffered as we had, I stormed into the crew's quarters, kicked Wignall's door off its hinges, and yelled, "If this boat isn't under way in ten minutes, I'm tying you to the propeller!"

I'll give Sidney credit. He showed great depth of understanding. The anchor clanked up, the ancient engine coughed up a cloud of black smoke through its stack, and the bow cut the water in eight minutes flat.

The wreck that Sidney thought might be the *Bonhomme Richard* turned out to be a cargo ship sunk by a German U-boat during World War I. And so the curtain came down on my introduction to the intrigue and adventure of hunting for shipwrecks.

Six months later, I was saddened to learn that the *Keltic Lord,* along with its entire crew, vanished without a trace in the North Sea during a winter storm. I'll bet the pubs in the seaport city of Hull haven't been the same since Gonzo's been gone.

Much to everyone's surprise, I got up off the mat and came out for the second round. I organized another expedition for the following year. Wayne Gronquist, Austin, Texas, attorney and eventual president of NUMA, suggested that for tax purposes we should incorporate as a nonprofit foundation. Wayne filed the papers in Austin, and we became a Texas not-for-profit corporation. Early on, the trustees wanted to call it the Clive Cussler Foundation. Humble Herbert I ain't. But my ego isn't quite that monstrous. I nixed the idea. So they decided it would be humorous to name it after the government agency that employs the hero in my books, Dirk Pitt. I was outvoted and the National Underwater & Marine Agency was born. Now I could say, "Yes,

Virginia, there really is a NUMA, a NUMA dedicated to preserving American marine heritage by locating and identifying lost ships of historic significance before they are gone forever."

This second attempt to locate the *Richard* was headed by former Navy Commander Eric Berryman. We covered ten times as much territory with a cost factor less than half the first effort. This trip I had the good fortune to meet and work with Peter Throckmorton and Bill Shea of Brandeis University, both of whom became trustees of NUMA. I also found a solid and comfortable boat called the *Arvor III*, a yacht that was strangely built to the specifications of a Scottish fishing trawler. An indomitable Scot by the name of Jimmy Flett was the *Arvor*'s skipper, and a finer man I've never met. Even with a top-rated team, we still failed to find the elusive *Bonhomme Richard*. We did, however, run onto and identify a Russian spy trawler that had mysteriously sunk a short time prior to our discovery. The Royal Navy was immediately notified, and they initiated a classified underwater investigation. I never did learn what secrets they found.

Someday, I'll give it another try. Gary Kozak once said, "Shipwrecks are never found until they want to be found." Hopefully, next time the *Richard* will be ready to show a beckoning finger.

NUMA was now a reality, and with very canny and respected people on board as trustees and advisors, including Commander Don Walsh, who made the ocean's deepest dive aboard the *Trieste;* Doc Harold Edgerton, the energetic and prodigious inventor of the side scan sonar and the strobe light; and Admiral Bill Thompson, who almost single-handedly directed the funding and construction of the Navy Memorial in Washington, D.C., we began an earnest program of shipwreck search projects.

After the unsuccessful '78 and '79 expeditions, we turned our ventures to home shores and made our initial try for the Confederate submarine *Hunley* in the summer of 1980. This preliminary search took in a small grid extending one-half mile from the inlet the *Hunley* sailed through outside

Charleston, South Carolina, before she torpedoed the Union sloop-of-war *Housatonic*. After the attack, she and her nine-man crew vanished, never realizing they had gone down in history books as the first submarine to sink a warship.

It soon became apparent, after research and initial probing into the seafloor outside of Charleston, that the *Hunley* had slowly become buried in the soft silt that covers the seabed off the coast. We found that the remains of *Housatonic* had also worked their way under the seafloor.

The only instrument generally used to locate a hidden object entombed under salt water and sediment is a magnetometer. If the side scan sonar is the right arm of any shipwreck search, the magnetometer is the left. The two metal detectors used most frequently for finding and measuring the magnetic intensity of a buried iron object are the proton mag and a gradiometer. Both basically do the same thing, but use different systems of measurement.

After finding no trace of the *Hunley* near shore, we realized the search grid had to be greatly expanded.

In 1981, we returned with an efficiently organized expedition. Alan Albright, chief marine archaeologist with the University of South Carolina, was most cooperative, loaning us a boat and a team of divers. Bill Shea operated his home-built proton magnetometer along with Walt Schob, who steered the search boat back and forth along the grid lines. A second vessel, a dive boat, followed behind to check out any interesting anomalies found by Bill's mag. The diving operation was headed by Ralph Wilbanks, the state archaeologist who represented the university.

To keep the mag survey boat in precise position at all times, the Motorola Mini Ranger Navigation Unit was used, with my son, Dirk, sitting in an oven-hot rental van on shore, staring at a graph and giving directions that kept Schob on a straight course while running narrow lanes of thirty meters.

Although we ran over five hundred miles of search lanes, we failed to pass over the grave of the *Hunley*. Our dive boat, however, discovered the remains of four Confederate blockade runners, the Union ironclad monitors *Weehawken* and *Patapsco,* and the dual-citadel ironclad, *Keokuk.* We were finally getting our act together.

After every expedition, we always take what we call a graduation picture of everyone involved with the project. As I studied the seventeen volunteers who worked so hard to find the *Hunley* and accomplished so much in the discovery of other Civil War shipwrecks, I wondered what a leaner and meaner crew could do.

In the spring of 1982, armed with the faithful Schonstedt gradiometer, always loaned to us by a wonderful and kindly man, Eric Schonstedt, who supported NUMA every inch of the way, Walt Schob and I set out for a wreck survey on the lower Mississippi River. Renting a station wagon, when they still built them, at the airport, we drove through New Orleans and down into the river delta until we reached the end of the highway at a town called Venice, the jumping-off point for supplies and crews heading for offshore oil-drilling rigs.

Here we charted a small sixteen-foot aluminum skiff that was owned by a taciturn Cajun fisherman. The first morning, he took my money and never spoke a word to us. By the third day he realized we were nice guys and began telling Cajun jokes. Because I had broken my right ankle two days before, and had a cast halfway to my knee, he kindly loaned me a lawn chair so I could sit comfortably in the bow, my plaster cast propped on the boat's gunnel, hanging out over the muddy water of the river like a battering ram.

During three days of magging, we found the Confederate ironclads *Manassas,* next to a load of iron pipe, and *Louisiana,* both later identified in an on-site study by a scientific team from Texas A & M. We also discovered the remains of the gunboats *Governor Moore* and *Varuna,* sunk during the battle of the forts when Admiral David Farragut's fleet of Union warships captured the city of New Orleans.

Walt and I then bade fond farewell to the fisherman and drove to Baton Rouge to search for the famous Confederate ironclad *Arkansas,* which is covered in more detail in a later chapter of the book.

This was truly a sublime shoestring operation. If nothing

else it proved that you can accomplish a lot if the commitment is there. The biggest expense of the entire project was the airfare. One thought to remember, if something is still missing after the passage of time ninety percent of the time it is because nobody has looked for it.

Also, unavoidably, time buries all memory of the location.

To embark on a search for a lost shipwreck, an Indian mound, gold bars, silver coins, or porcelain chamberpots, you don't need the backing of the government or a university. You don't need a truckload of expensive equipment. You don't need a million-dollar inheritance. All it really takes is dedication, perseverance, and a grip on your imagination, so you don't get carried away on a wild-goose chase. Some artifacts can never be found. Some were never lost to begin with, some were figments of somebody's imagination, and all too many are not anywhere near where they are supposed to be.

The Mississippi side-paddle riverboat *Sultana* is a prime example. She was a luxurious boat that carried passengers from New Orleans to St. Louis. Shortly after the Civil War, a greedy Union officer, receiving $22 a head from the shipping company for every military passenger, crammed 2,400 troops aboard. Many of them were badly treated prisoners recently released from the infamous Confederate prison camp Andersonville and heading home to their families. The *Sultana* also carried eighty paying passengers and forty mules. A photograph taken of her when fully loaded has an eerie look about it. All the shadowy figures clustered on the roof and crowding the decks, including the mules, look like phantom wraiths.

About fifteen miles above Memphis, Tennessee, at 2 A.M. on April 27, 1865, a boiler on *Sultana* exploded and turned her into a holocaust before she sank in a cloud of steam and smoke. At least 1,800 died, and perhaps as many as 2,100. The disaster still ranks as the worst marine tragedy in American history.

In the summer of 1982, Walt Schob and I worked with Memphis attorney Jerry Potter, the leading expert on the disaster and author of the book *The Sultana Tragedy.* Using the gradiometer, we ran search lines over several sites north of the city on dry land because the Mississippi River has considerably altered its course since 1865. Potter recalled that Mark Twain once wrote "that someday a farmer would turn up a piece of the old *Sultana* with his plow and be much surprised." Twain was very prophetic. The burned-out hulk of *Sultana* was eventually discovered within fifty yards of the position I had reckoned, two miles from the present banks of the Mississippi, twenty-one feet deep under a farmer's soybean field in Arkansas.

Research is the key. You can never do enough research. This is so vital I'll repeat it. *You can never do enough research.* Without a ballpark to provide reasonable boundaries to look, you'll be wasting time and money on an effort with the same probability of success as finding the Pied Piper of Hamelin and the town's kids on Mars. Sure you can get lucky, but don't bet your bank account on it. The odds can be a hundred to one, and yet there is still that slim possibility of victory. A thousand to one? Not worth the effort.

Research can either lower the odds or tell you it's hopeless. Many's the wreck project I filed away without making the slightest attempt to explore because the data showed that it was a lost cause. A ship that disappeared in the Gulf of Mexico, a ship that vanished on a voyage from Bermuda to Norfolk, a ship that sailed unobserved into oblivion somewhere between San Francisco and Los Angeles, forget them. Without a clue, you're looking at a search grid that could extend over a thousand square miles.

If and when they decide to be found, it will be purely by accident.

Threading the needle through investigation and study is my true love. I've often said that if my wife threw me out of the house, I'd take a cot and sleeping bag and move into the basement of a library. Nothing can match the intrigue and rapture of knowing you have pinpointed the location of a lost artifact and thus found the answer to a mystery thought unsolvable through the dust of centuries.

Many people think looking for a lost ship is exciting and adventurous. I can't speak for the big boys, the old pros like Bob Ballard and his Wood's Hole Institute team, but for the little guy it's no bed of orchids. The truth is, the actual search is the living embodiment of tedium. You're thrown hither and yon in a small boat by waves from dawn to dusk, sweating your pores out in a humid climate while fighting to keep from becoming seasick as you stare at little lines squiggling across graph paper. Still, when an image appears on the sonar recording or the marker sweeps across the aluminized paper of the magnetometer and you know you've got an anomaly or a target that matches the signature you're after, the anticipation becomes overwhelming. Then, when the divers surface and report that they've identified the object of your search, the blood, sweat, tears, and expense are forgotten. You're swept by a wave of triumph that beats sex any day of the month. Well, almost.

I receive ten to twenty letters a week from people volunteering their time and energies to NUMA. I deeply regret turning away their kind offers. Many think we're a big conglomeration with a ten-story building perched on pilings over the ocean. The truth is, we have no office, no employees, not even our own boat. We tried operating NUMA out of an office for a couple of years under the able management of Craig Dirgo, but there was little or no business to conduct and we closed it down. Expeditions only occur when I'm in the mood, which is seldom more than once a year.

Our crew of volunteers is small. Few are divers. Most are marine-history buffs and electronic technicians. When we go to a particular area to search for a lost ship, we charter a boat and invite local divers familiar with the waters we'll be working. Quite often we are joined by members of a state archaeology team.

Because most of our expeditions are funded by my book royalties without any type of donations or grants, my wife and accountant, and yes, the IRS, all think I require a frontal lobotomy because I indulge in all this madness for no profit or gain. This is actually the first time in nearly twenty years I've put my experiences down on paper. I'm new at writing in the first person, but it does provide an opportunity to mention and thank all the wonderful people who have supported NUMA.

If there were more peculiar persons like me out there willing to spend money without the slightest hope of a return, we could take on more projects. A few people have talked big about wanting to become involved with NUMA's search for legendary shipwrecks but never put their checkbooks where their mouths are. I wish I had a bottle of beer for every time someone offered to contribute to a shipwreck search only to back out at the last minute. I could open my own saloon on promises alone. Many have promised much, but with no pot at the end of the rainbow; not one ever came across with a dime. Too bad they'll never experience the excitement of the chase or the satisfaction of a successful discovery.

The only man I know who shares my love of the search and is willing to lay a buck on the line is Douglas Wheeler, an executive from Chicago. He generously comes through whenever NUMA launches a search for the unknown.

Eccentric that I am, I've never searched for treasure or taken artifacts NUMA has raised from a wreck site. All recovered objects are used strictly for identification purposes before being preserved and donated to museums. Nothing is kept. Visitors and guests are stunned to find no maritime artifacts in my home. My only mementos are thirteen models I've had built of the shipwrecks NUMA has discovered, the buoy tied to the *Hunley* when my team first dove on it, and a life ring from *Arvor III*.

Why do I do what I do for no financial gain and despite frequent failure? I can't really say. Curiosity maybe? A fanatical desire to achieve what is all too often the impossible? To find something no one else has found? There aren't many of us out there who are driven by the same madness.

Alan Pegler is one who dared to follow that faraway drummer. Mr. Pegler, a jolly man with thick burnsides whiskers, was the owner of a thriving plastics manufacturing company. One morning over breakfast, he read in the *London Times* that the *Flying Scot,* the famous crack express train that ran between Edinburgh and London during the late twenties and early thirties, was going to be sold for scrap. He contacted the chief director of the railroad and purchased the majestic old locomotive and its cars before they were destroyed. He then had the entire train immaculately restored to its former glory. Not content to let the train merely sit in a museum, Pegler took the *Flying Scot* on whistle-stop tours throughout England and the United States.

Unfortunately, the operation proved exorbitantly costly and drove Pegler into bankruptcy. He was, however, able to donate the *Flying Scot* to a nonprofit foundation, which currently maintains and operates it for the public. People, young and old, can still thrill to the sounds of a steam locomotive as they are carried through the countryside under a column of black smoke and white steam.

At the bankruptcy hearing, the rather stern judge admonished Pegler: "Your downfall arose from your unbounded enthusiasm for railways. The *Flying Scot* has been your folly."

Pegler, incredibly cheerful under the circumstances, answered, "Of course, I cannot say that I do not regret losing all my money, my house, my country manor, my villa in Italy, my Bentley and my Volvo, and being left with only what I stand up in. But I do not regret one moment buying the *Flying Scot.* It was saved and that is worth it all."

Obviously Alan Pegler is my kind of guy.

What follow are the chronicles of lost shipwrecks and the remarkable efforts by a group of dedicated NUMA volunteers, who worked long and hard to find them. The people who are portrayed, past and present, were and are real. The historical events, however, although factual, were slightly dramatized to give the reader a more focused insight into the action.

Part 1

The Steamboat *Lexington*

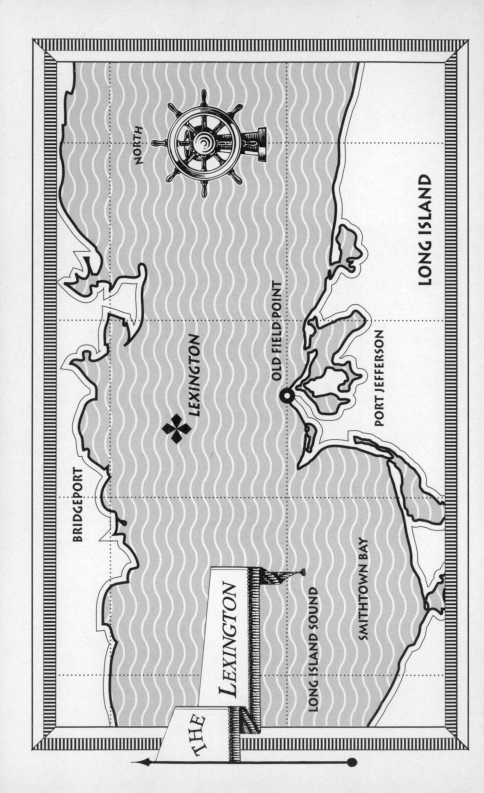

I

Through by Daylight

Monday, January 13, 1840

STEPPING FROM THE TWO-WHEELED HANSOM CAB, A TALL bearded man shivered from the bitter cold and buried his chin beneath the collar of his coat. He set his carpetbag on the icy sidewalk, reached up, and handed the fare to the cabbie, who sat elevated behind the carriage. The man paused to glance at his pocket watch. The Roman numerals on the gold timepiece told him it was two minutes past three P.M. Reassuring himself that his ticket was firmly in the breast pocket of his coat, he hurried through the terminal to the pier on the other side.

The bearded man had booked passage on the steamboat *Lexington,* bound from New York for Stonington, Connecticut, the terminus where passengers transferred onto the railroad to continue their journey to Boston. He was returning home there, where he was Smith Professor of Modern Languages at Harvard, after giving three lectures and selling his latest poem. He never considered remaining in the confines of a New York hotel longer than necessary. He rarely felt comfortable in the city and was anxious to reunite with his wife and children without delay.

Seeing black smoke surge through the steamboat's tall forward stack, and hearing the shrill sound of its steam whistle, he began running madly across the wooden planks of the pier, forcing his way through a wave of passengers who had disembarked from the steamboat *Richmond.* Apprehension mounted and quickly turned to frustration.

Too late. He had missed his boat.

The boarding ramp had been laid on the pier by dockworkers, and the ropes that had moored the boat to the pier were being pulled aboard by her crew. Only a few feet separated the hull from the dock. The man was tempted to jump the gap. But one glance at the ominous, frigid water and he quickly changed his mind.

The captain was standing in the open door of the wheelhouse, staring at the late arrival. He smiled and shrugged. Once a boat cast off and left the dock, no captain ever turned back for tardy passengers. He threw the disappointed ticket holder a brief wave, stepped into the wheelhouse, and closed the door, happy to return to the warmth of the potbellied stove beside the big steering helm.

The man on the pier stood there panting, his normally white face turned crimson. He stomped on the planking of the pier to shake the crust of ice from his feet as he watched Long Island Sound's fastest steamer slip into the East River, her side-paddle wheels churning the gray-green water. He failed to notice a dockworker, who moved beside him, puffing on a pipe.

The stranger nodded at the departing boat. "She leave without you?" he asked.

"If I had arrived ten seconds earlier, I could have jumped aboard," the stranded passenger answered slowly.

"There's ice forming on the Sound," said the dockworker. "A miserable night to be makin' a passage."

"The *Lexington* is sturdy and fast. I've booked passage on her a dozen times. I'll wager she'll dock in Stonington by midnight."

"Maybe so, maybe not. If I was you, I'd be thankful to stay warm on land till the next boat leaves in the mornin'."

The man gripped the carpetbag under one arm and shoved

his gloved hands deep in the pockets of his long coat. "Curse the luck," he said gruffly. "Another night in the city is the last thing I wanted."

He took one last look at the steamer making its way upriver through the cold, forbidding water, then turned and walked back to the terminal, unaware that those few feet between the dock and the hull of the departing boat had spared him an ugly and violent death.

"I'd have sworn that crazy fool was going to jump for it," said Captain George Child.

The pilot of the *Lexington,* Captain Stephen Manchester, turned without taking his hands from the helm. "A mystery to me why passengers wait until the last minute to board."

Child stepped to the front of the wheelhouse and peered at a thermometer that was mounted on the exterior window frame. "Barely four degrees above zero. She'll hit a good five degrees below before this night is over."

"We'll see ice before we dock in Stonington," said Manchester.

"The old *Lex* is the strongest boat on the Sound." Child pulled a cigar from his coat pocket and lit it. "She'll see us through."

A veteran ship's officer with four years' experience in steamboats traveling the Sound, Child routinely served as master of *Mohegan,* another of the passenger line's steamers. But this night he was substituting for the boat's regular master, Captain Jacob Vanderbilt. The brother of Commodore Cornelius Vanderbilt, who was in the early stages of amassing a fortune in ship and rail transportation, "Intrepid Jake," as he was called, had a reputation that bordered on the foolhardy. He often drove the *Lexington* on her runs across Long Island Sound at a furious rate. Fortunately for Jake, as it turned out, he was home with a nasty head cold and had no choice but to turn over his command to Captain Child.

Unlike Jake Vanderbilt, George Child was a cautious skipper who rarely took chances. He stood by Manchester as the pilot concentrated on navigating the *Lexington* through the dangerous tides of Hell Gate. From there, the tortuous narrows of the East River widened slightly until the boat passed Throgs Neck and steamed into the often treacherous waters of the Sound.

He left the comfortable heat of the wheelhouse and made a brief inspection of the cargo. The space beneath the promenade deck was packed with nearly 150 bales of cotton, some piled within a foot of the smokestack casing. For some strange reason Child failed to be concerned about the heavy concentration of inflammable cotton stacked so close to the casing that had caught fire only a few days before. So long as the necessary repairs had been made, he chose to ignore the potential hazard.

The rest of the cargo, in wooden crates, was stowed around the shields surrounding the engine. Satisfied the cargo was tied down properly and would not shift under the onslaught of heavy waves, he dropped by the cabin occupied by Jesse Comstock. The boat's clerk was busily counting the money taken in from the passengers, who paid for their meals in advance. Child did not interrupt Comstock's concentration, but stepped to a hatch and dropped down a ladder into the center section of the boat, where the engine and boilers were mounted.

The *Lexington* was powered by one of the most efficient steam engines of her day, built by the West Point Foundry. This was a vertical-beam engine, commonly called a walking beam, activated by a forty-eight-inch-diameter steam cylinder with an eleven-foot stroke. The engine's piston rod was connected to a long shaft that drove the forward pivot on the walking beam, converting the up-and-down thrust to the aft shaft that powered the crank that turned the *Lexington*'s big twenty-three-foot-diameter paddle wheels with their nine-foot sweeps. Her boiler furnaces were originally designed to burn wood but had now been modified to take coal. When a full head of steam approached the red line on her pressure gauges, she cut the water at close to twenty-five miles an hour, faster than most Confederate blockade runners two decades later.

Courtland Hemstead, the boat's chief engineer, was examining the quivering needles on the dials of his brass steam gauges when Child tapped him on the shoulder. "Soon as we pass Sands Point, Mr. Hemstead, pour on the coal," Child said over the roar of the boilers and the sound of steam. "I want a fast run."

" 'Through by daylight,' that's our motto," Hemstead said, pausing to spit a stream of tobacco juice into the bilge. "Too bad Captain Jake came down with the fever and you had to leave your fireplace for a run this night."

"I'd rather sail in January cold than a November storm."

"Cold is the last thing I worry about down here by the boilers."

"Enjoy it while you can," Child said, laughing. "When summer comes, you'll be sweating in Hades."

Hemstead turned and began shouting orders to firemen Benjamin Cox, Charles Smith, and two other stokers, as they shoveled coal into the fireboxes of the big boilers. Child enjoyed the warmth for a minute or two longer before climbing back up the ladder and making his way to the captain's cabin to wash up for dinner with the passengers.

Manchester turned the wheel over to his helmsman, Martin Johnson. He wiped the glass, which had begun to mist from the inside, and peered at the beacon on Kings Point. "Three degrees to port," he said to Johnson.

"Coming three degrees to port," Johnson acknowledged.

Manchester picked up a telescope from the forward counter and peered at a schooner that was approaching on an opposite course to port. He noted that she was heeled to the leeward from a brisk breeze. He put the telescope back and studied the Sound ahead. The sun had dropped behind Manhattan Island in their wake and darkness was settling over the water. What little ice he was able to see was caked mostly on the calmer surface around inlets of the shoreline. There was no apprehension as he stared over the blackening water. Now that they were in the open Sound, the trickiest part of the voyage was over, and he began to breathe a little easier. He felt safe on the *Lexington*. She was a stout boat, fast and ruggedly built for heavy weather.

Her keel had been laid by the shipyard of Bishop and Simonson of New York on a warm Monday in September of 1834. Unlike later steamboats that were designed by men who drafted detailed plans, a wooden model of the hull was carved and altered to the whims of Commodore Vanderbilt until he was pleased by the results. Then, using the model as a guide, full-size outlines were drawn in chalk. Next, carpenters, exacting craftsmen of their time, cut and joined her timbered framework.

Later renowned as a man who revered Ebenezer Scrooge, Cornelius Vanderbilt stepped out of character and went overboard in making the *Lexington* the finest passenger vessel of the era. He lavished a considerable fortune on ornate teak deck railings, cabin doors, staircases, and interior paneling. A fancy lounge and dining saloon comprised the main cabin. All deck lighting, curtains, and furniture were of superb quality and could have graced the finest mansions of New York City.

The Commodore personally scrutinized every inch of her construction, and conceived a number of advanced innovations in her design. He insisted on the finest seasoned white oak and yellow pine for her beams and floor timbers. Integral strength was assured by a stress plan lifted from *Town's Patent for Bridges*. The hull was super-strong, with a heavy box frame, unusual for most ships before or since.

No safety feature was overlooked. Her smokestack was well cased through the decks, and cinders were passed through a wide pipe fitted in the hull that expelled them into the sea. No exposed woodwork was installed near the boilers or steam pipes. The *Lexington* even had her own fire engine, complete with pumps and hose. Three large lifeboats hung in their davits behind the paddle wheels along with a life raft that was tied to the forward deck.

The boat went into service on Monday, June 1, 1835, and was an immediate success. At first, she ran as a day boat between Providence, Rhode Island, and New York. Two years later, she was switched to the Stonington run. Her passenger accommodations were advertised as luxurious and expensive. Lady passengers were especially courted,

Vanderbilt providing all the niceties they enjoyed. Food was superb and the service second to none.

Either Commodore Vanderbilt sailed under a lucky star or else he enjoyed an acute sixth sense. In December of 1838, Vanderbilt's toughest competitor, the New Jersey Steam Navigation and Transportation Company, made the Commodore an offer he couldn't refuse. They paid him $60,000 for the fastest boat on the Sound, and then spent another $12,000 refurbishing the interior and converting her boiler furnaces to burn coal. His brother, Jake, agreed to stay on as captain of the *Lexington* until the family's new boat was launched.

Manchester pulled a lever that rang a bell in the engine room and called down through a voice tube. "We're in the clear now, Mr. Hemstead. Your boys can shovel on the coal."

"As you wish, captain," the chief engineer replied loudly over the tube.

Smoke spewed out her tall stack, thickened and mushroomed. A white bone grew and arched up around the bows as the *Lexington* leapt forward. The water beneath her huge paddle wheels seethed and boiled. To Manchester, she was like an unleashed greyhound. He never failed to be stirred when the big engine flexed its muscle and hurled the hull across the water as fast as if not faster than any other boat ever built.

He checked the thermometer again. Already the pointer hovered at zero.

Not a good night to stand outside, he thought. He glanced down at the water skimming past the hull, spreading into the wake, and couldn't imagine the horror of finding himself immersed in it this night.

Most captains of the passenger boats plying the Sound were not comfortable mingling with the passengers and remained aloof in the wheelhouse or their cabins during most of the trip. But George Child was a warm and friendly man. He felt it was his duty to show courtesy to his passengers and reassure any, and there were a fair number, who were fearful of traveling on a steamboat.

As Child stepped into the main cabin fifteen minutes before the call to dinner was announced, he looked over the passengers, who were seated in groups, conversing sociably around the stoves. Job Sand, the tall, distinguished head-waiter, moved around the cabin serving refreshments. Although Sand was white, the other five waiters, the kitchen help, Joseph Robinson, the boat's esteemed chef, and Susan Holcomb, chambermaid, were all black.

Without checking the boarding list, Child guessed there were approximately 115 passengers who had paid the $1 fare, meals extra. Deck passage was 50 cents, but there were no takers tonight. Counting his crew of 34, there were almost 150 men, women, and children on board the *Lexington* for the run to Stonington. It was as though the boat held a miniature city.

Several card players were seated at the tables, quietly engrossed in their game. Two well-known Boston comedy actors, Charles Eberle and Henry J. Finn, kept the conversation lively as the cards were dealt. Never ones to ignore an audience, they had generously offered to act out a scene from their new play after the passengers had dined. Peter McKenna, a businessman from New York, won the first pot.

Mothers and fathers gathered on the sofas and entertained their young children with stories and toys purchased in the city. Mrs. Russell Jarvis, described as a woman of uncommon beauty, kept her two lively daughters occupied by counting beams from the lighthouses rising around the danger points of the Sound. James Bates scanned a newspaper while his wife read aloud from a book of poetry to their young boy and girl. Parents with two children seemed to be the rule on board the *Lexington* this Monday. William Townsend was giving his wife a holiday by taking their two girls on a trip to Boston.

On a more somber note, the funeral party of Harrison Winslow were sitting quietly off to one side of the cabin by themselves. His widow, Alice Winslow; her father-in-law,

William Winslow; and Harrison's brother, John Winslow, were accompanying the body, stowed in its coffin with the other cargo belowdecks, for burial in Providence. On the opposite end of the cabin, Mary Russell giggled happily with Lydia Bates, a young woman her age. Mary had been married the day before in New York, and was returning to her home without her new husband to break the news to her parents.

A party of merchants stood around the stoves discussing business and debating politics. Banker Robert Blake politely disagreed with business proprietors Abram Howard, William Green, and Samuel Henry over the New York bank's tightening of interest rates. John Lemist, treasurer of the Boston Leather Company, had nothing good to say about the bankers, who had recently charged his firm a high rate of interest on a loan to increase inventory.

The lounge was heavily attended this trip by sea captains, who had made port after months at sea and were traveling to their own firesides and their cherished loved ones. Captains J. D. Carver, Chester Hillard, E. J. Kimball, David McFarland, John Mattison, Theophilas Smith, and Benjamin Foster, who was returning from a three-year voyage to India, took turns swapping sea tales with each other.

Other notable passengers included Dr. Charles Follen, a respected professor of German literature at Harvard College, and Adolphus Harnden, of Harnden's Express, who was transporting $20,000 in silver coin and $50,000 in bank notes for the Merchants Bank.

Dinner was served at 6 P.M. by Job Sand and his staff of waiters. Chef Joseph Robinson and his assistant cooks, Oliver Howell and Robert Peters, offered passengers a choice between mutton with boiled tomatoes and baked flounder in a wine sauce with rice.

Amid the clink of glasses and the soft murmur of voices engaged in small talk, none of the 115 souls assembled around the dining tables could have known that, except for one man seated among them, this would be their last meal on earth.

*   *   *

Shortly after 7:30, the first mate, Edwin Furber, came to the wheelhouse door and alerted Captain Manchester that the boat was on fire. Manchester immediately stepped outside and stared aft. Flames were coming through the promenade deck around the smokestack casing. He scanned the darkened shoreline and took a quick bearing. The boat was well past the beacon at Eatons Neck Point and approaching the lighthouse on Old Field Point, both on the Long Island side of the Sound. The lights of Bridgeport to the north appeared farther away. He immediately took the helm from steersman Johnson and swung the wheel hard-a-starboard in a vain effort to turn the boat and beach her on Long Island.

Seemingly out of nowhere, Captain Child rushed into the wheelhouse. "We've a fire on board!" he shouted. "Set a course for the nearest land!"

"I'm bringing her about now," Manchester answered, "but the wheel is not answering the helm."

Together, the three men gripped the spokes and applied their strength in an effort to steer the boat toward safety four miles and twenty minutes away. Suddenly, the wheel spun out of their hands.

"She's not responding," Johnson muttered in dazed bewilderment.

"The fire must have burned through the port steering rope below the wheelhouse," said Child.

Now out of control, with the engines still turning, the *Lexington* began helplessly running in wide circles. Child leaned out the door and gazed toward the stern. The beautiful boat, once the pride of the Vanderbilts, was vomiting fire and smoke from her entire midsection. He realized with sickening certainty that his boat and everyone on it was lost.

Leaving Child and Johnson, Manchester ran outside and called to the deckhands to operate the fire engine and break out the water buckets. The deckhands appeared frightened and confused. They attempted to put the fire engine into operation but they couldn't seem to find the buckets. At that moment smoke poured into the wheelhouse. Child and steersman Johnson were forced out on the deck, choking and coughing from the deadly fumes.

Second Mate David Crowley rushed to the center of the boat and found flames leaping from several bales of cotton. At that point, the fire had yet to spread to the boat's woodwork. He organized the deckhands and the dining-saloon waiters into a bucket brigade and began throwing water on the growing holocaust. Short on buckets, they spilled the Merchants Bank's silver coins from their wooden crates onto the deck and hurriedly began filling the boxes with water and passing them on to the men nearest the flames. Their efforts made no headway as the flames spread with incredible speed. If cool heads had prevailed early on, the fire might have been contained. Now it became a moment born in hell.

Any hope of saving the boat had evaporated.

The blaze quickly forced Chief Engineer Courtland Hemstead and his men from the engine room before they were able to shut down the engines. Immune to the fire, the big steam cylinder kept the paddle wheels turning, making it impossible to launch the boats.

The *Lexington* surged on through the dark waters as if driven by some unearthly force.

The strength of the flames soon overwhelmed the firefighters. They retreated past the towering walking beam to the paddle-wheel guards. Since it was too late to make their escape, the crew on the forecastle deck were trapped by a wall of fire reaching up to the top of the smokestack.

To Captain Chester Hillard, who helped strip away the canvas covering the lifeboats, "The *Lexington* is a gone case."

Crowley stood by Captain Child and asked, "Sir, what is to be done?"

Child looked around at the fear etched on the passengers' faces and calmly replied, "Gentlemen, take to the boats." Then he walked aft to direct the launching of the lifeboats.

Twenty minutes before there were informal pleasantry and relaxed gaiety in the main cabin. Now the entire scene was one of horror. Utter confusion and terror swept the passengers. Calm gave way to the inevitable contagion of panic. As one, they made a frantic rush for the lifeboats, brushed aside the crew, who were attempting to ready them for launching, and took possession. Caught up in mindless panic, the passengers flooded into the boats as if they were lemmings; overwhelmed by mass frenzy, they unknowingly destroyed themselves.

Dangerously overfilling the boats, the passengers dropped them into the black water that was still swirling past, agitated by the thrashing paddle wheels. The boats, along with their helpless occupants, were immediately swamped and swept into the night.

The remaining passengers were left to fend for themselves, and none of them knew which way to turn. Few jumped into the water. Drowning was nearly as unthinkable as being incinerated. During the early nineteenth century, fewer than ten people out of a hundred knew how to swim. In any event they would have expired within minutes from hypothermia in the frigid water.

Captain Hillard rounded up a few deckhands and a small band of passengers, and directed them to throw overboard any cotton bales that had not caught fire. After a dozen were heaved over the side, Hillard and stoker Benjamin Cox climbed down and positioned themselves astride a bale, each facing the other. Their combined weight settled the cotton bale until only one-third of it was above the surface of the water. The wind was fresh and the current carried them away from the boat at a speed of a knot and a half.

As Hillard drifted around the stern, he noticed a lady, whom he took to be Mrs. Jarvis, shouting frantically over the railing. Somehow, one of her children had fallen overboard. The men passed the child so closely Hillard could reach out his hand and touch the little body. From its dress and long hair streaming in the water, Hillard could see it was a female. He also saw that she was already dead. Mrs. Jarvis beseeched him to pull her daughter from the icy water, but he was more concerned with saving his own life. This was a time when self-preservation prevailed before the cry of "Women and children first" became a worthy tradition of the sea.

Hillard turned away from the heartrending scene, pulled

out his watch, and calmly noted the time by the light of the fire. It was just 8 P.M.

The *Lexington* would take a long time to die.

An immense, billowing cloud of black smoke reached hundreds of feet into the sky, blocking out the stars. The main deck had fallen in, and the only parts of the boat the flames had yet to devour were the stern and bows forward of the capstan. Ten people still stood on the stern while thirty more milled around the forecastle, including Manchester.

"Shouldn't we jump or something?" a dazed Adolphus Harnden asked Captain Manchester.

"To do so would be to perish," replied Manchester.

"We can't just stand here and be burned to death."

"Every man for himself," Manchester said solemnly.

He turned away and lowered himself over the side onto a raft of debris. There were two or three other men on it already, and his added weight sank it under the water. He grabbed a piece of the railing that was underwater and used it to pull himself onto a bale of cotton that was floating nearby. He found that passenger Peter McKenna had climbed aboard the bale first. Harnden, still on the forecastle, shouted to Manchester.

"Is there room for another?"

Before Manchester could answer, Harnden jumped, knocking McKenna off the bale and falling in the water with him. Ignoring Harnden, Manchester hauled McKenna back on the bale. Then he found a length of board that was floating past and began paddling away from the blazing boat. As had Captain Hillard earlier when abandoning the boat, he checked his watch. It was just midnight.

Lexington had burned for four hours.

Second Mate Crowley also reached a cotton bale empty of life. He pulled himself aboard, and with surprising presence of mind stuffed his clothing full of cotton to ward off the frigid night air. He was luckier than the others who had reached the temporary safety of the cotton bales. Without the added weight of a second body, he was able to lie the full length of the bale without immersing his legs and feet.

Drifting with the current, he could do little but fight to keep warm and identify the different points of land as he floated past.

The most harrowing escape from the inferno was by stoker Charles Smith. He had just fallen asleep between shifts of firing the boilers when he was awakened by a friend, who informed him there was a fire. He quickly rushed to the engine room, attached the fire hose to the water and opened the valve. But he was unable to reach the end of the hose to spray water on the blaze. The smoke and flames drove him aft, where he intended to board one of the lifeboats. He found Captain Child standing by the davits that swung out the starboard lifeboat, and heard him shouting for Chief Engineer Courtland Hemstead.

In less than a minute, Hemstead appeared, his eyebrows and much of his hair singed away. "You wanted me, captain?"

"For God's sake, stop the engine," Child implored. "We can't launch the boats while we're under way."

Hemstead shook his head wearily. "The fire drove us from the engine room before I could shut down the pressure valves. There's no going back in the inferno. I'm sorry."

Child nodded. "You did your best. Take your engine-room crew and see what you can do to hold back the flames for as long as it takes to get everyone safely off the boat."

Hemstead vanished in the smoke while Child stepped over the rail and tried to steady the lifeboat as it was lowered with a full load of frightened passengers. At that instant, someone cut the stern line and the boat swung outward, its bow plunging under the turbulence from the rotating paddle wheels. Child fell into the boat. Passengers, Captain Child, and the half-sunken boat drifted away and disappeared into the night, joining the dead bodies already floating in the wake of the *Lexington.*

Soon after, the engine finally stopped and the boat began to drift. By waiting another few minutes the doomed passengers in the swamped boats might have been saved. Only four souls would survive.

Smith climbed over the stern railings, kicked in three

cabin windows, and using the sills as footholds, lowered himself on top of the rudder. After half an hour, a young boy climbed down beside him. Smith looked into the face white with fear. He pointed to a cotton bale floating nearby.

"If you want to save your skin, son, you'd better get yourself on that bale."

"I . . . I can't swim," the boy stammered.

"Hang on. I'll bring it closer."

Smith slipped into the freezing water, swam over to the bale, and got on top of it. Using his hands, he tried to paddle the bale close enough to the stern for the boy to jump aboard, but he could not make enough headway to reach the boat. At last, he regained the burning steamboat, and unthinkingly climbed back on board. This time, he found himself amidships, near the starboard paddle wheel. There he found a dozen people still hanging onto different sections of the smoldering remains. The flames had decreased to where the passengers were able to cling to the side by standing on the chines, an extended rib of the hull made of solid timber running fore and aft to keep the boat from rolling.

Smith found himself clinging next to Engineer Hemstead; Job Sand, the headwaiter; Harry Reed, a deckhand; and another stoker, George Baum. All around the burned hulk they could see the sea filled with a blanket of debris, ashes, and dead bodies of all ages. Smith clenched his jaws as he stared at the appalling reality of the tragedy. He choked off the bile rising in his throat and looked down at the water below his feet that waited patiently to engulf them.

At three o'clock, seven hours after the fire was discovered, the smoldering remains of the steamboat slipped beneath the cold waters of the Sound, accompanied by a great hissing sound as the cold water surged through the cremated interior of the hull. Steam mingled with smoke to create a pall that was slowly carried away by wind, and soon the flotsam drifted away, leaving the grave of the *Lexington* shrouded and unmarked by a merciless sea.

As the hull sank from under them, Smith, along with four others—Harry Reed; George Baum; the actor and comedian Henry Finn; and the boy who had taken Smith's place on the rudder—struggled onto a large piece of the paddle-wheel guard that had ripped away and bobbed to the surface after the ship sank. Like Manchester and Hillard before him, Smith also did his best to keep the others alive on the paddle-wheel guard. He shook and massaged them, and tried to force them to exercise, but overcome by the cold, the living had reached the limit of their endurance. They died one by one and rolled into the water.

Smith, a tough drinker and brawler when ashore, stared at the devil and shook his fist.

The unnatural glare of the fire across the dark water was seen from the Long Island and Connecticut shores. The flames shot up in huge columns, lighting the water for miles around.

William Sidney Mount, an artist of some renown for his paintings of Long Island country settings, witnessed the calamity and described how local mariners struggled to sail through pack ice clogging ports and inlets. Fishermen, thinking they might rescue victims while the steamboat was only two miles away, set out from their harbor in the bitter cold. But just when they thought they were within hailing distance of the flaming wreck, the winds and the tides shifted, sweeping the *Lexington* back into the middle of the Sound. Defeated by the whims of nature, the intrepid fishermen had no choice but to return home, the water being too rough for them to venture into the Sound.

Captain William Tirrell, of the sloop *Improvement,* sighted the burning pyre, but failed to offer assistance, claiming that he thought the steamer had her boats, and he was afraid that if he stopped he would lose the tide coming into the harbor. Like Captain Stanley Lord of the *California* seventy-two years later, who was accused of standing by while the *Titanic* sank, Tirrell was denounced as a cruel and heartless man. Because of his alleged indifference to the suffering of the passengers on the *Lexington,* he came within an inch of having his master's papers revoked. But later studies showed that he was a good twelve miles distant and facing a contrary wind. Investigators considered it doubtful that he could have reached the stricken vessel in time to save its ill-fated passengers had he tried.

Discovering the steamer on fire, Captain Oliver Meeker of the sloop *Merchant* tried to sail his vessel from the pier at Southport. But the combination of a shallow harbor and a falling tide caused the *Merchant* to run aground.

Captain Hillard and Benjamin Cox had drifted about a mile from the *Lexington* when she went down. A scattering of clouds strayed over the mainland and a bright moon illuminated the Sound. The night air was incredibly cold, and the men tried to keep warm by whipping their hands and arms around their bodies. They were as miserable as two humans could get. Then, as if ordained to multiply their agony, a large swell overturned their cotton bale. Plunged into the frigid water, Hillard and Cox struggled to climb on the opposite side. Losing the paddle was a double blow. Besides employing it as a means to keep warm through exercise, they had found it useful for steering against the tide. Now the bale became uncontrollable and rolled heavily under the onslaught of the waves.

Cox had abandoned the boat wearing only a flannel shirt, loose-fitting pants, boots, and a cap. An old mariner, Hillard had wisely worn his heavy woolen pea jacket. He gave Cox his vest, and then rubbed the passenger's arms and legs, beat him on the body, and made every attempt to keep his blood circulating.

"I want to die," Cox suddenly announced.

"You talk like a crazy man," said Hillard. "Do you have a wife and family?"

Cox nodded drunkenly. "A fine wife and six children."

"They will suffer miserably without their father. You cannot give up hope. Think of them waiting for you at home."

Cox did not answer. He seemed to have lost all desire to live.

Hillard did not realize it at the time, but his efforts at keeping Cox alive no doubt prolonged his own life as well. "Damn you, Cox," he snapped. "Do not let yourself die. Hang on for God and your family."

Cox appeared not to hear. He was beyond caring. The cotton bale slewed broadside in a trough before being struck by the next wave. Hillard somehow clutched the bale with hands numb of all feeling, fighting to hang on as the bale was pitched and tossed crazily.

His body limp with apathy and insensibility, Cox slipped off the bale and Hillard saw him no more.

Hillard's ordeal was very nearly an exact replay of the drama acted out on Captain Manchester's cotton bale.

Manchester's partner, McKenna, complained constantly about the bitter cold. Then as the icy water soaked his skin and the frigid air sucked the life from his body, he babbled about his wife and children, how he had kissed them the morning he left home.

"You'll be with them this time tomorrow," Manchester gamely assured him.

"No, I fully expect I'll die from the cold."

"Move about, man," Manchester implored, trying to encourage McKenna. "Get your blood flowing. Wave your arms, kick your legs, anything to keep warm."

"What good will it do?" mumbled McKenna. "We're both going to perish."

"Speak for yourself!" Manchester suddenly snapped. "I'll be damned if I'll give up."

Like Benjamin Cox on another cotton bale less than a mile away, McKenna appeared not to hear and went silent.

Manchester had heard many tales from ocean mariners about shipwrecked sailors who lost the will to survive. Discipline, they swore, was the key to survival. Too many mariners who were forced to abandon their ships expired out of lethargy and hopelessness. He could see it happening before his eyes. McKenna did not appear to care whether he lived or died. Staying alive to keep his wife and children from having to survive without a husband and father seemed the farthest thing from his mind.

Manchester could do nothing but watch helplessly as McKenna gave in to fate. He died shortly after the *Lexington* sank. His body fell backward, his head hanging partially in the water. The first heavy wave that struck the bale washed him off. For almost half an hour, he floated alongside Manchester, the moonlight reflecting on his white face and hands, before he finally drifted out of sight.

The agonizingly cold night came and passed, a night of torment that never seemed to end. With the coming of the sun, the sea turned smooth, and Captain Meeker of the *Merchant,* who had labored through to dawn, unloading cargo to lighten his vessel, was finally able to work his sloop off the sandbar with the incoming tide and set sail into the Sound.

Perched on his cotton bale, Hillard sighted the *Merchant* at about noon and wildly waved his hand to attract the attention of those on board. Captain Meeker smartly turned his sloop toward Hillard and came alongside. The helping hands of the crew pulled the half-frozen survivor over the side, where every courtesy was paid to him. He was taken below, where damp clothes were replaced with warm blankets, and he was placed in front of a stove while being fed cups of coffee laced with whiskey.

Next to be rescued was Captain Manchester. Nearly insensible from the cold, his hands frozen, he managed to insert his handkerchief between his rigid, unfeeling fingers and wave it feebly in a light breeze. Observed by Meeker's alert crew, he was soon thawing out beside Captain Hillard in the galley of the *Merchant.*

At two o'clock in the afternoon, fireman Smith, his hands and feet badly frostbitten, was barely conscious when he was spotted by Captain Meeker and picked off the paddle-wheel guard. All three men suffered from the effects of the exposure to extreme cold, but all recovered in time to testify at the coroner's inquest. Captain Meeker also retrieved two bodies from the water before heading back to Southport.

The most remarkable story of survival was that of Second Mate David Crowley. Luckily, his bale did not capsize or roll heavily with the sea, enabling him to burrow a nest into the center of the cotton. With his clothing stuffed with cotton until he looked like a fat snowman, he kept from freezing to death. Unseen by Captain Meeker's crew, Crowley suffered all day Tuesday and through the night. Not until nine o'clock Wednesday night did his floating home-away-from-home drift against an ice pack along the Long Island shore.

Afraid he might fall through into the frigid water, Crowley crawled across the ice on his stomach until he reached land. Then he stumbled nearly a mile to a house and rapped on the door with the last of his strength. The residents, Matthias and Mary Hutchinson, thought they were looking at a bloated dead body, dressed only in bulging light pants and a shirt, and with a bared head. They were astounded when the warmth of the house and their vigorous massage of his limbs brought Crowley back to life. He had suffered forty-eight hours of freezing cold on his floating cotton raft and had drifted over fifty miles.

Shortly after his miraculous survival, the owners of the cotton on board the *Lexington* presented Second Mate Crowley with the same bale that had carried him to land. He had it transported to his home in Providence, Rhode Island, where he kept it standing in his living room for many years. When the price of cotton skyrocketed during the Civil War, Crowley sold his bale for charity. From it sprang the famous Lexington brand of cotton cloth.

There were other intriguing sequels to the burning of the *Lexington.*

Lithography was becoming a popular profession in the 1800s. People throughout the country bought lithographs from their general stores and hung them in their living and dining rooms. For the price of a few pennies, the public came into the habit of changing the colored lithographs on the wall every week, especially when the subject that was illustrated struck their fancy.

Right after the burning of the *Lexington,* a young artist, struggling to launch a lithography studio, was contracted by the *New York Sun* to produce a lithograph of the disaster. Working night and day, he turned out his masterwork in just sixty hours, and splendiferously titled it:

THE AWFUL CONFLAGRATION OF THE STEAMBOAT *LEX-INGTON* IN LONG ISLAND SOUND, MONDAY EVE, 13TH JANUARY 1840 BY WHICH MELANCHOLY OCCURRENCE OVER 100 PERSONS PERISHED.

Appearing in the *New York Sun*'s extra edition, the portrayal of the frightful catastrophe became a sensation and hung in almost every home in America. Considered a breakthrough in journalism, the use of graphics to illustrate a hot news story quickly became a traditional style that is with us today in newspapers and magazines.

The young artist's reputation was made, and he went on to become world famous. If the tragedy of the ill-fated *Lexington* did nothing else, it gave the country the remarkable talents of Nathaniel Currier, who in seventeen years would join forces with another artist/lithographer, James Merritt Ives, to produce evocative color lithographs that became the illustrated soul of early America.

The man that arrived late at the dock and who wisely decided not to make an attempt to jump onto the *Lexington* read of the disaster in the extra edition of a newspaper late the next morning. He could not believe his luck. If he hadn't been delayed because of an argument with his editor, Park Benjamin, over editorial changes in his poem *The Wreck of the Hesperus,* set for publication in the *World* newspaper, he certainly would have been one of the 150 frozen bodies floating in the Sound.

He folded the newspaper, set it aside, and asked the waiter for a sheet of the hotel's stationery and an envelope. After the dishes were cleared, he began writing his wife and father to inform them their husband and son, Henry Wadsworth Longfellow, was still alive and well in the restaurant of a New York hotel.

Captain Joseph Comstock was appointed by the Transportation Company to proceed to the scene of the disaster and search for the bodies of passengers and crew, and to recover any luggage and company property. The steamboat *States-*

man, Captain George Peck commanding, was chartered for the recovery operation.

Comstock's first problem was to determine the approximate position of the *Lexington* when it caught fire and later sank. Witnesses to the flames on the water gave conflicting testimony. Some reported seeing the burning ship off Eatons Neck Point, others put it in the middle of the Sound off Crane Neck Point. The lighthouse keeper at Old Field Point claimed he saw the flames vanish about three o'clock in the morning about four miles to the north of the lighthouse and slightly west. The depth of water was judged to be twenty fathoms.

After two days of searching, only seven bodies were discovered, including the two pulled from the water by Captain Meeker of the *Merchant.* Numerous sections of wreckage washed up ashore. The nameplate on the wheelhouse, two feet in length with the entire word *Lexington,* and a swamped lifeboat, were found and retrieved, along with several pieces of luggage.

The weather during the search was intensely cold, the temperature holding at four degrees below zero. The sudden accumulation of ice along the shore rendered further efforts hopeless. Captain Comstock called off the search and ordered the *Statesman* back to New York with its pitifully small cargo of dead. The recovery operation was especially bitter for Comstock. One of those lost, whose body was never recovered, was Jesse Comstock, clerk of the *Lexington,* the captain's brother.

The coroner's inquest threw blame in every direction. The jury censured the steamboat's owners for maintaining a dangerous ship and denounced them for transporting inflammable cargo on a steamboat carrying passengers. They criticized the state steamboat inspectors for ignoring gross safety violations, and the dockworkers for loading combustible cargo next to a heat source. They accused Captain Child and his dead crew of the *Lexington* of dereliction of duty, while strangely exonerating Captain Manchester, Second Mate Crowley, and fireman Smith from all blame.

The verdict was that the *Lexington* was a firetrap. The

casing around the smokestack ignited a fire that was communicated to the cotton bales stacked around it. No one was indicted, convicted, paid a fine, or lost a license.

All that remained were hearts overwhelmed with grief. The burning of the *Lexington* left ninety grieving widows and nearly three hundred fatherless and motherless children. For all but five of the dead, there would be no tomb.

POSTSCRIPT

An item from a weekly paper, the *Long Islander,* Huntington, New York.

September 30, 1842. THE LEXINGTON. The wreck of this ill-fated vessel has been raised to the surface of the water, but, one of the chains breaking, she again sank in 130 feet of water. The attempt is again in progress. The eight hundred dollars recovered from her were not in bills, as before stated, but in a lump of silver, weighing thirty pounds, the box having been emptied on the deck to be used as a bucket for throwing water on the flames.

II

Enter NUMA

April 1983

I CAN'T REMEMBER WHAT INITIALLY SPARKED MY INTEREST in the *Lexington.* I believe it might have been an afterthought while searching the sand and surf of the Fire Island National Seashore in New York for the remains of the first steamboat to cross the Atlantic, the *Savannah.* She struck the beach during a fog in 1821, several years after her epic crossing. Although she was under steam for only eighty hours, her famous voyage stands unchallenged in the history books.

This type of search is usually the most frustrating because almost all ships that run aground on sandy shores or on the banks of rivers are covered in time and completely buried under a shroud of silt. You can easily observe this phenomenon while standing at the edge of a surf line. As the dying waves pass beyond you, your feet sink into the sand and are soon covered. The same thing happens to a ship, even a battleship, if given enough time. Another problem is that landmarks go through great change, and the sightings of contemporary witnesses seldom apply.

On a boat belonging to a pair of Long Island residents,

Bill Shea and I conducted a remote sensing survey with his proton magnetometer as close as we dared to the breakers on the Atlantic Ocean side of the island in hopes of detecting the magnetic signature of any iron left on board the *Savannah*. Although we had planned a mile-long search grid that ran parallel to the beach, we could not distinguish landmarks over the high sand dunes that run along the spine of Fire Island. Since the boat did not carry navigation equipment, this was imperative if we were to set our boundaries for running our search lanes in the water and on the beach.

I volunteered to swim to shore, climb the sand dunes, and take visual sightings in order to plot our search grid. Fifteen minutes later, I located the landmarks that I had plotted from a topographic chart that corresponded with the approximate site of the *Savannah*'s burial place. After marking the eastern boundary of the grid with a piece of driftwood that could be seen from the boat, I began pacing off a mile toward the west boundary.

Taking my terrible memory into consideration—when my wife sends me to the store for a loaf of bread, I always come home with a jar of pickles—I kept track of my progress by shifting ten pebbles one by one from one hand to another. The beach appeared totally deserted, so I merrily counted out the numbers aloud in a Mitch Miller sing-along fashion.

About halfway toward my western boundary, I noticed a figure approaching from the opposite direction. Drawing closer, I could see that it was an elderly man wearing a big-brimmed floppy hat on his head. I was so wrapped up in not losing my count I paid no more attention to him until after we had passed. Then a tiny brain cell told me that something wasn't quite right. So I turned around.

The old gentleman had stopped about ten paces away and was staring at me as if I were some nutcase who had escaped his padded cell. Amusement was etched on his suntanned face. He, no doubt, couldn't imagine why someone would walk down a deserted beach while staring at the sand and singing numbers to himself.

He couldn't have been more amused than me when I

realized that beneath the floppy hat the old guy was completely nude.

One of the practices I've come to rely on when looking for a particular shipwreck is to research other ships that went down in the same general area. Should my primary target prove too elusive or impossible to find within my time schedule, or luckily, I stumble on it early in the game, I can use the extra days to hunt for a second or third wreck. There is nothing wrong with being extra ambitious when you're given the opportunity of achieving an additional success by catching two or more fish on the same hook.

Unable to find a solid magnetic signature of the *Savannah,* I decided to give her a rain check, and I moved the crew across Long Island into the Sound for an attempt at discovering the steamboat *Lexington,* lost for nearly 150 years.

Bob Fleming, a nationally respected Washington, D.C., researcher and shipwreck scholar, who works with me on a regular basis, put me onto the track of the ill-starred steamboat. Fleming sent me the story behind the tragedy. Cursed with a vivid imagination, I could almost hear the cries of the *Lexington*'s victims begging for someone to find their tomb.

Margaret Dubitsky, a Long Island schoolteacher, who worked long and hard in compiling a remarkable research package from New York state and local archives, found references to the steamboat's being raised. One vague report claimed it was brought to the surface and towed away, suggesting it no longer lay on the bottom of the Sound.

This piece of information nearly sank the project before it began. It was known that occasional sea hunts through the decades had failed to find a trace of the steamboat. Could this explain why she was never located by either sport divers or fishermen? Everyone, it seemed, claimed that because she couldn't be found she must no longer exist.

I hated to give up on her. Much of my life people have told me I was wasting my time or engaging in an exercise in futility when I tackled a seemingly hopeless project. What is interesting is that they were right only 40 percent of the time.

Shoving all pessimistic thoughts aside, I felt strongly that it was conceivable the *Lexington* might still rest in the murky depths, forgotten and untouched for almost a century and a half. If so, the charred wreckage of what had once been the finest steamboat on Long Island Sound had now become a historically rich and archaeologically significant vessel.

Raising a two-hundred-foot vessel from 130 feet of water is a feat rarely if ever attempted today. Difficulties with weather, unpredictable seas, the heavy lifting equipment involved, and the expense can be enormous. Having the technology in 1842 to accomplish such an undertaking seems incredible. Hard-hat diving was in its infancy. Decompression tables were unknown. Did divers sling chains under the hull to lift her out of the water, or were cables dragged under the wreck by two vessels steaming side by side? And then there had to be a barge and a crane with the capacity to lift a 488-ton vessel to the surface. Even by twenty-first-century standards this takes a derrick almost the size of the one used by the *Glomar Explorer* to raise the Russian submarine. And yet it *was* accomplished, as eventually proven by NUMA in July of 1983.

Finding no insurance-company records of a raising, no credible, detailed accounts in contemporary newspapers of a charred hull brought into port, I forged ahead and formed an expedition to search for the wreckage I felt certain was still on the seabed. I was told by any number of divers that I was laboring in vain and pouring time and money into a sinkhole. To me, this was akin to telling MacArthur he couldn't invade the Philippines.

Working with Zeff Loria of Port Jefferson, Long Island, who agreed to act as project director, I began analyzing the historical material gathered by researchers Fleming and Dubitsky. The enigma? Where exactly was the *Lexington* when she finally sank? Ship captains sailing in landlocked waters did not navigate by latitude and longitude coordinates. Nor did they estimate their positions by the stars or dead reckoning. They used visual sightings. Log books from ships sailing the Sound simply contained entries stating that "Oak Neck Point was abeam at 9:35 P.M." Few other details on position were given.

The *Lexington* left few clues.

Of all the sightings from witnesses on shore, I placed my faith in the Old Field lighthouse keeper, who reported seeing the flames die about four miles north of the Point and slightly to the west. Figuring that he was a good judge of distance across water, I laid out an initial grid of four square miles in his approximate area, and the search was on.

The first attempt was spent primarily in studying the area, bottom conditions, run of the tide, and underwater visibility. Captain Tony Bresnah, with his boat, the *Day Off,* anchored us over a sunken barge and we made a test dive into the Sound. One to two feet of visibility was not unexpected, but the current was much stronger than estimated. We figured close to four knots, and all divers were holding on to the anchor chain while stretched horizontal like flags in a windstorm. We also discovered that half our search grid passed under the path of the Bridgeport–Port Jefferson ferry that ran between the mainland and Long Island during the summers. In continuous operation since 1874, it provided an excellent reason why fishermen didn't fish and divers didn't dive in the neighborhood.

For the second attempt, Zeff Loria assembled a first-rate crew. The *Mikado III,* captained by Mike Arnell, an experienced divemaster, was chartered. The dive team was led by Robert Wass along with Doug Rutledge and Sandy Zicaro. Equipment included a Schonstedt gradiometer to detect the presence of iron, a Klein Associates Inc. side scan sonar to record objects protruding from the sea bottom, and a Loran navigation unit, since made obsolete by newer Global Positioning Systems, utilizing satellites.

For once the tedium of running search lanes did not cause uncontrolled yawning. Tom Cummings, Klein's sonar technician, announced not one but three solid targets the first hour into the search. Subsequent runs over the targets suggested one large vessel broken into three sections. In one sonar recording the engine's walking beam and a large section of the guard from a paddle wheel could be detected.

Captain Mike Arnell then expertly moored the *Mikado III* directly over the wreck so the divers could descend on the anchor line. The bottom depth registered 140 feet on the boat's echo sounder and the diver's depth gauges. This time we waited for slack tide. The view inside a tunnel offered better visibility than what Wass found on the bottom, and they had to examine the wreck with powerful underwater lights.

Using a safety line, we made narrow sweeps of the central section of the wreckage. With the divers restricted to only ten minutes of bottom time, major exploration was severely limited. Wass brought up a few bolts and pieces of charred wood. He reported seeing one of the paddle wheels and more charred timbers and described the hull construction as looking like an egg crate, verifying the *Lexington*'s unusual box frame.

It is a pity you cannot stand on the sandy bottom, step back, and view the wreckage in its entirety. The length of the burned and broken hull, the great paddle wheels, the walking beams of the engines are more imagined than seen. The dismal green, murky water allows you only a few closeup glimpses of how the ship must have once appeared. You feel as if you're groping through a haunted house in the dead of night, glimpsing its ghosts from the corner of one eye.

Because of the many long hours of research, I felt as though I had walked the decks of the *Lexington,* watched the smoke pour into the sky from her smokestack, seen her passengers and crew. To the other divers, she was simply a pile of debris on the bottom. I saw her in my mind as she once was, a greyhound of the waters. And yet I was not sorry to leave her.

After we assembled the artifacts and cataloged them, I sent a piece of a timber to Robert Baldwin, a leading expert in wood science, who identified it as yellow pine, one of the woods used in the construction of the steamship.

Wass also described strands of a weird green wire that

looped around the wreck. Believing that the wreck *was* raised before breaking into three pieces, I did a bit of detective work by contacting Mr. Oliver Tannet, an executive with a wire cable company. As luck would have it, Mr. Tannet collected antique wire and was an authority on early cable. He stated that by 1840 engineers had not achieved the technology to extrude flexible wire cable. In order to make it curl, the iron strands were woven around a core of copper. After a century and a half of attack by salt water, the iron in the cables used to hoist the *Lexington* off the bottom had eroded away, leaving the green-patinaed copper core behind.

The lighthouse keeper was close to the mark. Instead of four miles north and slightly west, the wreck of the *Lexington* was found *three and a half miles north and slightly west.*

The artifacts recovered by NUMA (sorry, no silver) were donated to the Vanderbilt Museum in Centerport, Long Island, for display to the public. Talk of raising the steamship soon faded, as do most recovery projects when the costs are added up and no one comes forth to underwrite the funding.

Since NUMA's discovery, many divers have investigated the *Lexington*. Her resting place is now well known to the local dive boat captains. Perhaps someday an extensive archaeological recovery may be realized on her remains.

The greyhounds of the Sound have long steamed over the horizon. The *Lexington* is a time capsule of an era when the United States was just beginning to flex its muscles and cross the threshold of the industrial revolution. A time when we were turning more of our energies from manifest destiny to technology. A pity we'll never see their smoke or hear their whistles again.

A final word of caution. Diving the *Lexington* can be very dangerous. The tides are treacherous and can run as high as four knots. Ambient light is almost nonexistent and disorientation is a sure bet unless the diver makes good use of a guideline attached to the anchor chain. I highly recommend that you dive only during slack tide to avoid a nasty current.

Part 2

The Republic of Texas Navy Ship *Zavala*

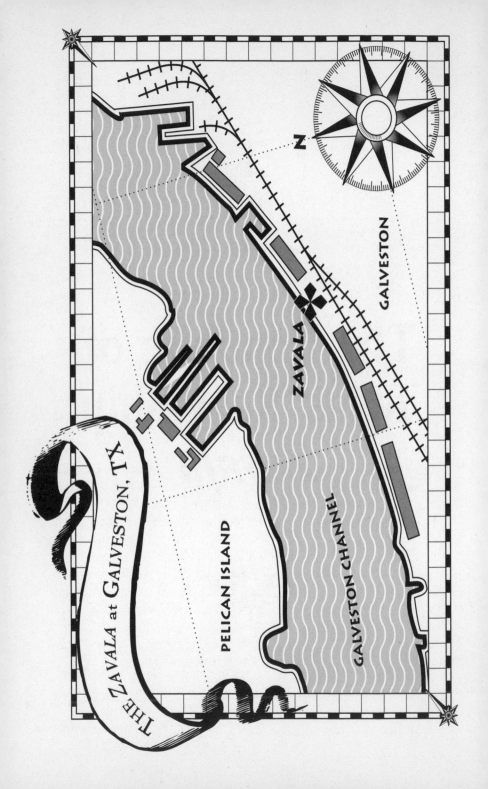

THE ZAVALA at GALVESTON, TX

Z

GALVESTON

ZAVALA

PELICAN ISLAND

GALVESTON CHANNEL

I

A Sweet-Handling Ship

1836–1842

BY EARLY MORNING, THE SUN WAS BLOTTED OUT BY BLACK, sinister clouds, and the wind gained in velocity with each passing hour. Lightning streaks were followed by the threatening rumble of thunder. A driving rain was accompanied by fast-rising seas as the worst storm in recent memory struck the mid-Atlantic coast in October of 1837.

Captain Henry May peered into the growing tempest from the wheelhouse of his ship, the steamship *Charleston*. The sea had turned from beautiful to ugly in less than forty minutes. A veteran of the run between Philadelphia and Charleston, South Carolina, May knew from experience that conditions were building into the worst storm he'd ever faced in his twenty-five years at sea.

"Better warn the passengers to tie themselves to their berths, Mr. Lawler. We're in for a nasty blow."

May's first mate, Charlie Lawler, forced a tight grin. "Nasty blow, captain? She looks more like the furies run amok."

"While you're at it, tell Chief Engineer Leland to mind

35

his fires. Judging from the rise in the waves, we'll be taking on water."

The full force of the storm fell on them without mercy. Within another hour, the seas became heaving mountains that rushed out of the sheets of pouring rain and curled down on the bows of *Charleston* as she took them head-on. The bulwarks and railings along the main deck were swept away along with the lifeboats. The shutters that shielded the lower windows of the passenger cabins were crushed inward by the force of the water.

May was blessed with an experienced crew, who fearlessly took to the decks to clear the damage and nail canvas and boards over the shattered windows. They labored under a drenching downpour that blocked out the sky and turned the sea into a boiling cauldron. Lawler's voice was lost in the howling wind, and he had to use hand motions to direct the crew to heave any wreckage overboard.

In the wheelhouse, May added his strength to that of the helmsman as they struggled to quarter *Charleston*'s bows into the wave crests before the steamboat dropped sickeningly into the troughs. "Help me bring her around," he ordered the helmsman. "We'll try and run her ashore."

"The waves will pound our broadside," helmsman Jacob Hill protested. "We'll never make it before being crushed to pieces."

"We'll sink if we don't!" May snapped.

Tall, broad-shouldered, with muscles raised for the task, Jacob Hill nodded in grim silence, murmured a short prayer, and took a new grip on the wheel spokes.

Slowly, too slowly, it seemed to Hill, the hull slewed broadside to the onslaught of the seas that smashed into the entire length of the helpless ship. She rolled on her beam ends until May could look out the side windows of the wheelhouse directly down into the menacing gray waters. *Charleston* was tossed like a helpless block of wood and buried repeatedly by the mountainous seas. After what seemed an eternity, the waves finally lifted, and dropped the stern as the great paddle wheels began churning with the current. She had incredibly survived the 180-degree turn without springing her timbers.

"Only God knows why," Captain May said, sighing, "but she's still sound as a dollar."

"She's a sweet-handling ship," muttered Hill. "I know of no other that could have done it."

At 569 tons, *Charleston* was a side-wheel steamer with a length of 201 feet and a 24-foot beam and was propelled by two walking-beam engines fired by two boilers and a smaller auxiliary. She was built in Philadelphia by the well-respected shipbuilding family of John Vaughan & Son in 1836. A fast ship for her day, she could make 16 knots.

Though *Charleston* was riding easier, the margin between life and death for her passengers and crew was still paper thin. Incredibly, the storm increased in its fury. The deck-houses were smashed in, as were the windows of the wheel-house. May and Hill found themselves fighting to keep the ship on a steady course while whipped and deluged by the driving rain.

Broken and confused, the waves surged up and under the sponsons, the wooden projections fitted under the guards of the paddle wheels and running the length of the hull, shoving the decks upward and allowing water to flood the ship's interior. All too quickly, the ship began to sink deeper in the twisting water.

Unable to spare any of his crew, Lawler beat on the doors of the cabins and ordered the male passengers to man the pumps and form a bucket brigade to bail out the water flowing into the cargo deck below. No man refused Lawler's demand. They kept at it for the next eighteen hours without rest, often helped by their wives, who insisted on lending a hand. Even the few children on board were pressed into service, to stuff rags and cotton around the sprung doors and windows of their cabins.

Just after twelve noon, the forward hatch cover was smashed in, and the water that poured in put out the fires of one of the two boilers. Thankful for the auxiliary boiler, Chief Engineer Leland stoked it to life. With the ship made nearly unmanageable by the mountainous seas, May ordered sails set in another attempt to run the battered *Charleston* ashore. But the vicious wind suddenly blew in from a new direction and tore the exposed canvas to shreds. For the moment it appeared that all hope was lost and the *Charleston* was going to the bottom, along with three other passenger ships that were pounded to pieces and sunk by the same tempest. But the contrary wind that dashed May's hope of grounding the ship in the safety of the shore began working in his favor, driving *Charleston* around Cape Lookout off the North Carolina coast and into more sheltered waters.

Once they were blown around the head of the cape, May ordered the anchors dropped. Now protected from the full fury of the wind and sea, the ship and her crew and passengers rode out the storm. The darkness came and passed. Though the danger of sinking had diminished, the night of torment never seemed to end. Gripped by her anchor chains, *Charleston* buried her bows into the violent and merciless waves. Dawn was a deliverance, but the exhausted crew and passengers, numbed by the cold and constantly soaked, never ceased bailing.

At the end of the second day, there was a noticeable easing of the wind and savage seas. The storm had veered northward. The rain fell off to a heavy drizzle and the swells flattened. A gull appeared and circled the steamboat, squawking as if surprised at seeing it still afloat.

Two hours later, Chief Engineer Leland informed Captain May that he had both boilers fired and enough steam to get under way. Now able to work his stove and oven, the boat's chef prepared the first meal the passengers and crew had eaten in nearly forty-eight hours. Wine and rum were poured by Captain May, and the crew and passengers toasted each other for their remarkable survival.

The next day, to the surprised stares of the town's citizens, who couldn't believe the sight, the battered and broken *Charleston* limped into the harbor at Beaufort, North Carolina. After temporary repairs, the steamboat triumphantly continued on to Charleston, where she was welcomed with cheers and a brass band.

*   *   *

"Well, we simply have to find the money," Republic of Texas President Mirabeau B. Lamar said forcefully in his office during the fall of 1838.

"We can try to raise more bonds," the state treasurer offered nervously.

"Just do it." Lamar paused. "If we cannot protect our shore, we cannot continue as a nation. With every ship of our original navy wrecked and sunk, we must replace them and build a new and better navy."

A light breeze blew the leaves of the oak trees outside his office in Austin and stirred the papers on his desk.

"Just do it," he repeated, before turning his attention to the problem of raids by the Comanches.

Somehow the money was raised, and in November of the same year Samuel Williams, the Texas commissioner to the United States, was dispatched to Baltimore. Standing on the deck of the *Charleston,* he quizzed the owner's agent.

"The engines?"

"Recently overhauled."

"The hull and fittings?"

"As you can see, the vessel is in excellent shape."

Williams stared at the agent. "How much?"

"Mr. Hamilton, the current owner, is asking only $145,000."

"Tell him the Republic of Texas will pay him $120,000."

The agent looked stunned. A spit-and-polish New Englander, he wasn't used to the candid ways of the wily Texans. "I doubt if Mr. Hamilton will consider such a low offer."

"One hundred twenty thousand firm, and I want her ready to sail next week."

"I'll submit your offer. That's all I can do."

Williams turned and walked down the gangway to the dock. Halfway, he turned and peered at the agent. "One more thing."

"Sir?"

"Get those damned pigeons off the rigging of *our* ship."

* * *

Renamed *Zavala,* in honor of Don Lorenzo de Zavala, the first Vice President of the Republic of Texas, the former *Charleston* had her deckhouses removed and replaced with an open gun deck, mounting four twelve-pounder medium cannon and one long nine-pounder. Her cargo holds were converted to crew's quarters. Predating any self-propelled vessels built by the U.S. Navy, *Zavala* had the distinction of becoming the first armed warship in North America.

The new commodore of the second Texas Navy, Edwin Ward Moore, sailed the *Zavala* to New Orleans to recruit new seamen. As a warship her complement became 126 men, three times the crew of the old *Charleston.* The pay was nothing to launch a bank. Marine privates were offered $7 a month, while experienced seamen drew $12. The higher grades drew more. A midshipman received $25 a month, boatswains $40, and lieutenants and surgeons an even $100.

Zavala was commissioned just in time. Trouble was afoot once again to the south. Mexico had proclaimed a blockade of Texas ports, and although the Mexican army was busy with a revolt in the Yucatán, the long-expected follow-up invasion of Texas after Sam Houston's decisive triumph over Santa Ana at San Jacinto was soon approaching.

President Lamar decided to assist the Yucatán rebels, who had revolted against Santa Ana, with his new fleet of warships and thereby draw the Mexican Navy away from the Texas coast. On June 24, 1840, the *Zavala,* accompanied by Commodore Moore's flagship, the sloop-of-war *Austin,* and three armed schooners, slipped out of Galveston Bay and turned south across the Gulf to the Bay of Campeche on the Yucatán peninsula.

Once they reached Mexican waters off Yucatán, Moore ordered his little fleet to begin regular patrols up and down the coastline. It soon appeared that President Lamar's plan to avert attack on Texas by sending his navy into enemy waters was working. Spies reported no immediate plans by the Mexican generals to send their armies north.

Zavala never fought a battle with an enemy ship during its service in the Bay of Campeche, but she proved indispensable for a daring expedition that Commodore Moore carried out in the fall of 1840. Under the command of Captain J. T. K. Lathrop, *Zavala* towed Moore's flagship, *Austin,* and the armed sloop *San Bernard* ninety miles up the San Juan Bautista River to the provincial capital of Tabasco, currently under the control of the Mexican government.

Anchoring his ships with their guns pointing into the city, Commodore Moore brazenly landed with a small shore party and walked into the main square. The small city was seemingly deserted.

Moore motioned to a seaman who spoke Spanish: "Shout that we want to see the town leaders."

The seaman nodded and yelled out the demand in Spanish. From inside a large brick building, a short, heavyset man with a red sash stretched across his broad stomach nervously stepped slowly into the street, holding a tree branch with a white strip of cotton tied to the top.

"Ask him who he is," Moore ordered.

The seaman questioned the man in Spanish. "He says he is the mayor. He also says the garrison troops have run away."

Moore smiled like a fox in an unguarded chicken coop. "Inform the mayor that unless he and his leading citizens hand over $25,000, we will level their city with our guns."

After the translation, there was no hesitation, no debate. The seaman glanced at Moore and laughed. "The mayor asks if it would be all right to pay in silver?"

Pleased that his gamble had paid off, Moore nodded. "Tell him that silver will be just fine."

That ransom paid the Texas sailors their wages and bought badly needed supplies for the always underbudgeted navy. In early February of 1841, the fleet returned to Galveston for repairs and provisions.

Before she saw Galveston again, *Zavala* very nearly became a drifting derelict.

On her way home, *Zavala* encountered a terrible storm that never seemed to end. For five days the sturdy steamboat fought her way through the heavy seas. With the deckhouses and passenger cabins removed when she became a warship, the sea surged over her now open gun deck without inflicting any damage. *Zavala* was no stranger to the savagery of turbulence. Her big paddle wheels stubbornly drove her on into the rampage.

"She can't take much more of this," the ship's first mate shouted to Captain Lathrop over the shriek of the wind.

Standing beside two helmsmen who struggled with the wheel, Lathrop shook his head. "She braved a blow worse than this in '37 when she ran between Philadelphia and Charleston. I heard tell ships sank all around her."

"She may be tough, but another five days of this weather and I'll bet my next promotion we'll all be walking on the bottom of the Gulf."

A fireman came up through a hatch from the engine room and approached Lathrop. "The chief engineer's compliments, sir, but he reports that we're down to our last ton of coal."

"Three hundred miles from home port." The first mate looked at Lathrop, apprehension in his eyes. "If we lose steam, it's all over."

Captain Lathrop stared thoughtfully at the deck for a few moments, the spray whipping into his beard. Then he looked up. "Please tell the chief engineer he has my permission to burn the ship's stores, bulkheads, and furniture. Whatever it takes to keep us under way."

Her interior gutted, *Zavala* survived the storm and arrived at Galveston four days later. When she crossed over the bar and headed toward her dock, her boilers barely produced enough steam for her paddle wheels to move her along at three knots.

After her one and only cruise as a warship, *Zavala* was laid up and allowed to deteriorate. Refusing to spend another dollar on the Texas Navy, newly elected President Sam Houston ignored pleas to save the finest vessel in the fleet. Unattended, she began to leak so badly that she was run aground to keep her from sinking. She was then stripped and abandoned. In time she became a rotting hulk at the upper end of the harbor's mud flats, settling deeper into the marsh until only the tops of her boilers and one of her two smokestacks remained in view.

By 1870, what was once the finest and most technically advanced ship in the Republic of Texas Navy had completely disappeared under the ooze and was forgotten.

II

Ship in a Parking Lot

November 1986

MY INVOLVEMENT WITH THE *ZAVALA* BEGAN INNOCENTLY enough when my wife, Barbara, and I visited NUMA president Wayne Gronquist, who has his law offices in Austin, Texas. During our stay, Wayne led me over to the capitol building and introduced me to then Governor White. After a short chat about lost shipwrecks, the governor presented me with a certificate signed by him, proclaiming me an admiral in the Texas Navy. I know I made some joke that I was probably admiral number 4,932. Then I really put my foot in my mouth when I said, "Now that I'm an admiral, the least I can do is to find myself a fleet of ships," never dreaming a Texas navy truly existed.

Like a great number of Texans, I was not aware that the Republic of Texas had put together a small navy, two as a matter of fact. The first navy was made up of four small warships, most of them sloops, that were destroyed by storms and enemy action between 1835 and 1837. The second navy, under the brilliant leadership of Commodore Edwin Moore and consisting of eight ships, lasted from 1838 until 1843.

The combined Texas navies left a remarkable historical legacy. The early ships harassed Santa Ana's supply line, capturing several merchant ships and sending their cargo of arms and supplies to General Sam Houston and greatly contributing to his victory at San Jacinto.

Despite their heroic and distinguished service, very little has been written about the exploits of the Texas warships. Only two books were written on the subject, many years ago, *Thunder on the Gulf* by C. L. Douglas and *The Texas Navy* by Jim Dan Hill. What few details have come to light since have appeared in articles of historic journals. As with most shipwrecks, their final graves were veiled and forgotten.

There is nothing worse than a cocky Clive Cussler. Masochistically hooked once again and compelled to uphold my pride, I called old pal Bob Fleming, my researcher in Washington, and launched plans to search for any Texan shipwrecks whose hulks might have somehow survived the ravages of time.

Of the twelve ships known to have served the Republic of Texas, all but three were either lost at sea, transferred to the U.S. Navy when Texas became a state and ultimately scrapped, or vanished from recorded history. The ships I concentrated on were the armed schooners *Invincible,* run aground in the Gulf after a battle with two Mexican warships; *Brutus,* wrecked in Galveston Bay after a hurricane; and *Zavala,* run ashore in the Galveston ship channel and abandoned.

Many extraordinary and friendly people in Galveston became swept up in the project and helped immeasurably. Adding to Fleming's research efforts, Kay Taylor-Hughes accomplished wonders by supplying local accounts of the ships. Mike Davis performed an outstanding job on *Brutus.* Bureaucratic red tape was cut by lovely Sylvia Jackson, Senator Chet Brooks, and Stan Weber. Wayne Gronquist coordinated the project, while Barto Arnold proved most helpful and cooperative.

Brutus was a schooner armed and commissioned in January of 1836. She was 180 feet in length with a 22-foot beam and carried a long 18-pounder swivel and nine short guns. In company with *Invincible,* she caused havoc with Mexican merchant ships along the Gulf Shore and Yucatán coast, capturing several prize ships. In her short career *Brutus* did her share to help Texas become independent.

In October of 1837, a tremendous gale swept the Texas coast, destroying a number of structures and wrecking a score of ships. *Brutus* was mentioned as being "considerably injured." Contemporary reports stated that she was left grounded near Williams Wharf.

After a survey of old records and a measure of the modern dock area off the city of Galveston, Mike Davis placed the *Brutus* at the foot of 24th Street and the end of Pier 23, under the Salvage Wharf Company warehouse 22–23, where her bones still lie today.

In the meantime, I concentrated on *Zavala.* She turned out to be a project that was fun and a challenge at the same time. I've always had a soft spot in my heart for her because she didn't make me sit on a survey boat, rolling in the waves, hearing the clack of the magnetometer and staring at dials and paper recorders for ten hours at a stretch.

The first clue that gave me a direction was a drawing that Fleming and Taylor-Hughes both turned up, portraying the capture of U.S.S. *Harriet Lane,* a Union war ship boarded by Confederates during the battle for Galveston during the Civil War. In the foreground of the pen-and-ink drawing, a triangular pier jutted into the harbor with several soldiers guarding a series of buildings perched above the pilings. The pier was labeled BEAN'S WHARF. In back of the structures, a black pipe protruded from the water. The artist identified this as the *Zavala.*

Now I had a ballpark.

In the Galveston Directory of 1856, we found the following information under the heading of "wharves."

Bean's Wharf—In rear of block 689 and opposite the "Shipper's Press," built the present year, by A. H. Bean and Nelson Clements, of New York, and con-

trolled by T. H. McMahan & Gilbert; has a front of
300 feet.

Any optimism that we were on the trail of the lost steamship was shot down by local historians, who believed that
Zavala sank outside the outer end of the pier in the channel
and was dredged out of existence many years ago. I couldn't
bring myself to write her off. I didn't read it that way. My
reasoning was based on the assumption that Bean would
never have built his wharf where the *Zavala*'s wreck could
hinder ships loading and unloading their cargo. It seemed
only logical that the wreck was either under or alongside
the old wharf pilings, certainly not outside in the channel.

Fortunately, I found the evolution of changes along the
channel was fairly easy to trace. Bean's Wharf was well
documented in old waterfront surveys from 1856 to 1871. It
began at the foot of 29th Street and extended 130 yards over
the water in an L shape, the outer docking area extending
west until it was adjacent to 30th Street. After I examined a
map of the waterfront from 1927, it became obvious that
years of landfill now buried the old wharfs that once traveled
over a broad marsh from shore. By overlaying the old maps
in chronological order a search grid was defined.

While the search team was assembling at Galveston, my
good friend and business partner Bob Esbenson, who became a character in my books and was described as a big
pixie with limpid blue eyes, and I drove to the site and
checked it out. My prime worry was that a structure of some
kind sat over the wreck. Warehouses, grain elevators, and
huge concrete dock facilities run continuously for two miles
along the channel. Incredibly, the site where Bean's Wharf
once stood was free of construction.

Our search grid was open because in 1971 a nearby grain
elevator exploded, killing nearly thirty people. A warehouse
over Bean's Wharf had been destroyed and the debris removed down to the dirt. It was now a parking lot for the
rebuilt grain elevator's workers.

I climbed to the top of the grain elevator and visually
lined up the streets shown on the old maps. Most of the

former thoroughfares that once crisscrossed the old dock area were now little more than weed-overgrown alleys. Far below, Bob Esbenson stood in the parking lot and moved about according to my shouted directions. Finally, when I was satisfied he was standing approximately where I thought *Zavala*'s remains were buried, he marked the spot.

The next step was a mag survey with the Schonstedt gradiometer. One very large target was recorded several feet under the dirt. Then I hired a well digger to core through the landfill. It was cold and rainy and miserable, but everyone stuck it out through the afternoon and long into the night. Each core was pulled out of the ground and studied for its contents.

On one of the first attempts the drill bit struck something hard and refused to penetrate. I hoped that we had struck *Zavala*'s boilers, but without a core there was no way of knowing for certain. We moved out and cored in three-foot grids, bringing up samples of wood, which could have been a ship or pieces from old pilings of Bean's Wharf. Small lumps of coal also appeared that indicated a bunker from a steamship. Other bits of debris surfaced that were too vague to identify positively with a ship.

Then, on the thirty-sixth attempt, we broke open the core and found seventeen inches of solid wood capped on the bottom by a copper plate. We had drilled through the keel of a ship and exited through the copper sheathing that was attached to the hull to prevent damage from worms and incrustation. But had we truly found the bones of *Zavala?*

With Barto Arnold's permission, Esbenson rented a backhoe and we began to dig. At twelve feet the scoop unearthed the twin boilers of a steamship. Additional excavation uncovered a side of the hull. The *Zavala* had been found.

Photographs were taken and a troop of boy scouts were lowered in the scoop inside the excavation so they could stand on the boilers, the first to do so in almost 150 years. Barto Arnold declared it a historic site, and the grave was re-covered.

Later, when Bob Esbenson was being interviewed by a

reporter from the Galveston newspaper, he was asked how I determined where the *Zavala* lay.

"Clive stood on top of the grain elevator and yelled down for me to move here, move there, until I was standing next to a 1967 yellow Mercury."

"Is that where you found the *Zavala?*" inquired the reporter.

"No, Clive missed it."

The reporter looked up from his notepad. "Are you saying he put you in the wrong place?"

Esbenson nodded sardonically. "Yeah, he had me standing a good ten feet off the center of the wreck."

The reporter stared at Esbenson, not certain if he had been conned, and ended the interview.

I wish I could miss them all by only ten feet.

During the following year, I commissioned Fred Tournier to build a pair of matching 1/8th-inch-to-the-foot models of the *Zavala*. Fred is a marvelous craftsman and the gentleman who built the dozen or more models of our shipwreck discoveries that I display in my office. One I kept, the other I donated to the State of Texas one memorable afternoon in the governor's office at the state capitol in Austin.

Craig Dirgo, good friend and longtime NUMA associate, arranged for the model to fly in the pilot's cockpit on our flight from Denver to Austin. I might add that the model was in a rather large glass case. Very carefully transporting it to the state capitol building in a cab and carrying it through the lobby and up an elevator, then around the rotunda to the governor's office left us flowing in perspiration. We were a few minutes late and a corps of newsmen were questioning the governor on some new legislative proceedings, really fascinating stuff.

As they left, I tried to get them interested in the *Zavala* and the Texas Navy. They scratched themselves and yawned when I told them that here was a symbol of a ship that represented and fought for the Republic of Texas, the only historical shipwreck at that time still accessible. They all looked at me as if I were trying to sell mineral water to a drunk. The newspeople simply have no grasp of history.

I was finally ushered into Governor Bill Clement's office, along with Wayne Gronquist and Barto Arnold, the very astute chief of the Texas Historical Commission. After Wayne made the introductions and presented the model, the governor looked at me and asked, "Did you build it?"

Politicians are not my favorite people. I always take great pride in marking No on my IRS return where it asks if I would donate a dollar to my favorite party. I recall voting in an election when I couldn't stand any of the candidates. So I wrote in John Dillinger, Baby Face Nelson, Pretty Boy Floyd, and Ma Barker for the nation's highest offices.

After I spent hundreds of hours researching the Texas Navy, standing all night in the rain coring for the *Zavala* in a muddy parking lot, and spending thousands of dollars for the actual project, the governor thought I was only some schmoe who built the model?

Maybe I didn't build it, but I paid Fred several thousand dollars so NUMA could present it to the people of Texas. Reduced to tears, I stood there in my sweat-stained Brooks Brothers suit, spurned by the news media, wondering why I get less respect than Rodney Dangerfield.

The governor didn't quite receive the answer he expected. I turned to Gronquist and Arnold and muttered, "That's it, I'm out of here."

And I walked out.

Poor Wayne Gronquist and Barto Arnold were embarrassed. The governor just shrugged and smiled and said, "I guess he's in a hurry to build another model."

Regretfully, the day may never come when Texas naval heroes such as Moore, Hurd, and Hawkins are as familiar as Travis, Bowie, and Fannin. But because it is so accessible, I fervently hope that the *Zavala* will someday be fully surveyed and preserved for public display as she lies. Perhaps what is left of her hull and machinery can point the way to a replica that can be built as she once was when she was the pride of the Texas fleet.

Now we turned our attention to the *Invincible,* which had run aground in the Gulf outside of Galveston in 1837 and was broken up by pounding surf. She proved to be the most elusive of the three, and we haven't identified her remains yet.

Part 3

U.S.S. *Cumberland* and C.S.S. *Florida*

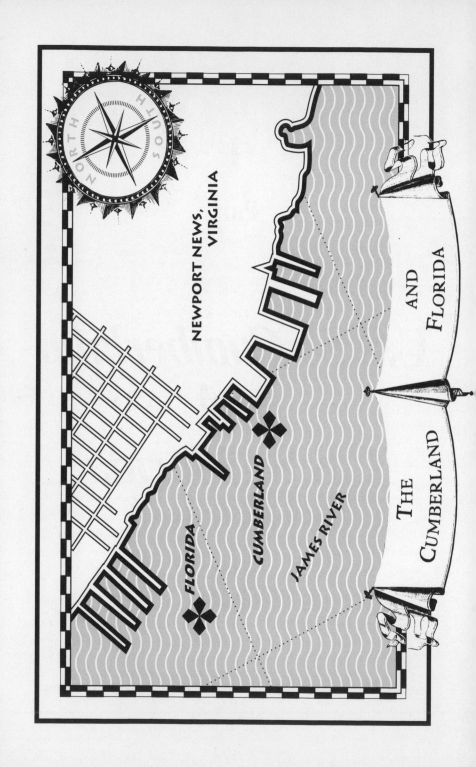

I

Her Flag Still Flying

March 8, 1862

SHE MOVED LIKE A MONSTER FROM THE DEPTHS OF A FOR-gotten Mesozoic sea. The bulk of her hull was concealed beneath the dark water, while her massive hump, with its iron-gray scales, rose into a morning haze, repugnant and repulsive. Her metamorphosis from a burned and sunken hulk into the world's most advanced murder machine had taken only ten months. When completed, no vessel in history looked as ominous and menacing. No warship in the world was thought to have the capability of sinking her. She was considered invincible.

Originally commissioned in the United States Navy as the steam-screw frigate *Merrimack,* she had been rebuilt by the Confederate engineers after their military forces captured the Norfolk Navy Yard from the Union Navy. Renamed C.S.S. *Virginia,* and captained by Franklin Buchanan, a crusty old navy man in his early sixties, who had been the first superintendent of the Naval Academy at Annapolis, the ironclad steamed toward its date with destiny.

* * *

The Union fleet of warships swung lazily on their anchors with the incoming tide that surged into the bay called Hampton Roads. Except for a low haze that hung over the water, the day had dawned cloud-free and blue. Blockading the mouth of the James River off the town of Newport News, Virginia, were the Union twenty-four-gun sloop-of-war *Cumberland* and the frigate *Congress,* mounting fifty-four guns. Three miles around the Newport News point were three of the Union Navy's mightiest warships, the huge steam frigates *Minnesota* and *Roanoke,* each mounting forty-four heavy guns, and *Cumberland*'s sister ship, *St. Lawrence.* Five ships that could have defeated almost any fleet in the world.

Cumberland was once the pride of the U.S. Navy. Built at the Boston Navy Yard in 1842, she had served as the flagship for both the Mediterranean and African squadrons. She was a ship artists loved to paint. With her raked masts and full set of white square sails set against a curtain of blue, her dark hull knifing silently through green seas, she was the last of her design. In two decades, fighting wooden ships would be replaced by drab vessels of iron and, eventually, steel.

Once mounting fifty-four guns, she had been modernized, razeed they called it then, by having her lower gun deck eliminated and her old weaponry replaced by fewer guns far more powerful. She mounted two ten-inch Dahlgren pivot guns fore and aft, twenty-two nine-inch new-model Dahlgrens on her broadside batteries, and one of the mightiest cannons built, a seventy-pound rifled gun. For a wooden fighting ship, she was as formidable as they came. But without engines she was an anachronism, an instrument of war beyond her time.

On board *Cumberland,* her crew were hanging out laundry and finishing their noonday meal in the galley. Shore boats rocked gently against the massive black hull near the ladder leading to the open gun deck. The crewmen with afternoon and evening shore leave pushed off for town, not knowing how lucky they were to be leaving the ship. The captain, Commander William Radford, had been ordered to preside over a court-martial near Fortress Monroe, and before the light of dawn had set off on his horse for the ten-mile ride.

Several sailors not yet picked for liberty were clustered on the aft deck. One of them was blowing a tune on his harmonica as a short, heavily bearded Irish gunner's mate danced a jig beside a thickly coiled hawser. The Irishman was happy with the thought that he would soon be able to drink in a local saloon and perhaps find a girl.

The weekly laundry, strung from the rigging to dry, gently waved in the light spring breeze. A young seaman, still in his teens, sat on the deck and scribed a letter to his loved ones at home. Finished, he sealed the flap with a dab of wax and placed the envelope in the pocket of his jacket.

On shore, soldiers from an Indiana infantry regiment and a battery of artillery were watching a wrestling match between the champions of two companies. Because of the unseasonably warm temperatures, a group of the soldiers were wading in the river close to the rocky beach. The few who knew how to swim paddled into the deeper water and taunted those who remained in the shallows.

Lying calmly, like a proud elk in the sights of a hunter's gun, *Cumberland* was blissfully unaware of the menace steaming toward her from across the bay. Her crew could not imagine the hell they were about to face, did not foresee how many would be maimed and killed in the next hour. Wood was about to collide with iron and the results would be catastrophic. Naval warfare was never the same again.

Under full steam, black smoke trailing from her single stack, the *Virginia* steamed down the Elizabeth River and headed into the waters of Hampton Roads. Sluggish as an overloaded barge, ugly as a tin bathtub turned upside down, she had suddenly become the pride of the Confederacy. The local civilians and soldiers, who had watched her being built and expressed great skepticism as to her potential, now crowded both sides of the river and gave her a rousing send-off. A crewman raised the Confederate flag of 1862 with its two horizontal red stripes separated by a white stripe, with thirteen stars in a blue field. Their cheers were accompanied by gun salutes from Confederate batteries guarding the mouth of the river.

The armament of the converted *Merrimack* consisted of a deadly assortment of old worn cannon that were hastily converted into more powerful rifled guns, numbering ten in all. There was no maiden voyage; there were no trials to train the crew or test the machinery. Old Buck Buchanan was an impatient man. With a makeshift vessel, knocked together with unskilled labor and a crew who had never set foot on board a naval vessel before, much less fought on one, Buchanan ordered the *Virginia* into battle while a gang of workmen still labored to finish her.

Unable to gather an experienced naval crew, Buchanan recruited 320 volunteers from infantry and artillery troops stationed at Richmond. So desperate was Buchanan for good men he accepted the services of Colonel J. T. Wood of the Confederate Army to come on board as an acting naval lieutenant.

As the ship moved ponderously toward the enemy, Buchanan assembled his crew and gave them a fiery pep talk. He ended his speech with the words "You shall not complain that I do not take you close enough [to the enemy]. Now go to your guns."

Lieutenant George Morris, *Cumberland*'s executive officer and acting captain during Radford's absence, stood next to Lieutenant Thomas O. Selfridge, Jr., and pointed to a column of smoke far in the distance.

"What do you make of it, Tom?"

Selfridge stared through a pair of binoculars. "That layer of haze over the water gives it the appearance of a mirage. I can't tell whether it's under way or motionless."

Morris laid a telescope on a railing to steady it and peered into the distance. "Looks to me like it's moving this way."

The two Union officers watched in silence for the next few minutes until the column of smoke loomed from the haze and revealed itself as spewing from a tall stack that protruded from the middle of a huge slope-sided vessel that plowed unswervingly across the water directly at *Cumberland* and *Congress*. Everyone in the Union Navy had known that their former ship had been raised and rebuilt and covered with a shield of iron. They had expected her to put in an appearance, but not so soon.

"It's the *Merrimack*," said Morris quietly. "She's coming out."

Selfridge stared through his binoculars at their approaching nemesis. "She's making for us and *Congress*."

"We're going to have a fight this day."

"Shall I pass the word to the other officers?"

Morris nodded solemnly. "And give the order for the drummers to beat to quarters."

The crew's wash was hurriedly pulled down, the sails spread for drying were furled, and the shore boats were rowed into the shallows away from the ship. Sand was spread over the gun deck to absorb the blood that was sure to flow. *Cumberland*'s guns were run out, loaded, and primed. A strange quiet fell over the ship as every man's eyes followed the progress of the iron beast moving inexorably toward them, estimating its speed and counting its gunports.

What they could not see beneath the water was the ten-thousand-pound cast-iron ram that was mounted to *Virginia*'s bow like the beak on a gigantic gargoyle.

"We'll ignore the steam frigates for now," said Buchanan to his second in command, Lieutenant Catesby Jones, "and concentrate on *Cumberland* and *Congress*."

Jones, about forty years old, stared at old Buck. "Isn't your brother on one of those ships?"

Buchanan nodded gravely, "McKean is paymaster on *Congress*."

"Which ship do you wish to attack first?" Jones asked.

"*Cumberland*. She has a seventy-pound rifled gun. I want to see what she can do against our armor."

Apprehension reflected in Jones's eyes. "A pity we didn't have a seventy-pounder of our own to test during construction."

Buchanan forced a tight smile. "We'll soon know how she stands up, won't we?"

Fifteen minutes later, *Congress* was the first to fire, unleashing an entire broadside, which bounced off the casemate of *Virginia,* as one Union sailor described it, "like hail off a tin roof." Then *Cumberland*'s batteries opened up in unison with the army's artillery on shore. Observers wondered at the smoke that erupted when a shell struck the Confederate armored casemate, ricocheted into the sky, and fell on the opposite side of the river. What they saw was the frying and sizzling of the animal fat Buchanan had ordered smeared on the sides of the ironclad's casemate to deflect Union shells. What he didn't count on was the sickening stench that was carried through the gunports and upper vents, washing over the crew like an evil wind.

The only damage sustained in the opening stage of the battle came from a shell of *Cumberland* that shattered *Virginia*'s anchor chain and drove it back through a gunport, killing one man and wounding several others.

The ironclad had the advantage. Because the Union warship was riding at anchor with the incoming tide and *Virginia* was approaching bow on, *Cumberland*'s gunners could not bring their broadside guns to bear. Reserving her fire until within easy range, *Virginia*'s forward seven-inch rifled gun was run out through the casemate and blasted away. The shot pounded through *Cumberland*'s side, bursting on the gun deck in a cloud of wooden splinters that killed and wounded a dozen marines. A fast reload and the gun's second round burst amid the crew of the forward ten-inch pivot gun, killing them all except the powder boy and horribly wounding gun captain John Kirker, who had both arms taken off at the shoulders.

As he was being carried below to the berth deck, where the ship's surgeon was already operating on the wounded marines, Kirker shouted, his arterial blood spurting from his shoulders, "Give 'em fits, boys, give 'em fits!"

Lieutenant Morris stood in the rigging, directing the battle, watching the destruction of his ship with helpless frustration as the *Virginia* plowed relentlessly ever closer to *Cumberland*. Then, unexpectedly, the ironclad swung around in a wide clumsy turn and pointed her bow at *Cumberland*'s starboard side. Only at that moment did Morris realize the iron beast meant to ram him.

"Steer straight for her and don't turn as much as one degree," Buchanan shouted above the gunfire to his pilot. "Strike her square abeam her forward mast."

"Wherever you say, sir," the pilot acknowledged.

A thick cloud of dusty black smoke poured from *Virginia*'s big stack as she closed the distance at a ninety-degree angle toward the doomed Union ship. Moving at her maximum speed of 5½ knots, like a giant fist punching through water, she broke past an outer layer of logs, erected around the hull of *Cumberland* as protection against just such an event. Her irresistible mass split the logs like toothpicks, and she crossed the remaining few yards to her target in seconds.

After the war, when Buchanan reminisced about the battle, he recalled that the most inspired order he ever gave in his long naval career came when he shouted down to the engine room half a minute before the impact. "Reverse engines!"

The big propellers stopped, reversed and bit in the river, as the massive ram, thrust by nearly a thousand tons of mass, crushed through *Cumberland*'s hull deep below the waterline just aft of the forward mast and below the berth deck, driving in timbers and opening a hole that some said later, "a horse and carriage could have driven through."

At the same time, the deadly bow guns of *Virginia* belched fire and shot directly through the side of the mortally wounded frigate, killing ten men belowdecks. The masts of *Cumberland* swayed back and forth like pendulums as water gushed inside the stricken ship. For nearly a minute the two ships were tightly locked together, the *Virginia* unable to break free from the frigate's grasp. *Cumberland*'s bow began to sink lower into the water. For a moment it looked as though the wooden frigate were going to drag the ironclad to the bottom with her. If Buchanan had not ordered his engines reversed before the collision, the *Virginia* would have surely embedded her bow more deeply in a death grip and gone down.

Fortunately for Buchanan and his crew, the immense ram was ripped from its mountings while held fast inside *Cumberland,* and the ironclad broke free. Then *Virginia* pivoted until the ships were side by side. The mauled crew of the frigate found sudden encouragement now that they could train all the broadside guns on their venomous adversary. The gunners got off three broadsides that shattered the muzzles on two of *Virginia*'s guns, smashed her smokestack, tore away her anchors and blew all but one of her lifeboats to splinters. Their fire was well aimed and deliberate, but an exercise in futility. Even at point-blank range, *Cumberland*'s fire caused little if any serious damage to her enemy.

On board the rapidly flooding ship was a scene of macabre horror. The gun deck was awash with the blood, entrails, and limbs of the decimated crew. There were so many dead scattered among the guns the living worked feverishly to pile them in heaps on the opposite side of the deck out of the way. The wounded, carried below to the berth deck to await medical attention, were powerless to save themselves as the water crept up from below and through the open hatches.

A gravely injured seaman named Winston Humbolt was waiting to be tended by a surgeon. His good friend and shipmate, Tom Lasser, who had had a wounded hand treated and was returning to the fight, stopped by to offer a few words of encouragement.

"Tom, are you going to leave me?" Humbolt whispered.

Lasser cradled his friend's head in his lap. "No, Winny, I won't leave you."

Lieutenant Morris was standing on the main deck as a final shot from the ironclad scored a direct hit on the stern gun crew nearby. The gun crew seemed to dissolve from the blast. Morris was struck dumb with shock. He stood frozen, splattered with gore and small bits of human remains, too dazed to move. The bile rose in his throat as he saw badly maimed gunner Karl Hunt, his legs shot off below the knees, crawl over to his gun and pull the lanyard for the last time, sending a shot against the ironclad that exploded in its smokestack.

Selfridge, seeing the horror, rushed over, and helped seat Morris on a hatch behind the mainmast. "Stay with us, George. We need you."

Morris grasped Selfridge by the arm. "I'll be all right in another minute. See to the guns."

He suddenly came unsteadily to his feet and pushed Selfridge aside when he recognized a voice calling to him through the roar of the guns to surrender. He staggered to a railing and gazed down at the ironclad only a few yards away. From a hatch in the upper deck of the casemate, Buchanan repeated his demand. "Surrender your ship!"

"Never!" Morris yelled back defiantly. "I'll sink alongside first."

His reply was punctuated by a shell from one of *Cumberland*'s nine-inch Dahlgrens.

Like a struggling scorpion that refused to die, the few operational guns on *Cumberland* kept firing away at the invulnerable *Virginia*. The forward slant of the deck caused one of the huge rifled guns to break loose from its moorings. Lieutenant Selfridge watched in quiet abhorrence as the cannon careered down the sloping deck, crushing a young sailor. His agonized scream was choked off as he was pushed by the gun through a railing into the river. His lifeless body rose to the surface, floating face down, a human marker to the devastation.

The guns were fired by their maddened crews until water came up the muzzles. The final shot of the dying warship was fired by seventeen-year-old Matthew Tenney as the river flowed around his knees. After his shell entered an open port of the *Virginia* and shattered the barrel of a gun run out to fire, Tenney attempted to scramble out through his own gunport. But the surge swept him back and he was never seen again.

Only when the bow went under did Morris give the order, "Abandon ship! Those who can, help the wounded over the side."

"The flag, sir?" a seaman asked Morris.

He looked up at the stars-and-stripes fluttering in the sun. "Leave it there for all to see." Then he turned and helped a badly wounded man over a shattered bulwark.

The rotund young drummer boy named Joselyn fearlessly remained at his station, beating the call to arms throughout the fight. Only now did he shove his drumsticks into his belt and leap into the water. Using his drum as a float, he began to dog-paddle toward the shore.

The ship rolled to port and slipped down into the river. Below, on the flooding berth deck, the cries of the wounded were quickly snuffed out. Tom Lasser, still holding his friend's head in his lap, closed his eyes and accepted the inevitable. He and Winston Humbolt drowned together.

Battered, beaten, but game to the bitter end, *Cumberland*'s keel sank into the muddy bottom of the James River, her masts still above water, her flag still flying, her fight forever over.

To a man, the crew of the *Virginia* agreed, "No ship was ever fought more gallantly."

Of the 326 men on board *Cumberland* at the start of the fight, 120 were dead.

Hearing the sounds of gunfire during the court-martial, the captain of the ill-fated ship, William Radford, left the proceedings, leapt on his horse, and rode the ten miles back to his ship like an army of ghosts were after him. Reaching the low cliffs above the James River, Radford dismounted his horse, which was frothing at the mouth and coated in a foam of sweat.

He stared in horror at the men struggling and drowning in the water. Nothing was left of his once proud ship except the masts rising from the water. He noted with no small degree of satisfaction that her flag was still flying.

Behind him, his horse wobbled unsteadily on rubber legs and began shaking like a leaf in a stiff breeze. Then the horse dropped to the ground, its tongue falling from its open mouth and its eyes becoming glazed, exhausted to the point of death by a wild ride that came too late.

Battered though his ship may have been after conquering *Cumberland,* Old Buck Buchanan and *Virginia* still had more than enough fight left in them. They now turned their attention to the next ship in line.

In a vain attempt to reach water too shallow for the iron-clad to follow, *Congress* ran toward shore and grounded, her stern facing the middle of the river. Buchanan merely stationed his impregnable ship a short distance away and hammered away at the helpless frigate until her captain was dead and his second in command raised the white flag and surrendered.

Buchanan lowered his only boat that would float and sent an officer to receive the surrender. But the crusty old commander of the troops and artillery ashore allowed that the ship may have surrendered, but he hadn't, and ordered his men to keep up their fire.

Standing with his officers on the casemate deck for a better view, Buchanan was seriously wounded, as were several other men near him, when he was struck by a rifle ball in the thigh. As he was carried below, angered that the shore troops had ignored the white flag of surrender from *Congress,* he ordered Lieutenant Catesby Jones to destroy the Union frigate.

"Burn the ship, burn her down to nothing!" he growled through the pain from his wound.

Jones took him at his word and shouted down to the gun deck. "Fire hot shot!"

The iron cannon shells were placed on grates above a furnace and heated until they were almost red hot. Rolled into buckets and carried to the guns, they were rammed down the muzzles and shot into the helpless frigate. Within minutes, *Congress* was blazing from stem to stern.

Through a gunport, Jones watched the conflagration with great satisfaction. The fire had reached the dying ship's guns, and they were discharging on their own, one by one, as if directed by the ghosts of their crew.

Nothing went right for the Union fleet that day. Raising her sails to go to the aid of her stricken sister ships, *St. Lawrence* ran aground. The mighty *Minnesota* suffered the same embarrassment. In an attempt to join in the battle, she too became firmly entrenched in the mud. And to add insult to injury, *Roanoke* lay impotent with a severed propeller shaft.

The final three ships of the Union fleet lay like tethered sheep, waiting for the appearance of a tiger.

Jones approached Buchanan, who was having his leg bandaged by the ship's surgeon. "Do I have your permission to resume battle, sir?"

Buchanan stared at the bandage around his thigh, which was already turning red. "I'm told *Minnesota* and *St. Lawrence* have run aground."

Jones nodded. "They appear to be stationary. Particularly *Roanoke*. Our spies report she has a broken shaft."

Buchanan stared through the door of his cabin at the light coming in through an overhead hatch. "It will be too dark to see in another half hour. I think it best we break off all action and head back to the dock. *Cumberland* put up a good fight and caused damage that requires repair before we attack again."

"I agree," said Jones. "They'll still be at our mercy tomorrow. We can finish them off then."

"Yes," said old Buck Buchanan, a foxlike grin on his face. "Tomorrow is soon enough."

Jones returned to the helm and directed the pilot to come about for Norfolk. Turning its stern on a scene of destruction never before witnessed in American waters, *Virginia* began steaming across Hampton Roads to her dock. Behind, she left some 250 Union sailors dead and over 100 wounded, at that time the largest single loss in United States Navy history.

Just after sunset, the fire aboard *Congress* reached her powder magazine, and she exploded in a fiery burst of fireworks before joining *Cumberland* on the bottom of the James River. Buchanan and Jones knew they had won a great victory, and looked forward to an even greater one the following morning. They had accomplished the unthinkable with a loss of only two men killed and eight wounded.

But unknown to them, their ultimate triumph was to be snatched away.

Before the black smoke from the *Virginia*'s shot-riddled stack drifted over the rays of the setting sun, and the final blast from the death throes of *Congress* rumbled across the dark water of Hampton Roads, a strange, ominous vessel materialized out of the mists creeping in from Chesapeake Bay.

In what has to be the most incredible coincidence in recorded history, the Union ironclad *Monitor* had arrived. On the following morning, the crew of *Virginia,* still called *Merrimack* in the North, were ready for another day's glory. They were stunned when what one of them called a "cheese box on a raft" steamed into view from behind the hull of *Minnesota.* The little Union ironclad made straight for the Confederate behemoth and fired her two big eleven-inch Dahlgren guns. *Virginia* replied, and the world's first battle between armored ships was launched. A few hours later, it ended in a stalemate. Neither ship absorbed much punishment and both claimed victory. History had been made and naval warfare was never to be the same again.

Barely two weeks after the epic battles of Hampton Roads, a salvage diver by the name of Loring Bates investigated the remains of *Cumberland* to discover if she could be raised and rebuilt. He found the wreck lying in sixty-six feet of water at a forty-five-degree angle and in complete disarray. He determined that she was too badly damaged to warrant the expense of raising her.

Sporadic attempts by salvors to recover supplies and

equipment of value and fights over who had the legitimate salvage contracts continued until the late 1870s. Despite the glory of her fight and the heroism of her crew, *Cumberland* and her grave in time became lost, unknown, and forgotten. It was not until 1980 that men came to find her bones.

II

She-Devil of the Confederacy

November 28, 1864

THE EVENING WAS CLEAR, WITH A FULL MOON, AND THE ship cast a spectral shadow over the water. One year and seven months had passed since *Cumberland* went down fighting only a few hundred yards downriver just off the town of Newport News, Virginia. The small crew of eight seamen who were guarding the ship did not expect trouble, and most of them were asleep. Only two assistant engineers, attempting to repair an auxiliary pump, were still awake. An army transport ship had accidentally sideswiped the moored vessel, the resulting collision loosing hull planks and causing minor leakage.

Shortly after midnight, a lone man rowed toward the ship from shore. He stared up at the black hull looming above him. Quietly riding into town, he had left his horse tied to a tree along the shore and "borrowed" a rowboat. No soldiers stationed nearby or civilian residents could witness the act he was about to perform. Climbing up the boarding ladder, a leather bag clutched in one hand, he moved like a wraith across the deserted deck of the ship. The guns did not seem ominous and menacing in the eerie moonlight, but looked like great dead beasts.

He stepped into the captain's cabin and admired the handsome mahogany doors and bulkheads. Then he walked through the wardroom and past the dispensary before dropping into the engine room. He saw the engineers laboring over the faulty pump and avoided them by moving around the backside of one of the big boilers. The intruder was an engineer and appreciated the ship's machinery. Running his hands over the brass gauges, he stared at the cold boilers.

"You're a beautiful ship," he said aloud, the soft-spoken words out of place on the silent vessel. "Forgive me for what I am about to do."

Heavy of heart, he opened the bag and retrieved a large wrench. Using it as a lever, he twisted the plugs from the valves that allowed the water to gush into the bilge. When he had removed the last plug, he dutifully waited until the water was gurgling and rising from the bilges. He listened as the ship creaked and groaned, her timbers flexing from the increasing internal weight. It was as if she were pleading with the engineer to save her.

The engineer closed his mind to the eerie sounds and struggled up the ladder to the engine-room hatch aft of the big seven-inch pivot gun. As he hurried across the deck to the boarding ladder, he deeply regretted his clandestine mission of sending the beautiful little ship to the bottom, but orders were orders.

Dropping down the ladder to his boat, he cast off and quickly rowed toward shore. After shoving the boat into the river, he watched it vanish with the current. Then he walked to his horse, untied it from the tree, and rode off without a backward glance.

Alarmed at the sudden increase of water in the engine room, the men who had been repairing the auxiliary pump awakened the chief engineer, William Lannan. After checking the rising water, he was stunned at the dramatic flow. Every effort was made to halt what appeared to be the ship's imminent sinking, but the water rose faster than it could be expelled.

A tug was called to tow the ship into shallow water, but it arrived too late. By 7 A.M. she was plunging down, her masts and yards clawing futilely at the sky. Her death song came as the air inside compressed from the pressure of the incoming water and hissed from the ports and hatches. Her hull vanished under a cloud of protesting bubbles. Then her keel sank into the soft bottom and the murky water became her death shroud.

History's first great raider of the seas was no more. She settled into the soft ooze to wait out time.

Two and a half years earlier, on March 22, 1862, Thomas Dudley, United States consul at Liverpool, England, stood on a seawall and watched as *Oreto* put out to sea. He wiped the lens of his spyglass with a handkerchief and peered at the ship through the drizzle of a March storm blowing from the north. He was always on the lookout for vessels built by British shipyards and then clandestinely sold to the Confederate States of America despite maritime law that banned the outfitting of warships for belligerent foreign nations.

Oreto was a beautiful vessel, allegedly built for the Italian Navy. With her sharply raked masts and twin smokestacks, she appeared to be moving while she was standing still. Designed as a fast cruiser, she incorporated several innovations. One was her screw propeller, which could be raised out of the water on a track to reduce water resistance when she was under sail to conserve coal. She seemed deceptively small for a Confederate raider, Dudley thought. Her overall length was just 212 feet with a 27-foot beam.

As he admired her lines, he decided that *Oreto* was too beautiful to be dangerous. He failed to picture her as one of the Southern States' most successful raiders.

Dudley watched as one of the harbor pilot boats pulled away from the hull of the ship as she slipped farther into the bay. "Appears to be only a trial run," he said to his aide, standing miserably in the heavy mist beside him. "Her captain, James Duguid, is British, with no ties to the Confederacy that I know of."

The aide, a skinny fellow barely in his twenties, pointed to the several women milling about on the deck. "The ladies are most certainly not in the Confederate Navy."

"The ship looks harmless enough," said Dudley. "But just the same, we'll keep a sharp eye on her when she returns to her dock."

"I'll be glad to take up that duty," the aide said, eying a nearby pub where he could escape the damp and warm up with a bit of whiskey.

Dudley stared at the retreating ship, then motioned to his aide. "Let's get back to the consulate. I want to make a report to our London Embassy."

Disappointed, the aide shrugged. "As you wish, sir."

Looking like a sleek thoroughbred of the sea, with barely a wisp of smoke trailing from her twin stacks, *Oreto* steamed past the buoys at the harbor entrance and increased her speed, heading on a course due west of Liverpool. Once land vanished in the heavy mist, Captain Duguid ordered the vessel stopped.

"The pilot boat is coming alongside," he said to his first officer. "Help the ladies across."

Walking to the lowered boarding ladder, he handed each of the women a five-guinea gold piece. "Thank you for your company, ladies," he said graciously. "I'm sorry to see you go."

A buxom lass with a dark beauty mark on her cheek flashed a wide smile at Duguid. "That's the easiest money any of us have made all year," she purred. "You look me up next time you're in Liverpool."

Duguid gallantly kissed her hand. "You can count on it."

He stood back and observed the transfer of the women to the pilot boat. He doffed his hat as the boat pulled away from *Oreto* and the women waved. Then he nodded to his helmsman. "Steer on a heading south by southwest until I can lay a proper course." Then Duguid turned to his first officer. "Raise the screw and hoist the sails. We have a long voyage before us."

* * *

One month later, Duguid and *Oreto* arrived in the port of Nassau in the Bahamas. He no sooner dropped anchor than the ship was shrouded in controversy. The United States consul had immediately filed a protest to the British authorities. He claimed that *Oreto* was being armed in British waters and demanded she be seized. The British, who were pro-Confederate, shrugged, and replied that the ship had no guns, nor was there any evidence that anyone planned to load them on board.

A stiff island breeze blew the curtains away from the window in the office of the governor of the Bahamas, C. J. Bayley. The simple whitewashed room was furnished with a large, copper-sheathed teak desk. Twin, stiff-backed wooden chairs, one occupied by a lean, hatchet-faced man, were positioned in front of the desk.

Samuel Whiting, United States consul at Nassau, was pleading his case. "The *Oreto* is a gunboat, pure and simple."

Bayley sipped at his china cup of pekoe tea. "Any ship with a cannon can be called a gunboat. We have no evidence the ship is armed."

"You know that she secretly belongs to the Confederacy," Whiting said angrily.

"I know of no such thing, sir," Bayley replied, his face reddening. "Furthermore, my office has not received word from London on any such assumption." The governor rose from behind his desk. "Now, if you will excuse me, I have a cricket match to attend."

Frustrated by Bayley's obvious prejudice toward the Confederacy, Whiting stormed from the room.

Not every Englishman sided with Jefferson Davis and Richmond. Suspecting skulduggery, a pro-Union commander in the British Navy seized the *Oreto*. But the governor pointed out that she was registered as a British ship and flew the Cross of Saint George. He gave orders for her immediate release. Charges and countercharges flew back and forth. The ship was seized again, and just as quickly released. A trial was held, giving United States agents another crack at condemning *Oreto*.

Feigning innocence, Captain Duguid testified that he knew of nothing irregular about the vessel. He agreed that she might make a perfect warship, but that without guns he saw her only as an ordinary merchant ship. The trial judge was satisfied and *Oreto* was released once again.

Quietly, Captain Duguid turned the ship over to John Maffitt, a dashing and successful Confederate blockade runner. Mission accomplished, Duguid caught the first steamer bound for England.

John Newland Maffitt was the son of a sailor, born at sea. Entering the United States Navy as a midshipman at age thirteen, he was especially fascinated by currents and underwater hydrography. After making the rank of lieutenant, he spent fifteen years on coastal survey of the Eastern and Gulf coasts. Maffitt knew every inlet and bay from the Portsmouth Naval Shipyard, Maine, to Galveston, Texas, like the palm of his right hand.

Maffitt was of average height and weight, but carried himself erect and gave the appearance of a much larger man. He had a strong chin covered by a thick, dark beard. There was a cockiness about him and a sparkle in his eyes, which always seemed to scan the horizon when he was staring directly at you. Intelligent, canny as a fox, John Newland Maffitt was second only to Raphael Semmes of the *Alabama* as a commerce raider, and was the most successful blockade runner of them all. He was, perhaps, the only Confederate skipper who never lost a ship. Feared and at the same time respected by his former friends in the Union Navy, he was a gentleman to the core.

Not about to wait for another seizure of his new command, Maffitt slipped out of the harbor, cleverly eluded a Union warship, and sailed to a small, uninhabited outer island off the Grand Bahamas Bank, where he rendezvoused with the *Prince Albert,* a coastal schooner that was carrying guns and munitions. As soon as the two ships anchored, the armament was transferred from the schooner to *Oreto.*

The haste cost Maffitt. He was forced to sail with a crew that was woefully shorthanded. He had so few hands that he and his few officers sweated alongside the ordinary seamen at getting the guns on board. But on August 16, 1862, mounting six six-inch and two seven-inch Blakely rifled guns and one twelve-pound howitzer, *Oreto* was officially christened *Florida* and commissioned into the Confederate Navy.

The first voyage of the C.S.S. *Florida* was a nightmare. Essential equipment required to fire the guns had not arrived on *Prince Albert*. The South's newest sea raider looked mean and had a big bite, but no teeth. Maffitt's situation quickly went from bad to worse. During the loading, his already undermanned crew was struck down by yellow fever. When he finally got under way and steamed away from the Bahamas, *Florida* carried the deadly scourge with her.

Maffitt ran the ship into Havana to set his sick ashore and recruit new crew members. But Cuban officials ordered him to sail before he infected the entire city. As Cuba faded in the distance Maffitt also felt the ache in his joints that signaled infection by the fever.

Maffitt lay in his berth most of the voyage, too ill to walk the deck. With a decimated crew (only twenty-one were still on their feet), he reckoned that his only hope was to run the Union blockade into a major southern port before a Yankee warship discovered and took advantage of his ship's impotent condition. An almost impossible feat under any circumstances, but made all the more perilous by his ship's inability to fight back. His decision made, he ordered his first officer, Lieutenant Jubal Haverly, to set a course for Mobile, Alabama.

Late in the afternoon of September 4, 1862, after a three-day cruise across the Gulf from Havana, Maffitt sighted the ruins of the lighthouse off the entrance to Mobile Bay near Fort Morgan. He also spotted three Union warships that were blockading the harbor. Still recovering from his bout with yellow fever and looking like a ghost, Maffitt was too weak to walk the deck. Propped up in a chair by a railing on the quarterdeck, his gaze traveled from the heavily armed enemy ships across the fifteen miles of water separating *Florida* from the protective Confederate guns mounted on Fort Morgan and the sanctuary of the harbor beyond.

Maffitt turned to Lieutenant John Stribling, who had served with Raphael Semmes on board the raider *Sumter,* and had volunteered his services so he could return home to South Carolina and see his bride.

"Tell me, sir, how would you describe our prospects?"

Stribling stared at the three warships bleakly. "We're a ship crewed by sick and cripples, we can't fire a gun. I'd say our chances of being blown out of the water in a matter of minutes are inevitable."

"You don't think it wise to make a run into Mobile Bay?"

"No, sir, I suggest we come about and make a try after dark."

Maffitt shook his head. "Blundering around in the dead of night while groping for the channel would put us aground on a shoal for sure."

"Either that, or run the ship ashore and burn her," Stribling said somberly.

Maffitt stared thoughtfully at the distant harbor entrance. Then he nodded bravely. "I'm a gambler who likes high odds. I do believe we can run a bluff."

"Sir?"

"We're the spitting image of a British gunboat. We'll run up the English flag and make straight for them."

In the little time remaining, Maffitt assembled the few of his officers who were still able to move under their own power. "We're going in," he announced. "Hoist the English colors. Every minute we can fool the Union ship captains saves us a broadside from their guns. The instant they get wise and open fire, give me a full head of steam. All men, including the sick, will be sent belowdecks. Only the officers will stay topside with me."

There was no word of protest. There wasn't a man who would hesitate to walk through hell with John Newland Maffitt.

"Mr. Stribling, will you do the honor of securing me to the rail?"

"But, sir, if the ship goes to the bottom . . ."

"Then we'll sink as one," Maffitt said with a grim smile. Then he talked to James Billups and Samuel Sharkey, *Florida*'s tough young helmsmen. "Gentlemen, I wish you to steer toward the largest ship in the Union squadron. Aim our bow directly at her beam."

"Aye, sir," replied Billups. "You say the word, and we'll cut her amidships."

The captain of *Winona,* the first Union ship approached by *Florida,* stepped to the railing and hailed the Confederate raider. "What ship are you?"

"Her Britannic Majesty's steamer *Vixen,*" Maffitt replied.

Taken in, *Winona*'s captain signaled the other Union warships that the stranger was friendly.

"One down, two to go," said Maffitt as *Florida* passed *Winona.* The captain of the second Union ship, *Rachel Seaman,* also took the bait and stood off to port while seeing nothing suspicious in the English ship, whose guns sat idle and unmanned. The last hurdle was *Oneida,* a big sloop-of-war, mounting ten guns, two of them huge eleven-inchers. Her captain, Commander George Preble, took no chances and ordered his helmsman to veer across the bows of the intruding Englishman.

Down in *Florida*'s engine room, unseeing of the drama above, the fever-racked firemen, their sweating bodies caked with coal dust, fed the fireboxes like men possessed. The new engines responded with a burst of speed that sent the ship's bow surging through the swells, throwing off great sheets of spray.

Billups and Sharkey grimly clutched the spokes of the helm and aimed *Florida*'s bowsprit directly at the hull of *Oneida.* Stunned at seeing the "Englishman" intent on ramming his ship, Commander Preble ordered his engines reversed. It had yet to dawn on him the stranger could be anything but British. She was a beautiful little ship, he thought, too innocent-looking to belong to the Confederacy. Seeing her captain at the railing, Preble hailed him as had the captain of *Winona.*

"Heave to! What ship are you?"

Maffitt stared as if in a hypnotic trance at the big eleven-inch guns, seeing their crews ready to fire. The point of no return had been crossed. There could be no turning back. The two ships were steaming parallel now, less than a hundred yards separated them. Preble ordered a shot fired across *Florida*'s bow, then a second shot splashed the water in front of the speeding ship. Maffitt had played his last card. At that moment, the war suddenly caught up with *Florida*. Her destiny was in the hands of fate.

At the command of Preble, *Oneida* unleashed a broadside. The blast devastated the fleeing Confederate ship. Luckily for Maffitt and his crew, *Oneida*'s gunners had aimed high. If the guns had been depressed, *Florida*'s career would have ended on the seafloor of the Gulf. Shells smashed her boats and railings to splinters, her rigging was shredded, spars fell on her open deck, narrowly missing Maffitt. In an instant, the once-beautiful ship was pounded into an unsightly ugly duckling.

Then the Union gunners lowered their aim and eleven-inch shells smashed into more vulnerable parts of *Florida*. One huge shell crashed through the starboard hull bare inches above the waterline, denting the port boiler, decapitating one man and grievously wounding nine others, before exiting the port side and leaving a hole as large as a horse before exploding. If it had burst a moment sooner, the resulting havoc would have plunged *Florida* beneath the waves.

As calmly as if he'd been watching a parade, Maffitt called out, "Mr. Stribling. It's time we showed them who we are. Haul down the British colors and raise our ensign."

Helmsman Sharkey leaped across the deck, grasped the halyards, and lost a finger to shrapnel. Ignoring his bleeding wound, he pulled the flag into the sky. When the emblem of the Confederacy unfurled over *Florida,* the officers on the Union warships realized how deeply they had been conned. To save their reputations they were determined more than ever to terminate the raider as quickly as their guns could be loaded and fired.

Winona and *Rachel Seaman* opened with every gun they

could bring to bear. A shell smashed into *Florida*'s galley as another exploded near her port gangway. Soon wreckage littered her decks and splashed into the water alongside. As if to add insult to injury, *Oneida*'s marines began sniping at any man who appeared abovedecks. Men that Maffitt sent aloft to set the sails were peppered with musket balls and shrapnel. Five were hit but managed to climb down after lowering the sails. They were helped below and laid out beside those stricken with yellow fever.

Drawing on every trick he could create, Maffitt dodged and maneuvered to throw off the Union gunners, gaining precious minutes as the faster *Florida* began to pull away from her pursuing hounds. Twenty-one eleven-inch shells struck the defenseless ship. An incoming broadside from *Oneida* seemed to lift *Florida* free of the water in a crescendo of detonations. The irony of battle. Ironic because none of the Union seamen could believe the impotent target they were pounding so outrageously was still surging through the sea in the face of inevitable defeat, shaking off her terrible injuries with no apparent show of surrender.

While concussions echoed and reverberated all around Maffitt and under him, he ignored the fiery storm and gave orders to his helmsmen in a voice utterly devoid of fear. Officers on board *Oneida* reported after the one-sided fight seeing a man sitting by the quarter rail as cool and commanding as if he were observing a horse race. They could not help but admire the bravery of the man who sat alone on the deck, gesturing to his helmsmen.

For a solid hour *Florida* was hammered and mauled by three enemies who could concentrate their aim without the distraction of incoming fire. As she raged ahead at fourteen knots, her superior speed was beginning to tell. Union crewmen had to elevate their guns after each shot now as their quarry pulled away.

Fort Morgan was drawing closer. On the ramparts, Confederate gunners cheered on their ship, their guns loaded and primed to fire the instant the Union ships sailed into range. They watched with growing optimism as they saw shells missing and splashing in the wake of *Florida* as they began to fall short.

Incredible as it seemed, a miracle had happened. Maffitt had gambled with fate and won. He watched as the Union warships, frustrated and outfoxed, came about and turned back into the Gulf as a shell from a rifled gun soared from Fort Morgan and dropped in the water between the hounds and their prey. *Florida* had reached safe harbor at last.

Maffitt untied the rope around his waist and rose to his feet, swaying weakly as his officers, who had stuck to their stations throughout the chase, surrounded him. "Gentlemen," he said, smiling broadly, "if our supply of rum wasn't destroyed, I propose we indulge ourselves." Then, staggering unsteadily to the helm, he shook the hand of James Billups, who had courageously steered the ship through the maelstrom of shot and shell. "My congratulations, Billups. You're a brave man."

"You don't know how happy I am to have been of service, sir."

"Mind the channel buoys and take her around Fort Morgan. We'll anchor there."

Maffitt ordered the engines reduced to slow speed as *Florida* proudly steamed into Mobile Bay, her flag taut in an offshore breeze. The men manning the guns of Fort Morgan gave her a mighty cheer as she limped past. Then the cannon began thundering as they gave the battered little ship a twenty-one-gun salute. Maffitt and his crew had achieved the impossible. Honors and tributes poured in from all over the South. England rang with praise for the ship they had built. People everywhere admired the underdog who beat the odds. Even enemies to the north could not help but be fascinated. Tough, hard-bitten Union Admiral David Porter was impressed with Maffitt's unparalleled audacity. He stated, "There was never a case where a man, under all the attending circumstances, displayed more energy or more bravery."

It took three and a half months to repair the more than fourteen hundred different injuries inflicted on *Florida*. Not until January 16, 1863, did Maffitt slip out of Mobile Bay during a rainstorm and thread his way through the Yankee blockading fleet. She then began her first cruise as a raider, which added a grand chapter to naval annals.

"She's flying the stars and stripes," Maffitt said, studying the graceful lines of a clipper ship under full sail. "Fire a shot across her bow."

A puff of smoke was followed by a loud blast, and a shell flew from the muzzle of the twelve-pound howitzer and splashed in the water fifty yards in front of the clipper ship's bow.

"Her captain got the message," said Lieutenant Charles Morris, Maffitt's second in command. "He's bringing her into the wind."

"She appears heavily laden," observed Maffitt.

As *Florida* pulled closer, a lone seaman on the deck of the merchant ship hoisted a white flag. "No chase this time," Maffitt said cheerfully. He turned to Morris. "Board her and recover the manifest."

"Very well, sir." Morris quickly assembled a crew and lowered the shore boat into the rolling waves. As he rowed over to the Yankee ship, he read the name lettered in gold on her port bow. The clipper was called the *Jacob Bell*. Bad luck, having a man's name, he thought.

Captain Charles Frisbee, a crusty New Englander, met Morris as the Confederate stepped onto the deck. "I won't say, 'Welcome aboard,' damn you," said *Jacob Bell*'s captain.

"I am Lieutenant Charles Morris of the C.S.S. *Florida,* captained by John Maffitt," said Morris in an official tone. "We are taking your ship as a prize."

"I have heard of your devil ship," snapped the New Englander, "and I've heard of Maffitt."

"May I have your cargo list, please?"

The captain handed Morris a sheaf of papers. "I knew you'd be asking for it."

Morris scanned the manifest. "I see you're carrying a full cargo of tea."

Jacob Bell's captain nodded. "Over a million and a half dollars' worth."

Morris's eyes widened at the incredibly high figure. "A great pity it will never see teacups."

"You're not providing me with the opportunity to post bond in a foreign port to get her back?"

"Sorry, captain, the risk of being intercepted by a Union warship is too great."

"You intend to sink her?" the captain muttered in outrage.

"We intend to burn her."

After food stores and any objects of value were transferred to the Confederate raider, *Jacob Bell* was set to the torch. John Maffitt was deeply saddened by the sight of the flames consuming such a beautiful clipper ship. An old seadog, he hated to see a ship, any ship, die. The fact that the *Jacob Bell* was to be the most valuable prize taken by any of the Confederate raiders during the entire war did not console him.

Florida's first cruise was successful beyond expectations. Maffitt had an uncanny knack at finding and capturing Union merchant vessels. In just six months he captured twenty-five cargo ships, whose combined cargo values approached $5 million. He set a record that was broken only by Raphael Semmes and his *Alabama*.

Two of the captured ships were given prize crews and operated as satellite raiders. One was commanded by the ubiquitous Charles Read, who had fought Farragut at the battle of New Orleans and manned the stern gun battery on *Arkansas*. Read captured twenty-one ships before he was caught during a daring raid in a New England harbor.

By August of 1863, *Florida*'s engines were badly in need of an overhaul, and her hull required the removal of several inches of marine growth. Although Maffitt preferred the work be done in a British shipyard, the political conflict between the United States and Britain made it impossible. So he sailed his ship into the French port of Brest.

The repairs on the raider were expected to take only eighteen days, but complications with the French stretched it to five months. During this time, Maffitt became ill with a variety of ailments caused in part by recurring symptoms from his bout with yellow fever. He asked the Secretary of the Confederate Navy to be relieved. Command was eventually given to his loyal officer Charles Morris.

With a new and inexperienced crew, Morris sailed out of Brest in February of 1864 and launched *Florida* on her second voyage. The pickings were slim because most of the ships of American registry were kept in their home ports by the high insurance premiums caused by *Florida* and *Alabama,* which was now also raiding the seas. After seizing thirteen ships, Lieutenant Morris sailed into the port of Bahia, Brazil, to take on supplies and coal.

Unfortunately for Morris and *Florida,* a Union warship was also at anchor in port, the U.S.S. *Wachusett,* captained by Commander Napoleon Collins.

"We *would* have to run into that devil in a neutral port," Collins said to the United States consul at Bahia, Thomas F. Wilson, who had rowed out to the Yankee warship.

"Can't you blow her out of the water when she sails from port?" asked Wilson.

Commander Collins studied *Florida* through a pair of binoculars. "Her speed is superior to mine. If she sneaks out on a moonless night, she'll be impossible to chase down."

"A damned crime, if you ask me," Wilson growled. "We fail to destroy her, and God only knows how many innocent merchant ships she and her crew of pirates will burn and plunder."

Collins did not reply. He seemed lost in his thoughts.

"You've got to take action before she escapes."

"What do you suppose Brazil would do to us if we attacked *Florida* here and now?" Collins asked.

"They'd probably threaten to blow you out of the water," answered Wilson. "But I doubt they would actually try it. Beyond that, I'd be recalled to Washington and censured, and you'd be court-martialed for creating an international incident."

Collins lowered his binoculars and smiled shrewdly. "A pity. She'd be easy enough to take. Most of her officers and crew have gone ashore. I hear Commander Morris and his officers are attending the opera."

"We have been presented with a golden opportunity, commander. Regardless of personal consequences, our duty is clear."

Collins turned to his first officer. "Mr. Rigsby."

"Sir?"

"Please find our chief engineer and order him to get up steam."

Rigsby stared at his captain, respect glowing in his eyes. "You're going after *Florida?* Sir?"

"I intend to ram and sink her on the spot."

A shifty grin crossed Wilson's face. "I'll be more than happy to defend your claim that it was an unfortunate accident."

Collins nodded toward the helm. "Just so they know who to hang, I'll steer us in myself with you at my side."

"I'd consider it an honor," Consul Wilson said without hesitation.

Before dawn the following morning, *Wachusett* quietly raised her anchors and steamed toward *Florida,* moored slightly more than a half mile away behind a Brazilian warship placed between the two enemy warships to discourage just such a situation. With Collins himself at the helm, *Wachusett* slipped around the Brazilian ship and headed on a collision course toward the unsuspecting *Florida.* A seaman standing deck watch sighted the Yankee ship looming from the predawn darkness, and gave the alarm. The cry came too late. Before the crew could spring from their hammocks and load the guns, *Wachusett* struck *Florida* on her starboard quarter, smashing her railings and bulwarks while shattering her mizzenmast and main yard.

In the darkness, Collins had misjudged. Instead of ramming his bow through *Florida*'s hull amidships and sending her to the bottom of Bahia harbor, he merely grazed her, causing minimal damage. As his marines sprayed the raider's deck with small-arms musketry, two of his broadside guns were fired in the heat of the action without his express orders. Taking advantage of the mistake, he shouted for *Florida*'s crew to surrender or be blown to pieces.

Lieutenant Thomas Porter, commander of the Confederate raider while Morris was on shore, had no choice but to concede defeat. His guns were unloaded, less than half the crew were on board, and *Wachusett*'s marines were shooting down anyone who moved. He conferred with the few officers who hadn't gone ashore, and all agreed that any defense could only result in a waste of lives. Reluctantly, Porter lowered the Confederate flag for the final time.

Collins ordered a hawser attached to the helpless *Florida*, and within minutes she was being towed out of the harbor. Alerted by the sound of gunfire, the Brazilian warship came to investigate. When its captain discovered the foul plan in gross violation of his nation's neutrality laws, he ordered his gun crews to fire at *Wachusett*. Collins ignored the inconsequential protest and refused to return a broadside. With the sun creeping over the horizon, he made the open sea, pulling his captive along in his wake.

Consul Wilson remained on *Wachusett* until it reached the United States. Fortunately for him, the decision to keep him on board was a sound one. Enraged by the wanton violation of neutrality, a Brazilian mob ransacked and burned the U.S. Consulate in Bahia. Had he remained behind, Wilson would have no doubt been strung up under a convenient light post.

Wachusett towed the illegally captured *Florida* into Hampton Roads and moored her off Newport News. Not long afterward, the Confederate raider mysteriously sank while at anchor. Rumors circulated blaming an army transport that rammed her in the dead of night. The true story didn't come out until one summer's evening in 1872, when John Maffitt was invited to Admiral Porter's home in Washington for dinner.

While enjoying brandy and cigars on the old sea dog's veranda, Maffitt looked at Porter and asked, "Admiral, will you give me a true account of the sinking of the *Florida*?"

Quite relaxed, Porter smiled shrewdly. "Certainly. Time enough has passed under the bridge."

"Then it was no accident?"

"No accident." Porter shook his head. "President Lincoln was quite upset about receiving a storm of protests from the nations of Europe over Collins's deceitful capture of the ship in Brazil. Lincoln insisted that we release *Florida* and return her to Bahia and the Confederates to avoid the reparation demanded by the Brazilian government. During the dispute, Secretary of State Henry Seward called me to his office."

Porter went on to relate the events leading to the demise of *Florida*.

"Seward paced the floor, his Machiavellian mind trying to find a way out that would appease the European community. 'To let loose this fearful scourge upon our commerce again would be terrible. It must be avoided.'

" 'What do you suggest, Mr. Secretary?' I asked.

" 'I wish she was at the bottom of the sea!'

" 'Do you mean it, sir?'

"Seward nodded grimly. 'I do, from my soul.'

" 'Then it shall be done,' I promised him. The next morning I sent an engineer under cover of night to the stolen steamer. My instructions were to open the sea cocks before midnight and not to leave the engine room until the water was up to his chin. At sunrise that rebel craft must be a thing of the past, resting on the bottom of the river." Porter paused to exhale a cloud of smoke into the humid Virginia evening. "I thought it poetic justice to scuttle her over the spot where *Merrimack* rammed and sank *Cumberland.*"

Maffitt listened in silence, staring at the brandy in his glass as if seeing his once proud ship resting in the eternal gloom at the bottom of the James River, where she would no more plague United States merchant shipping. No more would she haunt the navy that could only stop her with devious subterfuge. She would be enshrined in history along with her sister ship, *Alabama,* as the high-water mark of the Confederate Navy.

So ended the final chapter of the *Florida.* All that was left was her epilogue.

III

Where Did They Go?

April 1980

ONE MORE MANIFESTATION OF CUSSLER'S LAW, "EVERY man knows the location of a shipwreck that isn't there."

Sadly, it seems, man does not live by reason alone. All too often we live by drippy intuition and foggy reasoning with no sound basis in fact. You have to be on your guard to keep the two from gaining the upper hand. I've never known a shipwreck that was found through divine revelation or down-home guesswork.

Because they were known to lie within less than a mile of each other, I decided to combine *Cumberland* and *Florida* into one expedition. What I assumed would be a relatively simple search project, because the ships were reportedly in a fairly compact area, turned out to be a very complicated and difficult affair. Although *Congress* had exploded and burned to her waterline, she was immediately eliminated as a possible target because she was raised in September of 1865 and her hulk towed to the Norfolk Navy Yard, where she was sold and broken up.

Why *Florida* and *Cumberland* were elusive for so many years is a mystery. Both were known to have sunk between the James River channel and the shore along Newport News. Accounts of her epic battle and the final resting place of *Cumberland* varied widely. Like witnesses at an auto accident or murder, none give the same account. Though a number of investigators looked into the enigma and accumulated a stack of data from 1904 until 1980, no one individual or group had actively searched for the wreck sites.

I began working with researchers Bob Fleming and Dr. Chester Bradley, who was an authority on the sinking of *Cumberland, Florida,* and *Congress.* Salvage accounts, eyewitness reports, correspondence, and newspaper articles were assembled and studied.

Research revealed that after the war George B. West, the son of a farmer whose waterfront property was close to where the vessels sank, used to fish in and around the wrecks while they were being salvaged. West described how salvage divers attempted to find in the paymaster's stateroom of *Cumberland* an iron chest that reportedly contained $40,000 in gold coin. I frankly never bought the story of the treasure. Never have I heard of a soldier, sailor, or airman, from the Revolutionary War to Desert Storm, being paid in gold. Impossible to believe our benevolent government paid their fighting men in anything other than paper money or silver coin. Incredibly, the safe was found and raised ten years after the war, in 1875, by Clements Brown, but newspaper reports state that only $25 or $30 was discovered inside.

I've always found it interesting that two weeks after a ship sinks, any ship, be it a tugboat or an ocean liner, there is a rumor that it was carrying $10,000 in cash somewhere in its bowels. Twenty years later the rumor mill has increased it to $100,000 in silver. At one hundred years, the figure has grown to $1 million in gold. After two hundred years, salvors and treasure hunters will swear the ship was carrying ten tons of gold and sackfuls of precious jewels, all valued at no less than $500 million. Such is the mesmerizing lure of treasure.

The facts are that, despite the occasional big strikes like *Atocha* and *Central America,* more money has been thrown into the sea searching for riches than has ever been recovered.

George West located the site where he had observed the divers working on *Florida* as "off Pier 1 and Pier 2" near the Newport News beach front. He then described *Cumberland* as ". . . being sunk off Pier 6 about the middle of the channel."

I then calculated possible sites by overlaying a transparency from an old 1870 chart on top of the most modern chart. By comparing the landmarks from West's accounts I could see that Pier 6 now corresponded with the Virginia Port Authority's Pier C, while the Horne Brothers Shipyard pier now stood over what had once been Piers 1 and 2.

John Sands, curator at the Newport News Mariners' Museum, was most helpful in providing us with copies of watercolors and sketches by contemporary artists showing *Cumberland*'s masts protruding from the river between two piers, approximately three hundred yards from shore.

Now, we had our ballpark.

I decided it was time to reap the fruits of our labor. I broke open a jar of Laura Scudder's peanut butter. While making my favorite sandwich of peanut butter with mayonnaise and dill pickles, I phoned Bill Shea and Walt Schob and set up a date for all of us to meet in Virginia for a four-day cursory inspection to collect initial data for a later, more in-depth search.

The next step was to apply to the Virginia Marine Resources Commission for a permit to investigate underwater historic property. John Broadwater, head of the Underwater Archaeology Section, was most helpful and even provided a team of state archaeologists to come along and dive. Support was provided by members of a British Advanced Underwater Team, a bunch of really fun and jovial guys.

On the day that everyone assembled for the project, the officials of the Commonwealth of Virginia (the title *State* isn't good enough for them) were somewhat less than impressed with our methodology, a term archaeologists are fond of using; it has an academic ring to it, like *provenance* and *empirical data.*

There are workboats and there are workboats. But our NUMA crew operated off a hundred-foot luxury yacht that was built in the 1920s and whose decks had been walked by two Presidents, Coolidge and Hoover. She was called *Sakonit,* and abounded with teak decks and mahogany interior paneling. Her skipper, Danny Wilson, had spent long hours and a fair sum of money restoring her to her original state. He and his family lived on board.

One could sit on the spacious open rear deck under a colorful awning and imagine ghostly men in tuxedos and women in flapper dresses, stockings rolled down below knees red with rouge, drinking bootleg booze and dancing to a Dixieland jazz band, playing "The Varsity Drag."

Thinking the search for the Civil War ships might be a change of scene, Wilson chartered the *Sakonit* to NUMA for half his normal charge for five days. He offered me a stateroom and invited me to enjoy sleeping on the famous old yacht. The problem was I couldn't sleep. The *Sakonit* didn't have air conditioning, and Virginia in July is not cool, nor is it dry.

I lay there staring at the reflection of rippling water through a porthole while lying in an ocean of sweat, insanely envious of Bill Shea, Walt Schob, and my son, Dirk, no fools they, who were living comfortably in a nearby Holiday Inn, under a constant seventy-two-degree temperature while enjoying a cocktail lounge within spitting distance that served ice-cold beer.

My tongue wagged like a blind dog's tail in a meat market at the thought of joining them, but the Wilsons were such nice and hospitable people I braved it out.

John Broadwater, his staff of underwater investigators, and the British dive team were not sure we had the proper approach for archaeological survey. For some unfathomable reason they thought our survey effectiveness was severely limited. They found our equipment lacking. Not intending a full-scale exercise, all we brought along was our trusty Schonstedt gradiometer, our own expert archaeologist, Dan Koski-Karell, two cases of Coors beer, and four bottles of

Bombay gin. I'm a strong believer in "getting there is half the fun."

On reflection I can see that our philosophies clashed. Broadwater and his crew were dead serious and expected a full-scale effort, but I was there strictly to investigate site conditions, study landmarks, and make a little whoopie on the side. A more extensive search project would come later.

Settling down to business, we began running our lanes fifty feet apart and perpendicular (I love that word) to shore. When anomalies of consequence were detected, buoys were dropped and divers went down, swimming one-hundred-foot circular search patterns around the centers of the targets.

Because all targets were at depths in excess of seventy feet, bottom time was limited to a maximum of forty minutes, and repetitive dives did not exceed twenty-five minutes. And because English dive tables restricted bottom time to thirty minutes with no repetitive dives, the British team could probe the sites only once a day.

Swimming under the James River cannot be compared to sport diving in the Caribbean. There have been attempts to clean the water since we were there in '81 and '82, but in those days we had to contend with a dark, murky void containing every pollutant known to man: sewage, ketone, chemicals, and an E. coli count that would make an environmentalist cry. If that wasn't enough, there were the river's current and the tidal surge from Chesapeake Bay sweeping back and forth over the dive sites to contend with. Ship traffic was also heavy, and the moving hulls and thrashing propeller blades of tankers, freighters, tugs, and barges, which travel up and down the river, presented a constant source of peril to divers.

Walt Schob, who dove around the world and worked on the recovery of the *Mary Rose,* King Henry VIII's flagship that lay forgotten for four centuries until found and recovered, said conditions on the bottom of the James River were the worst he had ever encountered.

Our one benefit was the warm water temperature. Beyond that the only thing you looked forward to after diving through seventy feet of gloom to the ooze on the bottom was the joy of reaching the surface and sunlight again. Visibility was nil. Divers who wore glasses needed the services of an optometrist to grind prescription lenses in their face masks. Even with 20/20 eyesight, it's tough to focus on a vague object less than six inches away.

Leaving the lion's share of the diving to the young guys, I spent my time keeping a sharp eye on the water for passing ships and any signs of problems underwater. My other job was to field questions by dignitaries and news people. I was always amused when a visitor came on board the *Sakonit* to observe the operation and spotted an artificial leg lying on the deck. Their expressions were priceless. It belonged to Dick Swete, one of the Virginia Research Center archaeologists, who had lost a leg in Vietnam. Before they could ask, I told them the divers had found it while probing the river bottom. I don't believe Dick ever knew about the story I created and handed out to the gullible about the one-legged sailor who was urinating on the casemate of the *Virginia* when it rammed the *Cumberland*.

One reporter asked me, "Do you have a doctor on board?"

"Not in the strict sense," I answered. "I handle all medical emergencies myself."

"Did you go to medical school?"

"No, but I subscribe to the *Reader's Digest.*"

I'm constantly amazed at how the ladies and gentlemen of the news media can't take a joke.

Of the two targets that seemed the most promising, one turned out to be an old coal barge constructed from iron. The other target, however, revealed a lumberyard full of worm-eaten planking the archaeologists classified as coming from a nineteenth-century shipwreck. Could it possibly be *Florida*'s remains?

IV

Back with a Vengeance

July 1982

AFTER GIVING IT MY EARNEST CONSIDERATION OVER TWO
martinis one evening, I decided to make another attempt on
Florida and *Cumberland.* Somehow it seemed the only sane
thing to do.

Since we were reasonably certain where *Florida* rested,
and had a grid site no larger than a football field for *Cumberland,* I felt that, in keeping with my image as a good fellow,
salt of the earth, and the backbone of America, it was time
for a professional survey conducted by a team of hard-core
professional archaeologists.

Fortune smiled. I didn't have to call Kelly Girls or run a
classified ad under Help Wanted. Four of the archaeologists from the Commonwealth of Virginia, who dove with
NUMA in 1981—James Knickerbocker, Sam Margolin,
Dick Swete, and Mike Warner—had resigned and launched
their own organization, called Underwater Archaeological
Joint Ventures (UAJV). I couldn't have found a better team
if I'd offered a reward. Between them, they had amassed
over eight hundred hours of bottom time in the James River,
and despite god-awful conditions had achieved a proven

record of success in both search and survey and expedition.

The first hurdle was obtaining a permit from Virginia and the Army Corps of Engineers to excavate the wreck sites.

Having a nonchalant flair for trivial details, I found the procedures and ensuing hurdles thrown out by the bureaucracy, the restrictions, the consideration of everything from the threat to shell-fishing activities and cultural resources to the requirements for daily logs, dive logs, excavation and artifact registers, monthly reports, methodology (that word again), and a hundred other stipulations rather exasperating. What you could and could not do reminded me of watching a Three Stooges film festival without being allowed to eat hot buttered popcorn and Milk Duds.

Because of some genetic short circuit, I have not become a slave to the acquisition of historical artifacts, and so the permit was finally issued, thanks in large part to the patience of the UAJV gang, who plodded unflinchingly through a mountain of paperwork.

Before the actual survey began, UAJV interviewed local watermen, sport divers, clam and crab fishermen, charter-boat captains, anyone who might shed light on variations in the riverbed. They struck gold when veteran clammer Wilbur Riley offered his services and showed our team the site where, during an effort to retrieve his tongs, which had caught and hung on a submerged object, he had pulled up artifacts from the Civil War era.

Divers went down and discovered heavy concentrations of scattered wreckage of a large wooden ship, whose huge hull timbers rose out of the muck like ghosts frozen in the past. Almost immediately they observed the shaft of a large anchor, decking planks, and ordnance accessories used by the men who manned the cannon. Over a period of several days, a number of interesting artifacts were recovered from the ship that tenaciously fought a battle she could not win. One was an irregular frame that a sailor had fashioned around the broken edges of a mirror. Perhaps the most dramatic find was *Cumberland*'s large bronze bell, standing 6 inches high and 19 inches wide. When you stare at it, you can imagine it rung by an unseen hand, sending her crew to their guns at the approach of the *Virginia.*

The one object any maritime museum would give its curator's left leg to put on display is the ram of *Merrimack/Virginia* which still lies buried inside the hull of *Cumberland.* This is the most prized artifact of all, but its recovery calls for a very expensive and extensive project far beyond NUMA's means.

An enigma that plagued the search team was the constant loss of their site-marker buoys. On the progress report there is constant mention of "New buoys set." "Buoys missing." "Buoys relocated." "Buoys missing." The buoy anchor lines appeared to be torn from the bottom. Surely passing ships and fishermen did not sweep across our dive sites every night of the week. We could not help wondering if someone didn't like us. But with no suspects, and certainly none with motives, we wrote off the phenomenon to ghosts from the wrecks who love to play pranks on the living.

Having proven with little doubt the ship off Pier C was indeed the *Cumberland,* Warner, Margolin, & Company moved six hundred yards upriver to the site we had surveyed two years before off the Horne Brothers Shipyard Dock. A section of hull, 121 feet, was found and recorded. The length of wreckage that showed above the silt was 135 feet, with a width of 23 feet. A large number of artifacts were retrieved, including boxes of Enfield bullets, champagne bottles in their original box, ship's hardware, fuses for cannonballs, a shoe, rigging blocks and spikes, and a tall, ornate pewter pitcher.

The divers apparently came down on the ship's hospital and dispensary, and brought up an assortment of apothecary jars and bottles. One bottle, with its glass stopper firmly set, still contained the yellow liquid contents that had remained undisturbed for 120 years. A white ceramic pharmaceutical bowl displayed a red serpent curled around a palm tree. The inscription advertised a pharmacy in Brest, France, the port where Maffitt turned over command of the *Florida.*

With the wreck sites now proven to be the two famous Civil War ships, at least to me if not to certified, card-carrying archaeologists, who insist on finding an engraved plaque giving the name, serial number, blood type, and DNA, we dropped the curtain on our field activities and concentrated on the preservation of the artifacts.

For the time being, we rented a small garage and placed the recovered antiquities in holding tanks containing that good old James River water to keep them stabilized and prevent them from crumbling into dust. Not ones to squander their budget on hot dogs and beer, the UAJV team bought a dozen vinyl kiddie pools to immerse the goods.

Originally, the Virginia Historical Landmarks Department offered to take on the job of preservation. But after the artifacts were raised and stabilized, they backed out, claiming they had run out of funds for the year. Their solution? Throw the precious antiquities back into the river.

I looked up to God, and I asked him, "God, why am I fleeced and inconvenienced at every turn?" And he looked down upon me, and he said, "If you're not happy, why don't you take up stamp collecting?"

He finally sympathized with me. Enter Anne Garland of the Conservation Center at the College of William and Mary in Williamsburg, who offered to split the cost of chemically treating the recovered objects for eventual display at the Newport News Mariners' Museum. The deal was struck, and they did a remarkable job on over thirty different pieces. I've always had a soft spot for William and Mary, especially since when all was said and done they only charged me a fraction of the final cost.

Then the rug was pulled out from under everyone again.

John Sands, the curator at the museum, built a magnificent exhibit around the *Cumberland* and *Florida* artifacts. They were on display for nearly six months, when some Navy admiral and the curator of the Norfolk Naval Museum walked in, asked to see Sands, and contemptuously demanded he turn over, as they charitably put it, *"our* artifacts."

It seems the Judge Advocate of the Navy had a dream. He envisioned that my two years of research, the small fortune I spent on the project, and the indefatigable efforts of the UAJV guys were for the navy's sole benefit. He sanctimoniously claimed the Department of the Navy owned both ships and all bits and pieces thereof. In the case of the *Cumberland,* he maintained that whoever sold it for salvage after the Civil War did not have the proper authority. Normally the *Florida,* he conceded, as Confederate property belonged to the General Services Administration. However, naval research showed that *Florida* had been captured as a blockade runner and was appropriated into the Union Navy.

Demonstrating a definite lack of style and sophistication, the navy threatened to go to court in order to claim the antiquities, to whose recovery they contributed zilch. And because they stoke the economy of the Virginia tidewater area with nearly 30,000 jobs, the Commonwealth of Virginia rolled over and threw in the towel. John Sands's exhibit was dismantled and the artifacts trucked to the Norfolk Naval Museum, where they are now on display.

I could have called their bluff, fought, and easily won in Admiralty Court. The navy did not have a peg leg to stand on. I have copies of correspondence from the original *Cumberland* salvors, who were sold the rights by Gideon Welles, Secretary of the U.S. Navy. If Welles didn't have the right to sell the wreck for salvage, who did? The navy's claim on the *Florida* was equally ludicrous. They had the wrong ship. The vessel they referred to was not the famous Sea Devil raider, captained by the redoubtable John Maffitt, but a garden-variety commercial blockade runner that was captured and appropriated into the navy as a warship they named *Florida.*

It is times like this I'm tempted to take up psychedelic eyelid painting. Through the years I've had many dealings with the U.S. Navy, mostly beneficial to both sides. But there have been times when I wondered how in hell they ever won the war in the Pacific. So long as the artifacts went on display to the public at the navy's Norfolk museum, I decided not to create a fuss. If they had hidden them away in the basement, the U.S. Navy would have cursed the name of Clive Cussler, something they probably do anyway.

What thanks did NUMA and UAJV receive for their struggle to preserve our country's maritime heritage?

Several years later, I was visiting friends in Portsmouth, just across the Elizabeth River from Norfolk. I visited the naval museum one day and was admiring the fruits of our labor when a navy lieutenant came out of an office and passed by the exhibit.

"Odd that they didn't recognize the people who found the wrecks and recovered the artifacts with a token placard," I remarked aloud to no one in particular.

He stopped and stared at me. "Who are you referring to?"

"The team from the National Underwater and Marine Agency along with the Underwater Joint Venture archaeologists."

His face reddened. "Do you know Clive Cussler?" he brusquely asked.

"Cussler, yes, I've seen him," I replied, alluding to the million times I've looked in a mirror.

"Well, you can take it from me," the lieutenant snapped, "that son of a bitch and his gang of thieves didn't have a damned thing to do with what you see here. A Navy SEAL team salvaged all this."

"No foolin'?"

"Those assholes made false claims. This was an all-navy show."

Ingratitude, rejection, antipathy.

Well, that's life, right? No skyrockets. No parades. You just wind up thinking that stamp collecting might not be so dull after all.

The end of the story has yet to be written. A navy dive-salvage team has made several attempts at finding the *Virginia*'s ram, but until now they have been unsuccessful.

In March of 1990, the FBI raided a small Civil War museum in Virginia and a relic dealer. Armed with federal search and seizure warrants, agents seized an enormous number of artifacts that were stolen from the sites of the *Florida* and the *Cumberland*. The stolen objects included pieces of timbers, bilge pumps, cannonballs, musket ammunition, and assorted brass and leather items. Indictments were handed up, but no one was given jail time and fines were minimal.

If nothing else, knowing that the wrecks are monitored and any antiquity stolen from their hulls can be easily traced will make looters think twice before raping the sites. In time, we can but hope that funding will be found and proper archaeological excavation will take place. Who knows? Perhaps someday your grandchildren can look in awe at the big ram from the *Virginia.*

The stolen cache was appraised at over $60,000. If Captain Charles Frisbee of *Jacob Bell* had lived to the ripe old age of 165, he might have been happy to learn that a collector paid $3,000 for a spoon from his ship.

Part 4

C.S.S. *Arkansas*

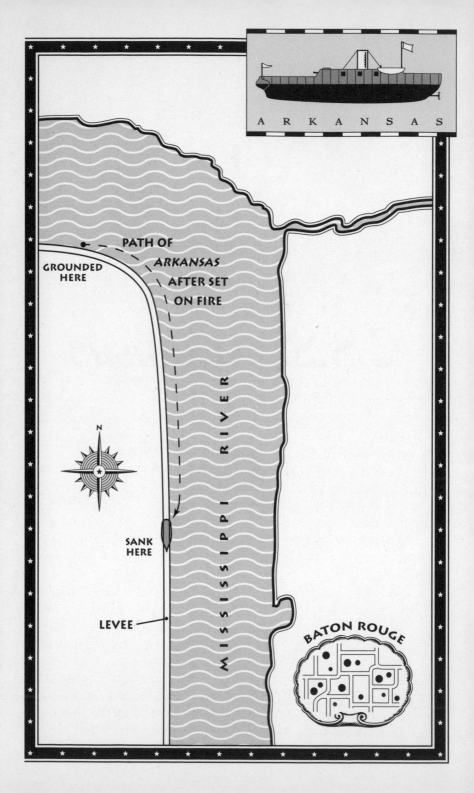

I

The Gauntlet

July 1862

ALONG THE MEANDERING COURSE OF THE YAZOO RIVER, the banks were lined with thick, tangled growth, a visible legacy from the rich delta soil. A succession of farms, now lying fallow, lined the banks. Their crops of cotton rotted in the fields, the men needed to oversee the picking off to fight for the Confederacy.

Near Satartia, Mississippi, Ephram Pettigrew sat on the tumbledown front porch of his home. He was old and weathered, in his late sixties, and he scratched out a living through sharecropping and fishing the river from his small wooden rowboat.

The few teeth he had remaining in his gums were stained brown from the plugs of tobacco he habitually chewed, and his thinning hair was stark white against his red scalp. He rocked slowly in his crudely crafted rocking chair and stroked a yellow tabby cat that purred in his lap.

He had heard the throb from the approaching boat's steam engine some minutes before it rounded a distant bend in the winding river. Scratching the cat's ears, he waited patiently until the vessel came into view.

Instead of the more common paddle-wheeled riverboats that passed by his front porch over the years, this was the strangest vessel he'd ever laid eyes on.

For a Confederate ironclad the hull rode high out of the water, its huge iron ram mounted on the bow spreading a white wake in the murky river. Rising in the center of the main deck was a rectangular casemate with sloping ends and uncharacteristic straight up-and-down sides, heavily armored with iron rails. A pilothouse, similar to a pyramid with the upper half cut off, protruded from the forward roof of the casemate.

A total of ten guns poked their sinister muzzles through the armored walls, three in the squared openings on each sidewall. The four guns in the forward and aft sections of the casemate fired through ports that were cut round. They were a strange mixture of 9-inch smoothbores, 8-inch 64-pounders, 6-inch rifled, and 32-pound smoothbores.

Unlike most other ironclads in the Confederate Navy, which were painted gray, this ugly vessel sported a dirty brown color scheme that almost exactly matched the exposed riverbanks. Drawing thirteen feet of water, C.S.S. *Arkansas* was as fierce and dangerous as any ironclad built by the Confederates, and she was heading down the Yazoo River, primed and ready for battle.

Farmer Pettigrew ceased stroking the cat as he saw a wiry man with a thick black beard standing beside the pilothouse with arms crossed over his chest, staring downriver. Spitting a stream of tobacco juice into a tomato plant alongside the porch, he rose from the rocking chair and went inside to skin the squirrel he had shot for supper.

He turned for a last look at *Arkansas* before it disappeared around the next river bend. "That's one bodacious boat," he murmured to his uninterested cat.

The captain of the ironclad dropped easily through a hatch on the casemate roof down to the lower gun deck. The air was stifling, the breeze created by the movement of the ship barely penetrating the vast interior.

Isaac Brown, no great believer in strict naval decorum,

removed his gray uniform jacket to relieve the summer heat-
Displaying his long-johns top and suspenders, he began a
tour of the ship's gun batteries.

As he walked toward the stern of the casemate, shielded
by three inches of iron rail track and backed by fifteen
inches of pine, Brown was met by Lieutenants Alphonso
Barbot and A. D. Wharton, his officers in charge of the side
gun batteries.

"Good morning, captain," Barbot greeted Brown. "You
look ready for action."

"I'm as ready as I'll ever be," Brown said, smiling as he
snapped his suspenders. "How are the army troops General
Thompson sent us from Missouri handling themselves?"

"A fine group of men, sir," Wharton answered.

"They took to the guns like old hands," Barbot agreed.

Brown nodded. "I'm glad to hear it. Stand ready and
continue with the drilling. We'll meet the enemy by this
time tomorrow."

A veteran of twenty-seven years in the United States
Navy, Isaac Brown looked at the two officers through eyes
dark with concern. They stood tall and ramrod straight. Both
believed devoutly in the cause and bore the optimistic out-
look of youth. But they had yet to witness the horrors of
war firsthand.

Wharton was twenty and had recently become engaged
to a lovely, genteel Southern lady from Nashville, while
Barbot, twenty-two, was already married with two small
children at home in South Carolina.

Brown glanced again down the gun deck. The newly
planked decks were swept and scrubbed with soapstone, the
wood now appearing polished. Near each of the big guns,
mounted on wheeled carriages, iron shot was stacked in
wooden racks with the swabbing rods and gunpowder to fire
them at close hand. He watched with satisfaction as the
crews of each gun ran smoothly through the firing drill.

"I'm going below to inspect the engine room. Keep the
men working at their guns."

Wiping tiny beads of sweat from his brow with the large
handkerchief he kept stuffed in his hip pocket, Brown de-

scended into the hellish confines of the engine room. At the captain's approach, Chief Engineer George City rose from his metal desk, which was bolted to a bulkhead.

City was approaching thirty, and his naturally ruddy complexion had turned almost purple red from the heat of the boilers. His hair was the color of mahogany, and unlike most of the crew he was clean-shaven, claiming truthfully it kept him cooler in the fiery atmosphere.

During the rushed construction of the vessel, the engine room had been designed to achieve negative pressure. When the hatches were set just right, they drafted air from the water and cooled the interior of the engine room. The problem today was that the air temperature on the river was close to ninety degrees and the disparity between it and the heat from the boilers was not creating much of a draft. The engines, hastily built in Memphis, were as balky as a team of unmatched mules.

Chief Engineer City's shirt was soaked completely through with sweat, and a large drop of the salty liquid seemed permanently attached to the tip of his nose.

"Morning, City," said Brown.

"And a warm morning it is," City acknowledged.

"How are your engines operating?"

"I've got my fingers crossed. The boiler that drives the starboard screw wasn't vented properly, and when the pressure dropped the beam would disengage. The bearings, I fear, are going to give problems."

Since the ship's initial trial run, one or the other engine had periodically stopped, causing only one screw to turn and sending the ship around in circles like a dog chasing its tail.

"I pray they don't fail us when we meet the Yankee fleet."

"I'll see they take us through to Vicksburg," City promised. "Or I'll carry the boat on my back."

Conserving her temperamental engines, *Arkansas* traveled slowly downstream. As night began to fall, the crickets that crawled over the vessel began a slow, melodious chirping.

In the deepening purple haze, men assigned to the forward guns put fire to the metal torches filled with turpentine that lit the muddy water ahead.

At regular intervals, the chief pilot, who went by the name of John Hodges, would call down to the engine room to halt their progress. Then two lookouts on the bow would take soundings of the river bottom, using a lead-weighted line. Comparing the recorded depths with the landmarks from shore, the pilot would mark the ship's position on a river chart before ordering the engine room to engage the engines again.

Captain Brown sat in the officers' messroom with Executive Officer Henry K. Stevens and Lieutenants John Grimball, George W. Gift, Alphonso Barbot, A. D. Wharton, and Charles Read. The remnants of a breakfast of bacon and mush were cleared from the table by the Chief Steward, Hiram McCeechum. Refilling the coffee cups, McCeechum then exited the messroom, leaving the officers to confer on the approaching battle.

"We'll be on the Mississippi by ten o'clock," said Brown. "And we have every reason to believe the Yankee fleet is expecting us." He paused and emptied his coffee cup, then set it aside. "Reports from our spies on the river claim that three Federal gunboats are already prowling above the entrance to the Yazoo. As soon as we make contact, I mean to ram and sink the lead vessel. Any questions?"

Every man shook his head in the negative.

Then Brown made the customary lecture. "Gentlemen, in seeking combat as we now do, we must win or perish. Should I fall, whoever succeeds to the command will do so with the resolution to go through the enemy's fleet, or go to the bottom. Should they carry us by boarding, the ship must be blown up. On no account must it fall into the hands of the enemy. Now go to your guns."

One by one the officers quietly set off to their gun stations. Brown sat for a moment, alone in deep thought, studying his river charts. Then he sighed, pushed back his chair, and walked to the ladder leading to the pilothouse.

Black smoke from the big stack curled low on the water and trailed behind the ship. Along the grassy slopes of the shore, river birds gripped the limbs of trees dripping moss, while in a clearing on the port side a small herd of milk cows lapped the muddy water and looked up silently as the ironclad steamed past. Brown hesitated before he entered the pilothouse, finding the scene deceptively peaceful.

Hands placed firmly at ten and two o'clock on the polished wooden-spoke wheel, Chief Pilot Hodges gazed at the river ahead, his eyes squinting through the slits in the armor plating. He spoke to Brown without turning his attention from the winding river.

"There's smoke rising over the tops of the trees around the next bend."

"Since we're the only Confederate ship on the river this day," said Brown slowly, "they must be Yankees."

Hodges touched a match to the pipe that was clenched in his teeth and puffed the briar bowl to life. "I'll bet my next pay they're planning a reception for us."

At that instant, almost before Hodges finished speaking, the Union ironclad *Carondelet* steamed slowly into view.

Spies from the Union Navy had watched as Brown built his odd-looking ironclad from scrap. They followed *Arkansas*'s construction, from the laying of the keel to the mounting of the guns. When the spies alerted Admiral Farragut to her departure down the Yazoo toward the Mississippi and her eventual destination of Confederate-held Vicksburg, he dispatched a small fleet of three ships to intercept her.

The advance flotilla was comprised of the fast ram *Queen of the West,* the lightly armed gunboat *Tyler,* and the ironclad *Carondelet,* which was under the command of Commander Henry Walke, an old friend of Brown's before the war. They had been messmates on an around-the-world cruise, and at one time were as close as brothers.

The instant the Union ships were spotted, *Arkansas* came to life. Stepping smartly back and forth across the enclosed gun deck, the drummers sounded the call to action as the gun crews stood ready to roll their cannons through the gun ports. The officers at each station passed out muskets, pistols, and cutlasses to the men in the possible event they had to repel boarders. Buckets of sand were spread on the deck to soak up spilled blood that was sure to flow from the coming battle. Most of the crew stripped to the waist and tied handkerchiefs around their heads. Like Brown, several of the officers removed their coats and performed their duties in undershirts.

From the pilothouse, Brown peered at the approaching ships. "They're coming at us three abreast," he announced. "Aim for the middle gunboat, Mr. Hodges, the big one. Try to strike her amidships."

On board *Queen of the West,* her only advantage, the enormous speed she could pull from her engines, was being reduced by the heavy river currents. She was without gun batteries, and her ability to ram was rendered ineffective. At the sight of the malignant brown Confederate ironclad, the *Queen*'s captain quickly decided to turn tail and run back downstream.

Staying on course straight up the river, *Carondelet* and *Tyler* made ready to fire their bow guns at the enemy. Their shots began to blast out of their gun muzzles but flew high, missing *Arkansas* as she relentlessly bore down on them.

"Shout across to *Tyler,*" Walke of *Carondelet* ordered his first officer. "Tell them we are turning and heading back downstream. The plan is to continue the fight with our stern guns and draw the Confederate ship along with us."

Spinning the helm, the pilot of *Carondelet* rotated the ship in the water, then called to the engine room for full steam as the stern gunners made ready to fire.

In response to the shouted instructions delivered by a brass speaking trumpet across the water, *Tyler* quickly reversed course in unison with her larger sister ship. With her shorter length and lighter tonnage, she quickly completed her turn and headed away from *Arkansas* at full steam. Her shots flew wide as she set off after *Queen of the West.*

Adjusting the wheel slightly, Hodges steered directly toward the Union ironclad bringing up the rear of the small fleet.

Standing beside the pilot, Brown studied the retreating *Carondelet* with his binoculars. Squinting through the smoke issuing from the Union guns, he turned to Hodges.

"I can see the white of fresh wood under her armor. Once we come within range, Lieutenant Grimball's sixty-four-pounders should be able to penetrate the casemate and sink her."

Grimball needed no order from his captain. He and his crew began firing, reloading, and firing again and again. In a rhythm of coordinated movement, the forward gunners settled into a routine. Grimball counted the shots as the recoil from his guns sent the bow of *Arkansas* seesawing from side to side. First one gun, then the other, each getting off one shot every three minutes.

Arkansas came menacingly downriver like a deadly serpent spouting smoke and fire at its prey. A flock of passenger pigeons burst from the trees along the edge of the river at the thunderous clap of her big sixty-four-pounders.

Below in the engine room, Chief Engineer City's stokers were furiously shoveling coal into the boilers from the nearby bunkers. The temperature continued to rise, and he shouted to his men over the noise of the guns and roaring boilers.

"The helm is calling for more steam! Shovel like the devil himself's after you!"

Inside the starboard furnace, the bank of red coals was already glowing like the fires of a volcano. Shoveling as if they were possessed, the crew hurled coal into the roaring flames before slamming the metal door and knocking the blackened latch closed with a board. Then they moved on to the next boiler and repeated the process.

"We're gaining on them, sir," Hodges said to Brown.

Before Brown could reply, a shot from *Carondelet* struck the forward shield of the pilothouse and bounced off, inflicting Brown with a severe contusion on his forehead as he was slammed against the hard iron wall. He lay there on the deck, feeling the throbbing of the engines underneath him, fighting off unconsciousness as he probed the source of the blood that flowed into his eyes.

"Sir?" Hodges called out. "Will you need the surgeon?"

Brown wiped away the blood with cool detachment until he could see again. Finding no gray that indicated brain particles, he thankfully replied, "I don't think so—"

His words were broken off as another shot from *Carondelet* struck one wall of the pilothouse and exploded against the armor. Part of the wheel was instantly sheared away and Brown was sprayed with a splash of gore that burst from pilot Hodges like juice from a crushed tomato.

The pilot crumpled to the deck, missing most of one shoulder and arm.

Another Yazoo River pilot, J. H. Shacklett, rushed up the ladder into the pilothouse to see if he could assist and was struck in the chest by the shrapnel of another exploding shell. He dropped to the deck on his hands and knees and tried to drag himself back toward the hatch ladder.

James Brady, a young Missourian who stretched six feet tall, had followed Shacklett into the pilothouse. Below on the gun deck when the shells had struck, he looked up and saw the carnage. Abruptly grabbing a midshipman, he yelled, "Send for the surgeon and three orderlies, quickly!" Then Brady climbed into the pilothouse over the bodies and gripped the splintered spokes of the wheel.

"Stay on a course toward the Federal ironclad," Brown ordered weakly.

Brady waited for an opportunity to ram *Carondelet,* but the river narrowed and prevented him from swinging *Arkansas* around on an angle. Any hope of ramming came too late. *Arkansas*'s superior speed soon brought her abreast of the Union ship. Broadside to broadside, the two ships raced downriver, pounding away at each other.

In the thick of the battle, the accuracy of the Confederate gunners improved markedly. Shell after shell tore into *Carondelet's* stern, scrambling her steam piping and disabling her steering gear. With pressure lost through the ruptured pipes, her speed greatly reduced and steering unmanageable,

Commander Walke reluctantly ordered his helmsman to head for the nearest riverbank.

At almost the same time Brady had assumed control of the helm, Chief Surgeon H. W. M. Washington entered the pilothouse and knelt over Brown.

"I'm not seriously injured," Brown muttered. "Tend to the others first."

The surgeon nodded and felt the vein on Hodges's neck. He shook his head and motioned to the orderlies. "Cover him and take him below." Then he moved to Shacklett, who, though nearly eviscerated, was still conscious. "Take him to my operating table, make him comfortable, and await my return."

After the orderlies carried out their grisly duties and removed the two pilots, Washington returned to Brown. "Captain, I must examine you."

Brown had struggled to his feet and was standing feebly next to Brady at the wheel. He stood in stony silence as Washington probed the gash on his forehead, unrolled a wide bandage, and wrapped it around the top of his head.

"You've a hard head," said Washington as he finished.

"So my father used to tell me," Brown replied with a taut grin.

By now *Tyler* had returned upriver in an attempt to help the crippled *Carondelet.* Lieutenant Commander Gwin, captain of *Tyler,* gave the order to a detachment of army sharpshooters that had been assigned to his boat. "Go out on deck and begin firing at that damned Rebel with muskets and pistols."

Like a terrier pestering a wolf, the gunboat audaciously pulled alongside *Arkansas* as the riflemen began raking the deck of the much larger ironclad with small-arms fire.

"Stay with the Yankees, Mr. Brady," ordered Brown. "I'm going below to direct the fire."

"I'll stick to them like molasses," Brady said gamely.

Brown dropped down to the gun deck, his boots scratching on the sand that had been spread to catch spilled blood. Just then, three of the broadside guns were fired in one huge burst. With a colossal roar, the shells hurtled across the water toward the disabled *Carondelet*. At the same time *Arkansas*'s bow guns swiveled their muzzles at *Tyler,* now only a few yards away. Brown watched the results of the point-blank barrage with grim satisfaction.

Pieces of *Tyler* exploded into the air as the little gunboat shuddered from stem to stern. At the same time, on the opposite side of the Rebel ironclad, shells smashed into *Carondelet,* heeling her starboard deck underwater and flooding her gun deck. At the same moment, a bullet from a pistol held by a Union officer on board *Tyler* cleanly entered the casemate through an open gun port and struck Brown in the temple, miraculously bouncing off and becoming lost in the smoke.

For the second time in less than half an hour, Isaac Brown fell to the deck nearly senseless.

Lieutenant Wharton, in command of the port broadside guns, shouted, "The captain's been hit! Take him to the surgeon!"

With the battle raging around him, Brown slowly opened his eyes, focused them, sat up, and looked around. As he began to pull himself to his feet, Acting Master Samuel Milliken ran over and grasped him by the arm.

"Sir, you should stay down. Your head is bleeding."

"I'll survive," Brown murmured. Shaking off Milliken, he staggered toward the bow gunports where he could see the effects of his ship's well-aimed fire.

Carondelet was a shambles: her armor shattered, engines disabled, and some thirty of her crew dead and wounded by the Rebel ironclad that until an hour ago was only a cursory report by spies. She sat impotent as *Arkansas* swept past. Clouds of steam billowed into the air from her severed pipes as her panicked crew leaped from every opening over the side into the muddy river.

Brown stepped out onto the roof of *Arkansas*'s casemate and called out to his old friend Henry Walke. It was never known whether Walke heard him or not, but there was no reply. Leaving the battered *Carondelet* hanging in the willows along the bank, Brown ordered helmsman Brady to pursue *Tyler* and *Queen of the West.*

Under ordinary circumstances the battle would have been considered the end to a fine day's job, but for the *Arkansas* and her crew it was only a prelude. As injured as his head might be, Brown's mind was still active and functioning. "I'm going below," he informed Executive Officer Stevens. "Don't let up our fire."

The bandage on his head stained a deep red, Brown made his way to the engine room. "Good God!" he gasped as he was struck by a wave of fiery air.

The temperature in the engine room was hovering at 130 degrees and rising. The firemen were stripped to the waist, their bodies blanketed with coal dust that adhered to their sweat, their faces beet red. Eyes watered nonstop from the heat. Every man felt as if his skin were scorched.

Stevens peered down through the hatch and yelled to Brown. "I've arranged for relief. We'll rotate the engine crew into shifts. The second group is coming down now."

Brown stared at Chief Engineer City, who had trouble keeping his head up as he bravely fought to keep from blacking out from heat exhaustion. "You're dead on your feet, Mr. City. You'd better go topside for a while."

City shook his head. "The breechings between the furnaces and the smokestacks have been shot away. We can't get any draft in here."

The injured captain helped the nearly prostrate engineer up the ladder toward the cooler gun deck above. After City emerged from the engine room, he collapsed. One of the sailors on deck splashed a tin ladle of water in his face to revive him. City sputtered, shook the cobwebs from his brain, and spoke down to Brown.

"One more thing, captain," he rasped as he struggled to inhale cooler air. "I can't give you more than twenty pounds of steam."

Arkansas had started out with 120.

"Tend to these men," Brown ordered Stevens. "No more than fifteen minutes down in that hellhole. And make sure they have an ample supply of fresh water. If you want me, I'll be in the pilothouse."

Clutching his throbbing head, Brown stepped into the pilothouse over the blood of the dead and wounded. He placed an arm on Brady's shoulder. "How goes the old *Arkansas?*" he asked.

"Still full of fight, captain. But we won't be ramming anyone. I barely have enough speed to make headway."

"No returning upriver then?"

"Absolutely not. If we weren't steaming with the current, a man could walk faster than we're traveling."

"Then we'll be entering the devil's sanctuary at a distinct disadvantage," said Brown, contemplating their reception by Admiral Farragut's combined river- and oceangoing fleet that waited around the final bend of the Yazoo only two miles ahead.

There would be no escape for *Arkansas*. Stretching from riverbank to riverbank, the thirty-seven warships of the Union Mississippi River Squadron sat anchored as far as the eye could see. Their black hulls, forest of masts, and endless rows of smokestacks formed an impenetrable gauntlet bristling with over a thousand guns.

"Oh, dear lord," moaned Brady at the horrendous sight.

Brown settled onto a high stool so he could peer through a slit in the shattered armor of the pilothouse. "Straight down the middle, Mr. Brady. We want to hit every ship we shoot at."

Brady's chin was trembling in fear at the shocking sight of so many ships with their guns aimed, in his mind at least, directly at him. Sweat ran down his face. Still, his hands remained steady on the splintered helm.

"Yes, sir," he said in a determined voice. "Straight down the middle."

The cry echoed from ship to ship within the Union fleet. "The *Arkansas* is coming!" The drummers on board began beating general quarters. Unable to make headway and maneuver into a position to fire a clear shot, the Union fleet, despite their overwhelming firepower, suffered a great handicap. Not believing *Arkansas* and her commander would dare take on the entire fleet, Farragut and his fleet were not prepared. They had been caught napping, without steam in their boilers and few guns primed and loaded.

Grim and dedicated, the men on *Arkansas* could only pray they could survive the coming holocaust of fire as the four-knot current carried them into the jaws of the monstrous fleet of ships lying on every side of them.

The Confederate ironclad soon pulled even with the first ship in line, Admiral David Farragut's flagship, U.S.S. *Hartford,* with her twenty nine-inch guns. The guns on *Arkansas*'s bow spat out a deadly blast of iron. The big, deep ocean-draft warship was caught unprepared and was immediately ravaged by the ironclad's well-placed shells. *Hartford*'s anchor, two boats, and several sections of her railings were blown away by the hail of iron as her crew ran for cover.

The gunners on *Arkansas* were free to fire from all sides without fear of striking a fellow Rebel, and they took advantage of the opportunity. Aiming at every point on the compass, their continuous fire could not fail but strike a target. It truly was a turkey shoot, Brown thought.

Next in line was the screw sloop *Iroquois,* then the river ironclad *Benton,* the steam sloop *Richmond,* and the armored ferryboat *Essex.* All were savaged by the mad Confederate ironclad as it steamed past, guns blazing from all ten ports.

The wind had died and the smoke from the three hundred cannon that could be trained on *Arkansas* soon created a dense black shroud that hung over the water. Unable to see, the Federal gunners were forced to use the muzzle flashes of *Arkansas*'s cannon to guide their shell placement. In the crossfire, they struck their own ships almost as often as they did the Confederate ironclad. A cry rose from the Union ships to cease firing until the air cleared.

* * *

On board the Union gunboat *Sciota,* her commanding officer, Reigard Lowry, ordered his eleven-inch gun to fire at the grotesque brown intruder. The first shot struck the Rebel's casemate, but bounced high off the armor and exploded harmlessly in midair above the stern. Lowry watched carefully as another shell crashed into the ironclad's side. The upper half of a body fell from a gunport. The man had been leaning out of the casemate, swabbing the gun barrel, when he had been blown in half by the blast.

Lieutenant Barbot was in charge of the battery of guns on *Arkansas* where the man was killed. He stared sickened at the sight of the lower half of the torso that was lying in a spreading pool of blood. Fearing the horrifying remains would demoralize his crew, already shaken by hours of continuous battle, he ordered one of his gunners to toss the carcass over the side.

"I can't!" the gunner cried loudly over the roar of the guns. "You see, lieutenant, that is my brother."

Barbot performed the ghastly duty himself.

Lieutenant George Gift, a stout Tennessean with a great breadth of shoulders, was directing the fire of the bow guns when a Union shell struck *Arkansas*'s armor just to the side of the port gun. "That was a near hit!" he shouted to his crew of gunners.

"Don't worry, lieutenant," said a young powder carrier, "they say that lightning never strikes the same spot twice."

The words were barely out of the lad's mouth when another shell burst through the port and exploded with ferocious force directly inside the gun deck. Gift's hat was blown from his head over the side, and his hair and beard were instantly singed to the skin by fire.

On the deck around him, lying like broken and cast-off wax figures, sixteen of his gunners lay dead and wounded. Most of them were dreadfully maimed by the splinters that sprayed from the wood planking behind the iron shield. The decks were set ablaze by the shell, and Gift quickly manned a pump and extinguished the fire. As he washed down the deck, his stream of water passed over the youth who just moments before had spoken to him.

The body of the boy was mutilated unmercifully, one leg blown completely apart at the thigh. His head was barely attached to his neck, by a mere thread of tissue. He had died before he struck the deck.

At the aft end of the casemate, Lieutenant Charles Read, already a veteran of the battle for New Orleans and destined for fame on the C.S.S. *Florida,* directed his crew who manned the twin thirty-two-pound guns that fired astern. Calm and collected, he stood whistling as if he were standing in line for a theater ticket.

He seemed amused as the solid shot struck the armor on the casemate and bounced away flattened, while shells burst into a thousand fragments.

Shells from *Arkansas*'s guns cut across the brief distance that separated her from the Union gunboat *Lancaster.* Although the captain of *Lancaster* had directed his crew to cover the boilers with chains to deflect cannon shot, the protection proved inadequate against *Arkansas*'s big rifled guns. Two shells penetrated the plate armor on the side of the ship and continued through the timbers into the boilers. Scalding water and steam burst throughout the vessel, boiling the men in the engine room like lobsters in a pot. A dozen men screamed in chorus from burning agony, their anguished cries heard aboard *Arkansas.* In the space of only thirty seconds, they fell dead, the flesh cooked from their bones. The remaining members of the crew, under a deluge of cannon fire, jumped into the river to avoid certain death by the superheated steam.

Brady the pilot clenched the wheel in helplessness as *Arkansas* charged through the Union sailors struggling to stay afloat in the muddy water, clinging to whatever debris they could find to keep from drowning. Brady never knew whether any of *Lancaster*'s crew were chewed up by *Arkansas*'s twin screws.

*   *   *

At last, *Arkansas* was through the worst of it. She was badly mauled, her armor punched entirely through in places and her engines barely operational, yet she was still afloat, making steam, her guns still firing in defiance.

Ahead lay but one solitary ship, a Union ironclad flying the square banner of a flag officer. It was *Benton,* commanded by Commodore David Dixon Porter, the last vessel in the Union gauntlet, and considered one of the most powerful on the river.

"I think I can ram this one," Brady said to Brown. "The current seems stronger through here and is pushing us at a fair speed."

Too late, Brown observed a lookout on board *Benton* frantically motioning toward *Arkansas.* With a sudden burst of speed, the Union ironclad slipped from the path of the avenging Confederate and swung toward the opposite side of the river.

"Pour a broadside into her," Brown yelled down to the gun deck.

The exhausted and bloody gunners gave their last measure of strength and blasted out their final volley. The Union ship was raked by a storm of shells. The crew on the gun deck of *Benton* were decimated, falling like grass under a scythe.

Admiral Farragut was furious that the lone Confederate ship had escaped the combined might of two fleets. He ordered the small, fast river steamer *Laurel Hill* to give chase. Quickly making steam, the heavily armed steamboat set off after the badly shattered ironclad.

The attempt came too late. Their quarry was free of the gauntlet at last.

Arkansas, looking for all the world like a bizarre barge heaped with iron scrap, navigated the dogleg bend in the river above Vicksburg and finally came under the protection of the Confederate Army gun batteries sitting high atop the rocky cliffs of the Rebel stronghold. Isaac Brown shielded his eyes from the sun and peered astern at the smoke from the advancing *Laurel Hill.*

"Shall we dawdle until she's within range?" he said quietly to faithful Brady at the helm.

Brady shook his head. "We'll be lucky to have enough steam to make it to the dock."

"Then take her in," Brown said, pounding the pilot's back. "We've fought enough for one day."

On the hills of Vicksburg, thousands of soldiers, joined by a vast mob of local citizens, greeted the weary brown ship with loud cheers. Alerted by the thunder of guns upriver, they had learned of the battle from a rider on horseback, who witnessed the spectacle from shore before racing into town. As *Arkansas* slipped alongside the dock, they ran down to the river to offer their heartfelt congratulations.

Led by three company bands, dispatched from the army in response to news of the glorious fight, the onlookers waved wildly at the gallant men who climbed dazed and exhausted onto the open deck of the ironclad. Begrimed with gunpowder and bleeding from wounds suffered from flying wood splinters, they stood mute and indifferent to the spirited reception.

"I want all hands who can still stand to carry off the dead and wounded," Brown ordered Lieutenant Stevens.

"I will see to it directly," Stevens acknowledged with a tired salute.

Within minutes, those of the crew who could still walk, many heavily bandaged, began to carry off their dead and near dead.

Like spectators at a grotesque carnival, the crowd on shore pressed close to the badly damaged ironclad and peered through the open gunports. Blood covered almost every inch of the gun deck. Severed limbs and body parts from the fallen crew were littered around the still-smoking guns. They stared in awe at the gaping holes gouged in the armor by Union shells. The brown paint was cracked loose in spots, revealing a coating of rust on the railroad armor.

Suddenly frozen in horror at the sight of the slaughter,

the spectators stood silent as the hospital and morgue wagons began to pull away with their pitiful cargo. The men who had carried off the bodies and the injured immediately returned on board, and without even a pause, they began to repair the damage.

"Ask the army for help in transporting coal to the dock," Brown ordered Lieutenant Harris. "I want the bunkers refilled as soon as possible."

Below Vicksburg, a small blockading force of Union gunboats began firing at *Arkansas*. They stayed far off, fearing the potent shore batteries, one of which was commanded by David Todd, President Lincoln's brother-in-law. The unenthusiastic barrage did little more than throw water on the coal dust that was coating the deck of the Confederate ironclad as her bunkers were loaded.

The mortified officers of the Union fleet, enraged by the death and destruction caused by the lone Rebel warship, pulled up their anchors and headed to Vicksburg to continue the fight. Their anger was well founded. Shot and shell from *Arkansas*'s guns had struck Union ships seventy-three times, killing forty-two men and wounding sixty-nine.

At seven that evening, they came within range of the docked ironclad. As the fleet passed by in formation, heading downriver, a hundred guns blasted away at the already trashed casemate of *Arkansas*.

The evening sky was ablaze from the furious bombardment, and sparks flew from the impact of Union iron against the Rebel's shielded walls. The inferno of cannon fire lasted throughout the night. In the morning light, Admiral Farragut and Commodore Porter stared anxiously through their binoculars, hoping to see that *Arkansas* was beneath the murky water of the Mississippi.

They were stunned to see that she was still floating stubbornly beside her dock and defiantly firing back.

"The Yankees don't know when to quit," Brown said with a smug grin. Not a man to shirk from a fight, he ordered his crew to take *Arkansas* on the offensive.

She was in no way fit for another battle against over-whelming odds, but she steamed toward the Union fleet as a storm of shot from the Confederate batteries on the hills thundered overhead in support. The besieged citizens of Vicksburg watched in rapt fascination as the battle-worn ironclad advanced to fight the entire fleet of Union ships for the second time in twenty-four hours.

Before she could strike a blow, *Arkansas* was struck by a 225-pound wrought-iron bolt from a big Union gun. In the shape of a dumbbell, the gigantic missile pierced the lower section of the casemate, passed through the armor, shredded the heavy timbers behind, and caused havoc in the engine room. Chief Engineer City was thrown against a bulkhead and knocked senseless.

"Help me get City above deck!" one of the firemen shouted.

Another stoker, barely visible in the cloud of steam that was filling the engine room, grabbed City by the feet. Together, they carried him up to the gun deck.

After the bolt had smashed into the engine room, disabling one engine, killing two firemen, and wounding several others, it then continued on through the dispensary, spreading a hail of fragments and splinters. In its wake it left a dead pilot, William Gilmore, who had volunteered to come aboard as replacement for the two pilots lost during battle with *Carondelet,* before lodging in the wood backing just short of the iron shield. James Brady, the brave pilot who had heroically manned the wheel during the run through the gauntlet, was wounded and knocked overboard into the water.

As the sun set, *Arkansas,* one engine barely turning, limped back to her dock below Vicksburg and once again unloaded her dead and wounded. Nor did the Union ships escape unscathed. Several were shot up by the Confederate's accurate fire and badly damaged. The dead and wounded more than equaled those of *Arkansas.*

The next few days passed slowly as much-needed repairs were completed. Captain Brown took great delight in harassing Admiral Farragut's crews. Every day at different times, he would order the boilers lit. As soon as smoke began to flow from her stack, the entire Union fleet, believing *Arkansas* was coming out again, would get up steam. Engine-room crews already sweltering in the summer heat, the heated boilers would raise the temperature on board their ships to an uncomfortably high level.

Undaunted, Farragut ordered another assault. At daylight on the 22nd of July, the Federal ships returned in force. The ironclad *Essex* took the lead and ran through the fire from Confederate batteries directly for *Arkansas*. A more opportune time could not have been selected, as all but twenty-eight officers and crew members of her normal complement of two hundred were in hospitals from wounds or sickness.

Muzzles of their guns only a few yards apart, the two vessels traded point-blank fire. The shots from *Essex*'s guns crashed through the armor plating in the stern and nearly split the barrel of the starboard after gun, killing eight Confederates and wounding six, fully half the remaining crew. Still, firing for all she was worth, *Arkansas*'s gunners disabled the Union ship and drove her away.

As the badly damaged *Essex* drifted downriver, her stack riddled with holes, steam pipes shot away, and gaping holes showing in her hull, the Confederate shore batteries found their mark and shredded her decks, cutting away her shore boats and anchor before wounding her captain.

The fast ram *Queen of the West* came charging out of the smoke and struck the Rebel warship's side. *Arkansas* shuddered from the impact, and for a moment it seemed as if her hull would give way. But she shook off the blow, righted herself, and poured a withering fire into *Queen of the West,* chasing her away as well.

To the frustrated Union fleet, it seemed the incredible Confederate vessel could not be bested. Admiral Farragut wisely called off the attack.

"You must have bed rest or suffer the consequences." The army surgeon who examined Isaac Brown spoke in a way that would harbor no objection.

"I have a ship and crew who need me," Brown protested weakly.

"You are of little use to them dead," admonished the surgeon, "and that's what you'll be if you don't follow my instructions."

Finally, after a futile argument, Brown was carried by wagon to Grenada, Mississippi. There, at an old friend's house, he was ordered to rest and recuperate from fatigue and his wounds. Unfortunately, any respite was short-lived.

"I'll be damned if my ship will sail without me," Brown argued upon hearing that *Arkansas* had been ordered to assist in the battle for Baton Rouge. "Engineer City is in the hospital, and without him overseeing the engines, there is no telling what disaster will occur."

He had left orders for Lieutenant Stevens not to move the ship. But under pressure and given orders by the ranking naval officer in the region, Stevens had no choice but to obey and cast off for the 300-mile journey downriver to Baton Rouge.

If there was one thing that Isaac Newton Brown was never short of, it was guts. Rising from his sickbed, he climbed aboard the first train toward Vicksburg. Barely able to move, he made the 180-mile trip aboard a pile of mailbags. Still racked with sickness, he hired a wagon to take him the rest of the way.

He arrived four hours too late. *Arkansas* had sailed on her final voyage without him.

The boat's executive officer, Lieutenant Henry Stevens, was now in command of the ironclad. Standing on the bow as the boat steamed downriver toward Baton Rouge, he stared at the muddy water with great apprehension. Although all damage had been repaired and *Arkansas* was as formidable as when she took on the entire Union fleet, without Brown the crew felt unlucky. And without Engineer City, any problem with the engines meant real trouble. The new man in charge of the engine room was a young army officer with no experience in marine steam engines. Already, before they were halfway to their destination, the ship had to halt while repairs were hastily made.

By the next morning, as the undefeated *Arkansas* steamed down the silt-swirled expanse of water, smoke lazily trailing from her crudely patched stack, Stevens could hear the faint rumble of thunder. He recognized the sound of battle as field artillery rocked the Louisiana countryside, and he realized the ground assault by the Confederate troops to retake Baton Rouge from the Union Army had already been launched.

Dropping through an open port to the gun deck, he descended the ladder to the engine room. "How are the engines holding up?" he asked.

"Not good, sir," the engineer answered truthfully. "They're thoroughly unreliable."

Predictably, five minutes later, the port engine inexplicably stopped.

"I have called this meeting to determine your feelings about continuing on to Baton Rouge," Lieutenant Stevens said to the group of officers assembled around the officer's messroom. "I've been assured the engines can be repaired and put back into running order. But for how long there is no guarantee."

"We could make better time if the crew took to oars," Lieutenant Charles Read muttered sarcastically.

Stevens glanced around the table. "In front of you are slips of paper. I want each man to write his opinion on whether we should continue on or turn back. Do not add your name. I want you all to give your honest assessment without fear of reprisal."

One by one, using the stub of a pencil that they passed from hand to hand, the officers filled out the slips and tossed them into a hat in the center of the table. Stevens filled his out last and then stirred the pile.

"Now let us see our fate," he said as he removed and unfolded the slips of paper and read them off. "Continue, continue, continue, Baton Rouge, continue, fight, continue . . ." And on it went until the last slip was read and the decision was made unanimous.

Stevens pushed back his chair and rose from his place at

the end of the table. "Resume your stations, gentlemen. We have an appointment to keep in Baton Rouge."

Stevens stared at the three Union warships advancing upriver from Baton Rouge. "There's our old friend *Essex,*" he said to the new pilot. "Ram her. Then we'll finish off the other two."

Arkansas was approaching the final bend in the river before entering a strait that ran past the city under siege as Stevens moved outside and stood on the deck of the casemate. He peered through his binoculars into the distance. He could see the Confederate artillery on the western shore making a game attempt at keeping the Union warships from firing on rebel troop positions. He had barely returned to the safety of the pilothouse when a grinding noise carried throughout the ship. The starboard engine suddenly went dead and the port screw swung *Arkansas* in an arc, running her aground on a shoal.

The replacement engineer reported the problem. "The crankpin shattered," he explained. "We've set up a forge on the gun deck and the blacksmith will hammer out a new one to insert in the rocking shaft."

"How long before we can get under way?" asked Stevens.

"About dawn." The engineer wiped his brow, blackened with grease, on a dirty rag. "That's my best guess."

As promised, the engine was turning over at sunrise, and *Arkansas* immediately began to heave herself free of the shoal. For fear of running onto a shoal, the Yankee gunboats had not attacked during the night.

"Make for the *Essex,*" Stevens ordered the pilot.

Arkansas backed out into the river and was about to turn toward Baton Rouge when suddenly the port engine rattled and came to a dead stop. Powered only by the hastily repaired starboard engine, she once again swung in a half circle before shoving her ram into the muddy shore.

"I'm sorry, sir," said the engineer, defeat etched on his face. "The port engine is beyond repair."

"Then it's over," Stevens murmured despairingly. With great remorse, he gave the order to abandon ship.

As word passed among the crew, they headed for their quarters and began removing what little they could carry off. All were cheerless and saddened. They could not believe their beloved warhorse would die without a fight. As if in a funeral procession they solemnly stepped off the bow onto shore.

Stevens motioned to one of his officers. "Lieutenant Wharton."

"Sir?"

"Once everyone is on shore, I want you to take command of the men and assemble them in an orderly fashion."

"And what of you, sir?"

"I will torch the ship."

A flowing line of men waded through the shallow water and congregated on dry land. The taller men helped the shorter ones find footing. They were a ragtag group, half-dressed and dirty. In their arms they carried what few belongings they could save: a rifle, soiled clothes wrapped in a bundle, letters, and pictures from home. Only Stevens and Read remained on board.

"The men have loaded and primed every gun," Read reported.

"Good," said Stevens. "That should give her a rousing send-off. Is the powder trail laid?"

Read nodded. "Right into the magazine."

"Very well. You'd better head for shore now."

With tears streaming down his face, Stevens set ablaze the gunboat that he had commanded for less than three days.

The crew solemnly stood on shore and stared at their ship. Smoke began rising high in the air above her as fire flashed over her decks and out the gunports. *Essex* had moved in closer and was firing shells across the bend in the river into the sides of *Arkansas*. Then came a deafening roar as the powder magazine exploded. Water surged in and ran toward her stern. The bow lifted and the ironclad slid off the shoal and began drifting down the river, her casemate an inferno of flames, her guns firing in a final display of defiance. Soon after, she exploded in a mighty blast and sank out of sight.

No enemy ever walked her decks, no Union ship or fleet of ships defeated her. She gave better than she took and fought to the bitter end, defying the best of the best. Few ships in history ever fought against such incredibly high odds and survived. Constructed in haste with shoddy materials that had to be scavenged, during her short life she had accomplished the impossible.

The extraordinary career of *Arkansas* spanned only twenty-three days.

Strangely, *Arkansas* never received the historical acclaim awarded her sister ironclads. *Merrimack* or *Virginia,* depending on which side your sympathies lie, is far better known. The terrific fight put up by *Tennessee* before its surrender at Mobile Bay is more widely recorded. Books have been written on *Albemarle* but none on *Arkansas.* Perhaps her lack of notoriety stems from the fact that she caused so much grief for the Union Navy, and the victors always write the history books.

Arkansas lay buried under the mud of the Mississippi, lost and forgotten, and as far as it can be determined, never salvaged. Her only mention came sixty-five years after her destruction, and then she was misidentified as the Union Navy frigate *Mississippi:*

FROM AN ARTICLE IN THE BATON ROUGE NEWSPAPER, JUNE OF 1927.

A quantity of shells and human skeletons believed to be the last remains of the flag ship in command of George Dewey, later the hero of Manila Bay, have been pumped up by the Thompson Gravel Company a few miles north of Baton Rouge on the west side of the river.

A three-inch shell presented to James R. Wooten of the Louisiana Highway Commission by P. A. Thompson of the gravel company had been fired from a Confederate gun, according to Major J. C. Long, of the

United States Bureau of Public Roads, who has had training in this line of work. He says the appearance makes it evident that the shell was fired and that it was of the type used by the Confederates.

The ship commanded by George Dewey, who was going up the river with Admiral Farragut, was disabled by Confederate guns below Port Hudson. It drifted down the river and finally came into the bank a few miles above here where it caught fire, the majority of the occupants escaping. It is believed that the human skeletons and shells were from that ship, the Confederate shell possibly having become lodged in the rigging after it was fired. One of the shells weighed 102 pounds.

II

Go Down to the Levee

November 1981

WHEN I LAUNCHED OUR SEARCH FOR ARKANSAS, I thought I'd make an attempt to find another adventurous soul who would throw caution to the winds, and match my effort and expense. So I took a page from Ernest Shackleton, the renowned British polar explorer. He once ran an advertisement in the *London Times* for volunteers to join his expedition to the South Pole. He received over a thousand replies. I paraphrased his ad and ran my own in the *Wall Street Journal:*

Men wanted to fund search for historic shipwrecks. Some danger. Much frustration. Long, tedious hours at sea. Failure often possible. Return on investment unlikely. Great personal satisfaction when successful.
                    Contact Clive Cussler
                    National Underwater & Marine Agency
                    Austin, Texas

I received two replies from people who were only curious and no offers to help with the funding.

130

Over the years I had learned that begging for bucks was a lost cause and decided it caused less frustration to pay for NUMA's expeditions out of my book royalties—a wise decision I've never regretted. It was either that or leave the money for the kids.

I suppose I could keep a mistress on what I spend in looking for sunken ships, but it wouldn't be fair to my lovely wife of forty-one years. Besides, the satisfaction that comes from discovering a long-lost artifact of historical significance has a more lasting value than mere sex. Granted, there are no few men and a fair number of women who might find fault with my opinion, but then I was never accused of being normal. It's just me against the world, and all too often the world wins.

With only Colonel Walt Schob and the Schonstedt gradiometer, I hunted up and down the Mississippi River in Louisiana on a limited budget and discovered the Confederate ironclads *Manassas; Louisiana,* sunk during Admiral Farragut's capture of New Orleans; and the unconquerable *Arkansas.* The latter was especially satisfying because of its amazing record, mostly unknown to all but dedicated Civil War Navy enthusiasts.

The best piece of advice I can give anyone who is looking for a historic site in a small town is to head directly to the sheriff or police chief's office. Explain what you are hoping to accomplish and ask for his help and blessing. By being straightforward and honest, I have yet to encounter problems and have always received a warm welcome and friendly cooperation. Too often, strangers poking around a small town's river or fields are treated with undisguised suspicion by the local residents, but if you tell them the sheriff is behind your project, you're always greeted like an old friend.

After driving up from New Orleans in a rainstorm, Walt Schob and I arrived in West Baton Rouge Parish to search for the site of the Confederate ironclad *Arkansas.* We went straight to the parish sheriff's department (Louisiana has parishes instead of counties). After a short wait, we were called into Sheriff Bergeron's office. He was a big friendly man who smiled and spoke in a soft southern drawl. Warm and humorous exterior aside, you somehow knew this wasn't a man you'd want tracking you down a backcountry road or through a bayou.

After we explained our intentions, Sheriff Bergeron graciously loaned us the department search boat, a well-crafted aluminum vessel that had been designed and built by a prison trusty. Our only obligation was to pay one of his deputies to operate the boat.

I've also found that almost every town or city situated on or near water has a boat owned by either law-enforcement officials or the fire department. This craft, we soon discovered, was used mostly in dragging for drowning victims. The following morning, we soon gathered a small crowd of gawkers along the levee while we towed our gradiometer back and forth. Seeing the cable stretched over the stern, they constantly shouted out questions over the water. "Who drowned? Anybody we know? How many died?" Not a one believed us when we yelled back that we were searching for an old shipwreck.

The nice thing about searching in a river versus the open ocean is that you have something to look at besides water. The surface is also much smoother, the only waves coming from the wash of a passing towboat with a string of barges. The craft loaned to us by Sheriff Bergeron had a comfortable little cabin that kept out the sun and rain. Another great enjoyment that comes from working with people who have grown up and live in the surrounding neighborhood is that they tell fascinating stories. Strangers are perfect repositories for local gossip, mysteries, and secrets. I'm always more than happy to listen. I never know when I'll hear a plot inspiration for my next book.

The deputy sheriff, appointed by Sheriff Bergeron, steered our nifty little prisoner-built boat up and down the river without complaint. He sat through the ordeal patiently, making course changes as directed by Schob, who kept one eye glued to his range finder. Only once did the deputy turn to me and ask, "Just what is it we're looking for?"

"An old Civil War shipwreck," I replied.

He looked at me funny. "Why for?"

I didn't think "Because it's there" would satisfy him, so I said, "It was the only Confederate boat that kicked hell out of them damned Yankees."

His eyes suddenly shone like a beacon. "Hey, I like that."

It was then he passed around a thermos of coffee. I must say one thing about southern down-home brewed coffee with chicory. If you have worms, you'll never have them again.

I wish someday to lie back in a hammock as the day drags on and the gradiometer sings its song while drinking Dom Perignon and dining on cold roast pheasant and caviar. It never hurts to think big. I usually have to settle for a baloney sandwich washed down with a bottle of geriatric fruit juice. I tell myself I must be doing something wrong.

We began our search above Free Negro Point at Mulatto Bend Landing (they have rather odd names for places along the river), four miles north of Baton Rouge. This was recorded as the site where *Arkansas* was run aground by her crew before she was put to the torch. The only question was, how far did she drift around and below the bend before she eventually sank?

As with most disastrous events, there were many eyewitnesses to the destruction of *Arkansas,* but no one recorded exactly where she blew up and sank. One account that made fascinating reading came from a book called *A Confederate Girl's Diary* by Sarah Morgan Dawson. As a young teenage girl, she stood on the levee and watched the Rebel crew burn and evacuate the ship. She described *Arkansas* as "a clumsy, rusty, ugly flatboat with a great square box at the center, while great cannon put their noses out the sides and front. The decks were crowded with men, rough and dirty, jabbering and hastily eating their breakfast. That was the great *Arkansas!* God bless and protect her, and the brave men she carries."

As teenage girls are prone to do, Sarah, her sister Miriam, and two friends excitedly met and flirted with the young men of the ironclad's crew after they abandoned their ship. She was especially smitten with the naval hero Charles

Read, who laughed in the face of death but who blushed with shyness when talking with the young, vivacious Sarah. Her account put the ironclad precisely on the west bank at the river's bend when the crew set it on fire.

I accepted her version as gospel while discounting the old newspaper report of the Union Navy frigate *Mississippi*'s being found at the gravel company site because contemporary accounts emphatically claimed *Mississippi* blew herself out of existence and slid under the water far to the north of downtown Baton Rouge.

One of the U.S. Navy's original steam frigates, the *Mississippi* grounded and burned while attempting to run the guns of the Confederate-held fort upriver at Port Hudson, a good fifteen miles from *Arkansas*'s final resting place. George Dewey, of Manila Bay fame during the Spanish American War, was not the captain but the ship's executive officer. After being abandoned by her crew, the frigate drifted down the river ablaze until her powder magazines exploded and she went to the bottom of the river that gave her its name.

It became obvious to me that the report of workers' finding a Civil War vessel at the Thompson Gravel pit indicated the site that belonged to *Arkansas,* and certainly not *Mississippi,* which couldn't possibly have carried that far. Its shattered hulk still lies deep beneath a vast swamp where the river once ran just below Prophet's Island. The shells that were found were obviously from the ironclad's guns. The human skeletons are a mystery, since no bodies were left on board the *Arkansas,* and almost all the crew was known to have escaped the *Mississippi.*

The problem was to sift vague rumor from straight fact. One report had the *Arkansas* drifting downstream for an hour or more before she exploded. Allowing a maximum river current of four knots, Walt and I took no chances of missing our target, and extended our search lanes from a mile above the point where *Arkansas* was known to have struck the west bank to a point four miles below Baton Rouge, a good two miles beyond where she should have traveled in an hour and a half.

My own gut feeling was that the time/drift estimate included the interval between the moment Lieutenant Stevens left the burning vessel to when the stern, heavy with incoming water from the scuttling operation, sank a few feet and lifted the bow off the bank. Only then did she float free and allow the current to carry her around the bend and down toward Baton Rouge.

Right or wrong, I've always had this insane urge to launch my search lanes from the farthest point and work in toward my prime target area. Most wreck hunters, on the other hand, are impatient and begin their search in the middle and work out. Who's to say who's right? Like gold, shipwrecks are where you find them.

Beginning a mile above Free Negro Point, we worked around the bend and traveled south for nearly five miles before turning 180 degrees and beginning the upriver grid lane. So that no stone was left unturned and we wouldn't accidentally miss our wreck site, we started running our grid lanes on the east bank and worked west toward the most promising location. Except when we crossed over an occasional oil or gas pipeline, the magnetic readings were generally insignificant. The weather was balmy and the river lazy. The only traffic consisted of six-story-high tugboats pushing huge barges. I used to watch them thread the needle between the pilings of bridges spanning the river, hoping they'd scrape the sides. But they never came close.

Naturally, the only anomaly that blew the gradiometer off scale we struck on the final run along the west bank. Stupid? Perhaps. But if we hadn't found our target, we at least knew where we didn't have to search again. It's called, *not knowing where it is, but knowing where it ain't.*

Arkansas lies under a large rock levee. Schob walked the entire area, setting plastic bottles where his magnetometer detected the presence of iron. The readings were indicative of a huge mass. When Walt finished he had almost a perfect outline of the old ironclad—165 feet by 35 feet. Not enough hard evidence for a positive identification, but the clincher came later.

Shortly after we turned over our findings to Louisiana

State archaeologists, a noted historian with a strong interest in *Arkansas,* prominent Baton Rouge attorney Fred Benton, led an elderly minister and longtime resident of Baton Rouge to the top of the tallest building in the city's center.

"Reverend," asked Benton, "can you show me where the Thompson Gravel Company used to be?"

The reverend nodded and raised his hand. "Right about there, on the west bank of the river."

Benton saw that the reverend's finger was pointing at the exact spot where Walt Schob and I found the one and only huge magnetic anomaly for seven miles along the river.

Walt and I rested our case.

5

Part

U.S.S. *Carondelet*

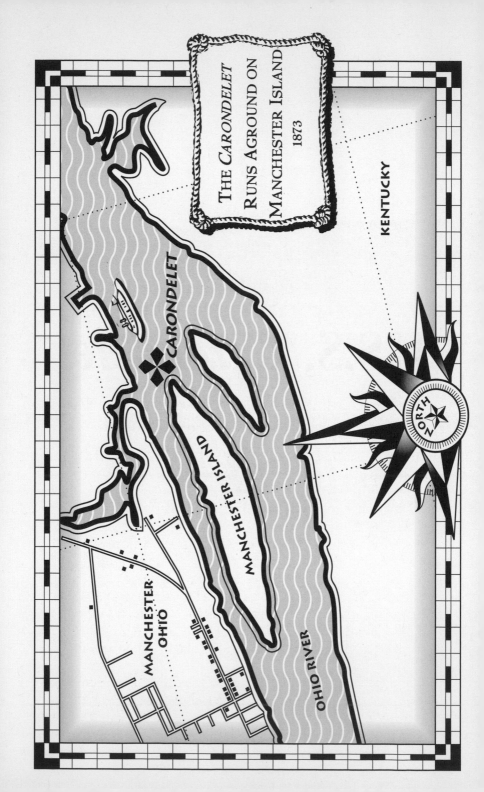

THE *CARONDELET*
RUNS AGROUND ON
MANCHESTER ISLAND
1873

KENTUCKY

CARONDELET

MANCHESTER ISLAND

MANCHESTER
OHIO

OHIO RIVER

NORTH

I

The River War

February 1862

"GUNS, PREPARE TO FIRE," COMMANDER HENRY WALKE ordered the officer who directed the gun batteries on board the U.S.S. *Carondelet*. Walke watched warily as his ironclad gunboat pulled into range a mile below the Confederate stronghold at Fort Donelson.

Alone, *Carondelet* closed the distance. The other gunboats of the Union Mississippi River Squadron that were ordered by Commodore Porter to support the attack on the fort were still miles downriver. Walke gave the command to open fire, and the three eight-inch smoothbore guns on the front of the armored casemate spat a hail of iron shot across the broad reach of the river. Soon they were joined by the thirty-two- and forty-two-pounders on the starboard side. For two hours, the lone boat kept up a constant barrage, firing 140 shells into and against the walls of the Confederate fort.

Situated in an ideal defensive position, Donelson was built on a rock bluff some 120 feet above the west bank of the water. She commanded a perfect line of fire for 180 degrees up and down the Cumberland River in Tennessee.

Three heavy gun batteries aimed their muzzles at the water, one at the crest, the second fifty feet below, and one a mere twenty feet above the shoreline. Sixteen guns in all, and every one threw their shot at *Carondelet.*

For a long while, the Union ironclad seemed immune to the missiles that exploded in the water around her. Then the $2^{1}/_{2}$-inch armor began to be pummeled and dented by the fort's barrage. A great roar issued from the fort as a 128-pound shell hurtled through the air and crashed through the casemate into the engine room.

The concussion of the blast in the boiler area felled fireman Albert Floyd. He struggled to his knees and stared dazedly at his partner, William Jeppsen, who lay facedown on the deck next to him.

"By God, Billy, I'd swear that shell was chasing our boiler crew."

Not a sound came from Jeppsen.

Floyd raised his voice, fearing the hiss of escaping steam from a severed pipe had drowned out his words. "Billy, did you hear me? It was like the shell was coming after our boys."

Still no answer.

Floyd reached over to shake his partner and friend, and finding no resistance, rolled Jeppsen over on his back.

Jeppsen was missing most of his chest. His stomach was opened up like a can of worms, exposing the organs inside. His facial features were horribly distorted. A spray of wooden splinters from the shattered timbers stuck in his skin like quills from a porcupine. To Floyd, his friend looked like a grotesque and bloody scarecrow.

He stumbled in shocked terror to the nearest ladder, vomited, and escaped from the engine room, howling like a banshee.

"Pull back!" Walke shouted to Chief Pilot William Hoel, as the hysterical fireman ran screaming across the gun deck.

Spinning the wheel, Hoel steered the boat away from the fort. Low on steam from the ruptured line, the center paddle wheels barely pushed the ironclad over the surface of the river. A second 128-pound shell from the big rifled gun on the bluffs severed *Carondelet*'s huge anchor, snapping it like a twig. Then the shell bounced over the forward pilothouse and smashed off part of the smokestack before falling in the river. Choking fumes began spilling into the gun deck, sending the crew to the open ports to breathe in fresh air.

As the gunboat retreated, the barrage continued without letup. The entire complement of lifeboats were blasted out of their davits; sections of armor at the waterline were punched completely through. Water flooded into the hold from several holes. The iron plating looked as though it had been ripped open by a giant chisel.

"The shells flew across the water like skipping stones," Walke recalled later. He ordered all available steam, which wasn't much.

While they were slowly pulling out of range of the fort, one of the guns on the port side exploded, wounding twelve of her crew. Red-hot pieces of the shattered gun flew through the air and embedded in the wooden deck, starting a fire.

Simon Grange, a seaman who had been assigned to load the gun that burst, was only slightly wounded by the blast. He immediately ran to man the water pump to extinguish the fire. Grange was only a few months past seventeen years. His hair was sandy-colored and his attempt to grow a beard and look like a proper mariner was failing miserably. He had a strong chin and a crooked smile, and his eyes still held the innocence of youth.

Grange was furiously working the steel handle of the fire pump when a final Confederate shot entered the open gunport. In horror, he saw three of his shipmates' bodies fly past him, their heads shattered by the blast. They landed at his feet in one big bloody heap.

The gun deck of *Carondelet* suddenly took on the look of a slaughterhouse. Metal fragments, wood blown off the casemate, and mutilated bodies all shared the same space. Grange stared in disgust at the spreading streams of blood that mixed with the water from the fire pump before disappearing in the cracks between the deck planking. By the time he had put out the fire and begun helping the wounded, his eyes were hard and cold from the sight of death.

That night, *Carondelet's* dead and wounded were removed from the boat and crude repairs hurriedly carried out. By next morning, she was joined by the rest of the fleet. The ironclads *St. Louis, Pittsburgh,* and *Louisville* accompanied her back up the river to Fort Donelson. Following them were the wooden gunboats *Tyler* and *Conestoga,* the latter captained by Lieutenant Thomas Selfridge, former second officer of the ill-fated *Cumberland,* sunk by *Merrimack.*

At dawn, the battle began anew. Admiral Andrew Foote, commander of the squadron, ordered his boats to close with the fort. It was a grave miscalculation, which would cause unnecessary destruction.

With the boats positioned beneath the Confederate guns, enemy shells no longer had to arc to hit their targets. Instead, they plunged straight down and, with the added momentum of gravity, slammed through the weakly armored roofs of the Union fleet.

St. Louis, Foote's flagship, was struck by a shell that killed the pilot instantly, jamming a spearlike splinter through his chest, then sheared away the wheel and wounded the admiral, breaking his ankle. *St. Louis* drifted downriver, disabled, out of the fight.

In almost the same moment, *Pittsburgh*'s tiller ropes were severed by shore fire. Also out of control, she drifted with the current until she was out of range of the shore batteries. *Louisville* suffered as well, taking a well-aimed Confederate shot below the waterline, and immediately began to sink in the middle of the river. Only a few watertight compartments kept her afloat as she struggled to retreat, handicapped by the weight from the river flooding her hull.

At the sight of the fierce, one-sided fight, unarmored *Tyler* and *Conestoga* quickly steamed away, leaving *Carondelet* alone once again to suffer the full effect of the fort's fire-power.

* * *

"Stay the course," Walke shouted from the gun deck to the pilothouse above.

With smoke from *Carondelet*'s guns fouling the air and cloaking her from eyes on shore, the solitary boat kept up her fire. But soon the wages of war became due again. A shell in the forward port gun misfired, peeling back the end of the muzzle like a banana skin, killing its entire gun crew and pressing the nearby armor outward as if a large boil had formed on the casemate.

Whistling through the smoke, shells from the Confederate gunners splashed the river all around *Carondelet*. Eventually a light breeze cleared the air enough for them to walk their fire onto the target. Projectiles began raining on the boat with great accuracy.

One struck the pilothouse and killed the pilot who had relieved Hoel. The iron onslaught cut away the Union flag and chipped the armor from the casemate like an axe hacking bark from a tree. After another hour of seeing his boat battered to pulp a second time without any sign of damage to the enemy, Walke reluctantly gave the order to steam out of range.

Over the past two days, his boat had taken fifty-four direct hits, forty of his crew were either killed or wounded, and the survivors were bleeding from the ears from the constant concussions.

Walke came across a wounded sailor huddled under blankets near a hole smashed in the casemate beside his gun station. "How are you doing, son?" he asked softly.

"I'm a little cold, sir."

"Go down to the boilers and warm up for a spell."

"I can't leave my gun station, sir," the young sailor murmured.

"You can if I order," Walke said, smiling. "Now go."

The sailor needed no further urging. He limped off toward the engine room.

Henry Walke did not look like a tough, hardened naval hero. He was tall, thin, and gaunt, and there was a lost, vacant look in his dark eyes. His hair was as black as ebony, thick and oddly receding in a straight line back of his forehead. He wore a goatee and could have passed for the twin brother of Benjamin Disraeli, Great Britain's Prime Minister.

Walke finished his damage inspection, climbed into the shattered pilothouse, and spoke to the pilot, William Hoel. "Tie up to the main dock in Cairo. I want the wounded on shore and in the hospital as soon as humanly possible. After they've been removed, we will take the boat up the river to the Mound City, Illinois, boatyard."

"She's damaged pretty severely, captain," said Hoel. "Is there enough left for the carpenters to fix?"

"She can be fixed," Walke replied firmly as he stared at his battle-wasted gunboat.

He was proud of her and his crew. *Carondelet* had been the first in and last out of the battle. She was badly scarred, but she would live to fight again.

A few days later, the commander of Fort Donelson surrendered to Ulysses S. Grant, who was happy to admit he owed a debt to the gunboat, once he saw how considerably reduced the defenses were from the heroic fire of *Carondelet*.

Malcolm Chesley worked as a shipwright in the yards at Liverpool, England, before the war. In 1860 he had immigrated to Chicago, seeking work as a cabinetmaker. When the war broke out and it became evident that the Union would need trained carpenters at the Mound City boatyard, he volunteered.

He stood on the dock beside the heavy cherry-wood case containing his precious tools, some nearly a hundred years old and passed down from his grandfather. As he waited for help in carrying them on board, he stared at the odd-looking vessel he had been assigned to repair.

Carondelet was one of seven ironclads built for the river war by a brilliant civil engineer by the name of James B. Eads, who in 1874 built the first triple-arch steel bridge across the Mississippi River, which is still in use by auto traffic today.

As the clouds of war threatened, Eads proposed building a

fleet of ironclad, steam-powered warships to operate against southern opposition on the western rivers. The United States government eventually approved his proposal, and Eads completed the massive project in record time. Working four thousand men in round-the-clock shifts, he finished the novel vessels in one hundred days, several months before the *Monitor* and *Merrimack* duel in Hampton Roads. *Carondelet* and her six sisters became the first ironclad fleet in the world to enter combat with enemy warships and land fortifications.

Her lyrical name came not from an exotic place but from Baron de Carondelet, the last Spanish governor of Louisiana. His name had been given to the small town where Eads had built her.

Not pretty, but tough and extremely efficient, the Eads ironclads or "Pook Turtles" as they were sometimes called because of their sloped sides, spearheaded General Ulysses Grant's offensive from Fort Donelson to Vicksburg. They fought up and down the Mississippi and on every river from Tennessee to Texas. As if striving for a gold star on an attendance report, *Carondelet* was present at nearly every engagement from 1862 until late 1864.

Chesley thought the boat unlike any he had ever seen. The hull was rounded on both ends, 175 feet in length and some 50 feet wide. The displacement was 512 tons, and to maneuver in the shallow waters the boat drew only six feet of water. An oblong casemate sat atop the flat hull. Angled at thirty-five degrees on the sides and forty-five degrees on bow and stern, it was topped out with a flat roof. Near the front of the boat was an octagonal pilothouse plated with iron and level on the top. Tiny square ports were cut in the iron to see through.

Aft of the pilothouse, twin smokestacks vented the smoke from the six boilers that powered two horizontal, high-pressure engines. Beyond the stacks toward the stern was a rectangular structure with a rounded top that housed the twin interior paddle wheels. Four boats hung from davits, two on each side. Twin rudders were hung for steerageway.

The sloped, armored casemate had gunports with protective shields that could be opened and closed. Through the openings poked thirteen guns, three in the bow, four along each side, and two in the stern.

Chesley studied the heavy damage to the boat by Fort Donelson's guns. It was a bleeding wonder, he thought, she still floated. To his mind, they might as well start over.

A junior carpenter started across the boarding ramp to the forward deck of the boat, and Chesley yelled across to him. "Give me a hand with my tools, will you, mate?"

The man returned and lifted one end of the heavy case. He nodded toward the jagged holes in the armor. "This should keep us busy until next Christmas, don't you think?"

"Maybe even Easter," Chesley grunted, lifting his end of the case.

Ten days later, *Carondelet* rejoined the fleet.

Henry Walke reached into his pocket and withdrew a worn old pipe. He filled it from a sealskin pouch containing his favorite Ohio Valley tobacco. Then he began an inspection tour of the engine room. Finding everything in first-rate order, he turned to his chief engineer. "Are the repairs to the steam heaters to your satisfaction?"

"They seem fine, sir. As the other boilers are fired, I'll open the vents and the boat should begin to warm up."

The bell in the engine room rang loudly. "That's the pilot," said Walke. "We've cast off from the dock."

The engineer nodded. "A quarter back," he ordered one of the crew, who immediately gripped a brass lever and notched it downward.

"Inform me if you meet with any problems," said Walke.

"I shall, captain," the engineering officer said smiling. "You'll be the first I'll complain to."

Walke nodded silently as he lit his pipe.

"May I ask where we're headed?" asked the engineer.

"Island Number Ten," Walke said over his shoulder. "Where we'll stare the devil in the eye."

The Confederate stronghold at Island Ten was the key to the upper Mississippi. The borders between Kentucky and

Tennessee were constantly changing, the line on the maps held hostage by the whims of a river that did not recognize state-designated lines. At the time of the battle for river supremacy, Island Ten was inside Tennessee, but just barely.

The island fortress sat almost smack dab in the middle of the Mississippi, barring the Union Navy from unimpeded access around it. At the outbreak of the war, the Confederates had wisely constructed a vast complex of forts on the island, eleven in total. Multiple batteries mounted nearly sixty guns.

In addition, a sixteen-gun man-made floating battery, with pumps to raise and lower its platform, floated above the fortifications. These powerful batteries, along with a complement of some seven thousand soldiers on the eastern bank, allowed the Confederates to hold deadly control over the upper river.

To win the river war, the taking of Island Ten by Union forces was an absolute necessity.

Below the fortifications, a long line of Union mortar boats had been towed up the river and placed along the bank, hidden by trees along the water's edge. A mortar boat was little more than a floating raft with sloping sides and a huge mortar in the center of the deck. Piled on all sides were shot and drums of powder. A small hoist lifted the immense projectile into the stubby barrel.

The men assigned to them would load the massive shells, touch the fuse with fire, and then run out a door and crouch behind a wall on deck. With mouths agape to prevent their eardrums from blowing out and hands cupped over their ears, they would await the blast. Even with such precautions, most of the mortar raft crews went deaf.

At sunrise, the entire Union force opened fire on the island batteries.

Days passed as the assault continued from land and river. The Confederates, who the Union believed would surrender when the gunboats arrived, were comfortably holding out, returning fire whenever they spotted a target.

Union Major General John Pope, in command of an army of twelve thousand men, was encamped on the west side of the river below the island. He thought that if he could transport his troops across river and attack the island from the south, the Confederates would be cut off and have no choice but to fold, placing control of the river in Union hands. It was a sound plan, but he needed a gunboat to run past the great mass of guns on the island and silence any field artillery that might stop his crossing.

Rear Admiral Foote, in command of the Union gunboat flotilla, was adamantly opposed to the idea. He believed the Confederate guns would tear to pieces any of his boats that made the attempt to run around the island forts.

Only one gunboat captain disagreed with Foote's prediction of doom.

Under a canvas army tent beside the river, the discussion was heated.

"We have to find another way," Admiral Foote argued.

"The mortar barrage is having little or no effect, admiral," General Pope stated truthfully. He sat on a camp stool and rubbed the soles of his black leather boots against each other, flaking off the dark mud, while he stroked his thick beard and sipped from a tin cup containing his favorite tea. "We need support from the navy. Only then can my troops take the island."

"If I lose any of my boats by their failure to run past sixty guns, then what help have you received?" Foote's fractured ankle from the battle at Fort Donelson was giving him great pain, and his overall health was fading fast from the pressures of command.

Several of his gunboat captains listened carefully without commenting.

Walke also sat listening, staring at the ground, deep in thought. Then suddenly he looked up and spoke slowly with purpose. "I'm certain I can get *Carondelet* around Island Ten, admiral. My crew is the most experienced in the fleet. They're no strangers to enemy fire. If we pass in the dead of night, we stand a good chance of success."

"At least someone in the navy has some spirit," Pope said acidly.

Rear Admiral Foote ignored the remark and stared at Walke. Foote was a kindly-looking man with soft brown eyes. He had worked his way up the ladder to flag officer through experience and wise decisions. He was well respected by his fellow officers and superiors. His hair remained dark and natural, but his bristling beard had turned gray. He was weary from the war that was scarcely a year old.

He leaned forward and clasped his hands. "Your fellow officers do not believe it can be done. Why should I risk the chance of losing you and your crew?"

"Carondelet is a lucky boat, admiral. She's fought in every river battle from here to Belmont and survived. If any boat can do it she can. I predict that when this war is won she'll still be afloat. I swear to you that if you allow me to make the passage I will get through."

Foote stared at Walke long and hard, then said quietly, "If I've learned anything during my many years in the navy, it's not to second-guess my commanders. If you feel your boat can make it when every other officer here believes it is madness, then it is a madness I share. But I have faith in your fervor, Henry, and your dedication. You get your boat safely past that damned island. Do you understand?"

"Yes, sir. You can rely on me."

"Good," Foote grunted. "Give them hell."

"Amen," General Pope sighed. "Amen."

By the fourth of April, preparations were complete.

In addition to the reinforced casemate, a huge barge laden with coal and cotton bales was lashed along the port side as protective shield from the island's guns. *Carondelet,* already homely by design, now looked like a floating derelict on a journey to nowhere.

"Issue the men pistols, rifles, and cutlasses to repel boarders," Walke ordered his first officer, Charles Murphy. "And check to see if the hoses from the boilers are in place."

Walke had ordered the shipwrights to rig lines directly from the steam boilers to the upper decks. If the ship became disabled and the Confederates tried to board and take the boat by hand-to-hand fighting, they would be sprayed with streams of boiling water.

Satisfied he could do no more, Walke gave the order to cast off the mooring lines attached to trees along the riverbank.

At ten o'clock that night, the moon had already set and the river was pitch black, the stars blanketed by thick clouds. A massive spring thunder shower, with drops as large as a baby's fist, splattered onto the decks of the boat as she pulled from shore.

As if it were an omen, an intense lightning storm tore the sky. Bolts flew from the black heavens in jagged shafts, first blue, then yellow, then white. To the Union observers on shore, *Carondelet* appeared and disappeared like some ghostly apparition without substance or body.

On the open top deck, the crew gathered around their captain as he stood with Bible in hand, leading them in prayer. He, too, took on the look of a wraith as he was briefly illuminated by the lightning.

"There she goes," Foote shouted excitedly through his speaking trumpet to the boats moored beside his flagship.

As word passed through the fleet, the mortar rafts let loose a curtain of shells to cover the sound of *Carondelet*'s steam engines. The only light inside the gunboat as she gathered speed on the dark river was a single lantern deep inside the engine room. The rest of the boat was as black as a crypt as she steamed toward what many thought was certain destruction.

"We're getting close," Walke said to First Master Pilot Hoel, who stood at the wheel, using every bit of his experience to keep the boat in deep water and away from shoals. It was a nearly impossible job in the dead of night, and the pilot was thankful for the occasional flashes of lightning that showed him the riverbanks.

"We'll be coming alongside the north end of the island about now," said Hoel.

The steam vent that kept the dust in the stacks moist had been diverted into the paddle-wheel housings to silence the loud hiss. As *Carondelet* passed the Confederates' floating battery, the dry stacks suddenly flared with flame and sparks.

"Man the pumps and extinguish the fire!" Walke shouted down from the pilothouse.

With fire blazing from her twin smokestacks like an erupting volcano gone mad and lit by the flashes of lightning, the boat steamed within range of the mighty Confederate gun batteries. And yet there was no sign that *Carondelet* had been discovered. No flash of cannon fire cut the night.

Hoel suddenly yelled, "Hard aport!" and furiously twisted the wheel. With only three feet to spare he had saved the boat from running aground on an obstruction the rebels had secretly constructed in the river channel. But in doing so, he had brought *Carondelet* directly abreast of the island just as she was fully revealed by a nearby lightning strike. Seeing the Union gunboat suddenly materialize from the darkness, the Confederates rushed to their guns.

A sporadic storm of shot and shell was unleashed across the water, aimed at the protective coal barge the Confederates thought was the side of the Union vessel. The barrage produced no effect. Not one piece of iron struck the gunboat's casemate.

With sparks still shooting from her stacks, paddle wheels whipping the water in a frenzy, and a jubilant Walke yanking the chain on her steam whistle in a defiant gesture, *Carondelet* steamed around a bend into the clear and vanished in the night.

A few miles below Island Ten, the lucky gunboat eased along the shore to the cheers of Union troops, elated that her big guns would soon support their assault on the Confederate works.

Two nights later, encouraged by the success of Walke and *Carondelet,* a second gunboat, *Pittsburgh,* made the hazardous passage. Soon, General Pope's troops were ferried across the river to attack the Rebels' back door. On April 7, surrounded by overwhelming ground and river forces, Island Ten surrendered.

* * *

Three months later, Commander Walke was summoned on board Admiral Farragut's flagship, *Hartford,* recently arrived after running his fleet upriver from New Orleans past the Confederate works at Port Hudson.

After offering him a glass of port, Farragut said, "Commander Walke, our spies report that the ram the Confederates have been building up the Yazoo River is nearly completed. I'm told she is armored with railroad iron. I would like you to take your boat up the Yazoo and investigate."

"Am I to engage her?" asked Walke.

"Destroy her if you can."

"Hard to believe the rebels found enough materials to build a warship."

"Queen of the West and *Tyler* will accompany you," Farragut continued. A permanent little grin seemed fixed on his congenial features. David Farragut was every naval officer's ideal. He also looked like everyone's grandfather.

"What do the Rebels call the ram?"

"They say it goes by the name *Arkansas.*"

"Any information on who her commander might be?" inquired Walke.

Farragut nodded. "A former United States naval officer, Lieutenant Isaac Brown. I understand he's an old friend of yours."

"Isaac Brown is no stranger to me. We were very close before the war."

"If you cannot sink *Arkansas,* give me ample warning to prepare the fleet to meet her should she make an attempt to reach Vicksburg."

"You can count on *Carondelet,* admiral."

Farragut shook Walke's hand. "Good luck to you, commander."

As Walke was rowed back to his gunboat, he could not imagine just how formidable the Confederate would be.

"Bow guns fire," Walke ordered his chief gunnery officer from the pilothouse. He stared through the viewing slits in the armor at the sudden appearance of *Arkansas.* The rebel ironclad had rounded the far bend and was steaming directly toward *Carondelet.*

"She looks like the work of desperate men," Walke muttered at the unholy sight of his former friend's gunboat. "Leave it to old Isaac Brown to paint his boat brown."

"Brown or gray, she means business," said Pilot Hoel at the helm.

"Is there enough room in the river to pass and catch her in a crossfire between us and *Tyler?*" Walke asked.

"The width of the river is not the problem, sir," his pilot answered. "If we try, she'll ram us for sure."

Walke turned and saw that *Queen of the West* had already turned and was heading down the Yazoo River for the Mississippi. "It seems we have no choice but to show the Rebel our stern and fight a running battle."

After his intentions were shouted across to Captain Gwin of *Tyler,* and the two Union gunboats made reverse turns, Walke instructed his stern guns to commence firing. Within seconds, the two thirty-two-pounders at the aft end of the casemate opened up on the rapidly approaching Confederate ironclad.

"That should give old Isaac a jolt," Walke said excitedly as a shot from *Carondelet* slammed into *Arkansas*'s pilothouse.

"Our guns are right on the mark," said Hoel as a second Union shell slammed into the Rebel boat's pilothouse.

On the stern gun deck of *Carondelet,* the gunners were firing their cannon as fast as they could reload and torch the fuse. *Arkansas* had drawn so close they couldn't miss, but the ironclad relentlessly came on, taking hits but showing little damage.

"Port guns prepare to fire," Walke shouted down onto the gun deck at seeing the *Arkansas*'s superior speed closing the distance between them. "Can you give us more speed?" he called through the speaking tube to his Chief Engineer, Samuel Garrett.

"Steam pressure is in the red now," Garrett's disembodied voice replied through the tube.

Ominously, *Arkansas* pulled alongside until they were

blasting away at each other hull to hull. The two ironclads were so near one another that Walke thought he caught a glimpse of Isaac Brown. His old friend looked to be standing beside a shell-torn opening on the side of his pilothouse, directing the fight. It appeared as though he had a bandage around his head.

With a thunderous roar across the narrow gap of water, *Arkansas* launched a wall of solid shot into *Carondelet*'s casemate.

"I've lost the wheel!" Hoel shouted. "She doesn't respond."

A midshipman burst into the pilothouse, his face white as a sheet. "Captain, they've hit the boilers!" he gasped breathlessly. "Some of the steam pipes are destroyed! The chief engineer says our steam is dropping fast!"

"Run back to the gun deck and report to Lieutenant Donaldson," Walke said calmly. "Tell him the steering gear is disabled, and I need him to tie the rudders to port. We're going to run the boat onto the bank."

Helpless while his gunboat was pounded unmercifully by the heavy Confederate cannon, Walke waited patiently until his orders were carried out. Already, the casemate looked as if it had been assaulted by a giant can opener.

"She's coming around," announced Hoel.

"Run the bow squarely into the mud, Mr. Hoel. Our anchors are shot away."

As *Arkansas* began pulling ahead, Walke saw Isaac Brown standing on the roof of his casemate, cupping his hands and shouting across the water. "Better luck next time, Henry!" Brown yelled.

The bastard has nerve, thought Walke. He made to shout a reply, but instinctively ducked as a broadside from *Arkansas* smashed into *Carondelet* and rolled her over on a twenty-degree angle that allowed water to rush through the gunports onto the deck. At the same time, the Union gunboat's bow slid up on the bank, coming to a stop as the mud gripped her hull. Walke was thrown against the wall of the pilothouse, badly bruising his shoulder.

After he struggled to his feet and stepped out of the pilothouse to answer Brown, it was too late. *Arkansas* was already pulling away, locked in a fight with the brave little *Tyler.* Walke could only shake his fist in frustration.

Carondelet's famed fight with *Arkansas* was over, and she had taken the worst of it.

"Carondelet," Rear Admiral Henry Walke recalled many years later, "was a most successful craft." Under seven different skippers throughout the war, U.S.S. *Carondelet* fought in more battles against the enemy (over fifteen engagements) and came under more fire than any other vessel in the Union Navy. From Fort Henry through her battering at Fort Donelson, her incredible run past Island Ten through the siege of Vicksburg and the fight with the durable *Arkansas,* and to the battle of Memphis, the defense of Nashville, and the Union campaign up the Red River, *Carondelet* ran up a battle record that would not be surpassed until World War II.

During continuous service from early 1862 until the end of the war, she was struck by enemy shot and shell over 300 times, 37 of her crew were killed and 63 wounded. She suffered 35 casualties from her drubbing by *Arkansas* alone.

A week after the close of the war, *Carondelet* cast off on her final voyage and steamed up the Mississippi River to Mound City, Illinois, where she was decommissioned. A few days later, all her guns and stores were removed, her crew was paid off, and her officers transferred to other commands. The career of the grand old fighting lady of the western rivers was finished. In November of 1865, she was auctioned off to Daniel Jacobs of St. Louis for $3,600.

For the next few years, *Carondelet*'s fate is shrouded in mystery. It was presumed she was sold by Jacobs and taken to Cincinnati, where it was rumored she was to be demolished for scrap. But for some reason she managed to survive. Her whereabouts from 1865 until 1872 are unknown.

Late in 1872, she was recognized as a wharfboat at Gallipolis, Ohio. Her owner was a Captain John Hamilton. A photo taken at the time shows her much modified, but still afloat.

At Gallipolis the old gunboat deteriorated until Hamilton decided to burn and scrap her for what iron remained in her hull, estimated at $3,000. But, before he could tear her apart, the spring flood of 1873 snapped her mooring lines and washed her 130 miles down the Ohio River. *Carondelet* finally came to rest at the head of Manchester Island, where she eventually settled into the soft silt and disappeared.

After twelve years of hard service and undying fame, *Carondelet* was no more.

II

Some Days You Can't Win

April 1982

A SMART PERSON ONCE WROTE, "AN OBJECT LOST AND hidden, waits and whispers." I'm remiss for not recalling the author. I hope he or she forgives me, but the phrase comes to mind because of the many lost shipwrecks that have whispered to me through the years. *Carondelet,* it seemed to my imaginative mind, whispered the loudest. It was as though she called out through the mists of time, 110 years in the past, begging to be found. Sadly, like the cavalry troop that arrives after the wagon train has been burned by marauding Indians, I rode on the scene too late.

I've always had a soft touch for Civil War ironclads because their design was so radically different from that of any ships that came before and after. The rough, often crude vessels constructed by the South were marvels of expedience and improvisation. Some built in ironworks, some knocked together in cornfields, their trademark sloping sides were a necessity, owing to lack of heavy-metal-forming machinery and the shortage of iron, a commodity that went mainly to build cannons for the Confederate Armies. Their armor plate was often train rails slotted together to form a shield.

The United States Navy ironclads, predominantly based on the monitor design, revolutionized naval warfare with their revolving gun turrets, flush decks, and total lack of sails and rigging. So successful were the monitor-class vessels, the U.S. Navy built and commissioned fifty up until 1903. The last monitor was not stricken from navy rolls until 1937.

It can safely be said that the original *Monitor* was the grandfather of the giant battlewagons that followed and fought in five wars.

Learning that the famous old warhorse of the river battles was sold for scrap after the Civil War, and later became a wharfboat on the Ohio River at Gallipolis, it became a simple matter for me to trace her route after the spring floods swept her 130 miles downriver to Manchester Island. Even if her owner, John Hamilton, had burned the derelict for whatever iron was left in her bones on Manchester Island, experience taught me that a considerable amount of her lower hull and timbers should still be intact.

There are two islands in the river off the town of Manchester. The smallest is named Manchester Island Number One, the largest, Number Two. The dilemma? On whose shore did *Carondelet* run aground? The solution came with researcher Bob Fleming's penciled overlay sketch from an atlas of Adams County, Ohio, circa 1875. Before the turn of the century, the smaller piece of land in the middle of the river was called Tow Head Island. The Manchester Island that held the remains of *Carondelet* was now called Number Two.

Enlarging Fleming's sketch to the same scale as the modern chart and performing the old overlay trick, I quickly determined the 1982 head of Manchester Island was now two hundred yards downstream from where it split the river in 1873. This gave me a search grid not much larger than a soccer field.

Armed with enough data to inspire an attempt to find *Carondelet,* Walt Schob and I flew to Cincinnati, Ohio, along with our Schonstedt gradiometer. We rented a car and drove along the Ohio bank of the river across from Kentucky. The valley carved by millions of years of flowing water is quite scenic. Rolling hills, thickly forested, drop onto picturesque farms, most of them growing tobacco.

Suddenly, I called out to Schob, who was at the wheel. "Stop the car and turn around."

He looked at me questioningly. "Why, did I run over something?"

"No," I answered excitedly. "There's a barn back up the road. I have to get a closer look at it."

"A barn?"

"A barn."

Walt dutifully made a U-turn and followed my directions until I motioned for him to stop.

Feeling as if I were carried back in time, I walked about fifty yards down a small, dusty road until I stood beside a fair-sized barn with dark gray, weathered walls. A man was standing on a ladder, painting a large sign across the vertically laid boards.

"Well done," I said to him. "You do nice work."

He turned around, stared down at me, and grinned. "I've been doing it for forty-five years, so I kinda got the hang of it."

I studied his handiwork. "I didn't think they still painted Mail Pouch tobacco signs on the sides of barns. I thought Mail Pouch outdoor advertising went the way of the Burma Shave highway signs."

"Nope, they're still in business, and I'm one of a dozen guys still painting them."

After a short chat, I returned to the car. "What was that all about?" asked Walt.

"When I was a kid in Minnesota, I used to watch for Mail Pouch signs on barns when my dad took the family for drives through the country. I thought they'd become extinct."

"Do they smoke Mail Pouch?"

"They chew it."

Walt made a face. "Nasty habit. Rots your teeth."

Poor Walt, he just didn't have any romance and sentiment in his soul.

* * *

Reaching the town of Manchester late in the afternoon, we stopped at the sheriff's department and asked to see the sheriff. He turned out to be a large, smiling man by the name of Louis Fulton. Although his department didn't have a search-and-rescue boat to work the river, a nice fiberglass outboard for that purpose was owned by the local fire department. Naturally, the sheriff's good fishing buddy was Fire Chief Frank Tolle, and before you could say, "It pays to have influence," we had ourselves a search boat, and early the next morning we were cruising the beautiful Ohio River, with the boat manned by fireman Earl Littleton.

There was a small catch, however. As a favor to Sheriff Fulton, we agreed to use our magnetic search gear to look for a woman who had inexplicably vanished three years previously.

The enigma was classic *Unsolved Mysteries* material. The story told to us by the sheriff concerned a widow in her late sixties. One afternoon, while she was roasting a chicken in the oven, she left her house and made a quick trip a mile or so into town to buy a few groceries. After leaving the store, she was never seen again, nor was her car ever found. When investigators learned she was missing, they immediately searched the house. Except for a chicken roasted to a crisp, nothing appeared out of place or missing.

Since the lady's house was situated on a road that sloped down toward the river, the sheriff's investigators speculated that she might have been approaching her house when she either blacked out or suffered a heart attack. A brick-enclosed mailbox appeared damaged at the entrance to her driveway, suggesting the car might have struck it a glancing blow after she became unconscious. Now out of control, the car rolled down the road into the river and sank out of sight, or so the theory went.

Divers swept the river with no luck. The lady and her car remained lost.

A sucker for a good puzzle, I gladly offered to help with a search before tackling the hunt for *Carondelet*. With the sheriff and two of his deputies on board, curious to see how we went about searching for a sunken object, Walt and I began running search lanes back and forth in the water below the end of the road. After covering a hundred yards downstream and nearly thirty yards out into the channel, we came up empty. We struck no magnetic anomalies that suggested the mass of an automobile.

I have a strong antipathy to searching for an object when totally unprepared. I suggested we return to the boat ramp and knock off for lunch. This gave me time to check out a few details. I walked the road from the main highway past the lady's former house and down the hill to the edge of the river. Then I asked the sheriff what month the lady went missing.

"Early December," he answered.

I looked at him. "The weather must have been cold."

"That time of year the temperature gets below freezing."

"Then it stands to reason that she'd have the windows on her car rolled up."

He nodded. "Sounds logical."

"What do you figure the speed of the river current?" I asked.

"About two to three miles an hour until spring runoff. Then it can hit four to five."

"Close to the pace of a walking man."

"I suppose so."

I pointed up the road past the house. "The grade is a good ten percent. A fairly steep slope. If she blacked out before she could turn into the driveway and the car continued another eighty yards down the road with her foot still on the accelerator, she could have driven into the river at over thirty miles an hour."

"A safe bet," the sheriff agreed. "Actually, our estimates were closer to thirty-five."

"All things considered," I said, "we're looking in the wrong place."

"You don't think she's near the end of the road?" he asked.

I shook my head. "The momentum and speed would have sent her almost to the middle of the channel. And because she must have rolled up her windows against the cold, water seeping in would have taken several minutes to fill and sink the car. Enough time for the current to carry the car a good hundred yards or more downriver."

"It's been three years," said the sheriff. "I can't recall exactly whether we swept that far. I do know the divers had a hard time fighting the current and covered only the primary area around the end of the road."

This was a situation similar to the drowning of Susan Smith's two boys in Union, South Carolina. Though that tragedy took place in a lake and not a river, visibility was so poor the divers' first search missed the car. A second attempt found the boys farther out and deeper in the lake.

Underwater search is seldom a cut-and-dried affair.

"What do you suggest?" Sheriff Fulton asked.

"I propose we extend the search farther offshore and downriver."

Half an hour later the gradiometer was trailing behind the boat ten feet beneath the water surface. While Walt kept a sharp eye on the instrument readings, I tied a float to the end of a rope. Next, I slipped on a pair of work gloves I usually carry on expeditions and dragged a grappling hook across the riverbed. If we were lucky and it hooked a piece of the car, the gloves would keep the palms of my hands from being rubbed raw, and the float would mark the spot.

Nearly two hundred yards from the road, Walt hit a target with a large magnetic mass. We crisscrossed it several times and received the same high readings. However, the grappling hook refused to catch its prongs in anything but river silt.

"Whatever is down there is big and it's buried," I said.

The sheriff looked up the river. "Sure seems a long way off."

I shrugged. "Perhaps, but it's the only credible target you've got between here and the end of the road."

"You couldn't snag anything with your hook?"

"After eight passes over the site and no prize, I think it's safe to say the car is buried over its roof in silt."

The sheriff looked thoughtful for a few moments. "Then

I guess we'll have to get some divers and a dredge in here and see what we've got."

Walt and I left for home the next day. We never did learn whether the missing lady and her car were found in the river at our target site.

Since we still had five hours of daylight left, we deposited the sheriff and his deputies at the boat ramp and headed upriver to where I suspected *Carondelet* might lie. As we rounded the head of Manchester Island, the biggest dredge boat I've ever seen loomed over the river. It had the appearance of a massive rectangular building with corrugated metal walls and a seemingly endless row of great steel buckets with jagged teeth that marched into the water and re-emerged, filled with tons of riverbed silt. I felt as if I were about to lose a jackpot lottery on a technicality when I estimated that the dredge was working no more than a hundred yards from my prime search grid.

Without bothering to drop the gradiometer in the water, we headed straight for the dredge, and pulled alongside. The superintendent in charge stepped from his office and invited us on board. A tall, florid-faced man with about the same dimensions as a phone booth, he held out a beefy hand in greeting. I took his grip and heard my knuckles crack.

"What can I do for you?" he asked with a wide smile.

I explained that we were on a survey for a sunken gunboat and inquired if he was working his way downriver. If so, I wanted to stop his insatiable dredge before it ate any remains of *Carondelet*.

His smile faded. "We're not working downriver," he said. "We're working up."

Cussler's little world teetered on the edge of the abyss. There was still a chance the trench carved by the big buckets missed the wreck. I pointed to my prime search location. "Did you dredge over in that area?" I asked.

The superintendent nodded. "We dredged through there no more than four hours ago."

"Do you know if you brought up any wood?"

"Sure did. Even saved some of the pieces. Would you care to see them?"

Without waiting for a reply, he disappeared inside a door of the dredge and returned after a minute carrying the remains of a wooden beam, brown and slimy from long years of being immersed in water, a fire brick that could have come from a steam engine, and several pieces of heavily rusted iron that included a bracket plate, long spikes, and fragments of a steam pipe.

Walt and I exchanged looks of agonized defeat.

"What kind of a boat did you say this was?" inquired the superintendent.

"One of the most famous warships of the Civil War," I answered.

"No kidding? My boys and I thought we dug up an old barge."

Wanting to confirm that the dredge had indeed pulverized the hull of *Carondelet,* Walt and I set up our search grid with buoys and dragged the gradiometer from one end to the other, finishing up just before dark. We extended our search lanes far beyond the former head of Manchester Island as added insurance. The only anomaly we found came at precisely the same site as indicated by the dredge boat superintendent where he pulled up debris. We received a number of small magnetic readings at a depth of eighteen feet. A few dives revealed the scattered remains of a large wreck. The excavation buckets had not quite dredged it all. The shattered lower hull and keel of *Carondelet* still appeared to be strewn about under the silt.

With nothing more to accomplish, Walt Schob and I drove back to Cincinnati, checked into a hotel, and caught a plane to our hometowns in the morning.

There has been many a night when I lay awake and stared at the ceiling, wishing we had gone straight to the selected search site instead of spending several hours hunting for the missing lady and her car. I'm almost certain we could have arrived in time to save the old gunboat's remains from being chewed to shreds by the ship-eating dredge.

A great pity we failed. It seems incredible that after nearly 110 years our attempt to find and rescue *Carondelet*'s historic remains literally missed the boat by only a few hours. Walt and I were there, no more than a mile away, when she was destroyed.

I'll always regret that I answered *Carondelet*'s whisper too late.

Part

The Confederate Submarine *Hunley*

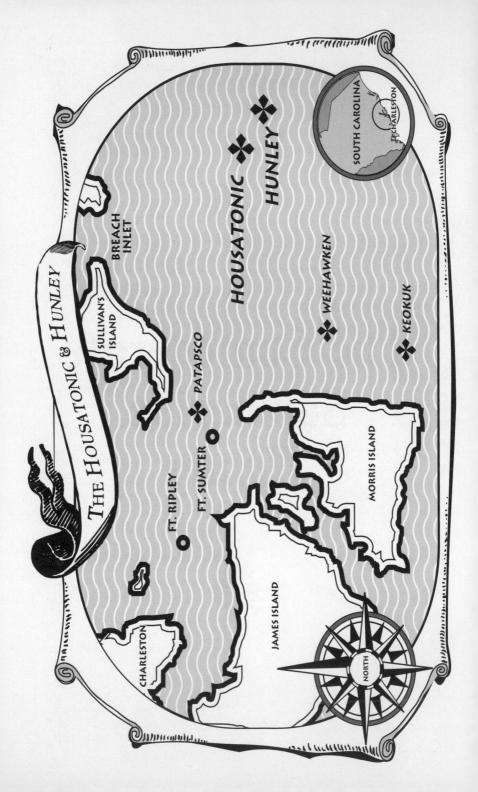

THE HOUSATONIC & HUNLEY

SOUTH CAROLINA

CHARLESTON

HOUSATONIC

HUNLEY

WEEHAWKEN

KEOKUK

BREACH INLET

SULLIVAN'S ISLAND

PATAPSCO

FT. RIPLEY

FT. SUMTER

CHARLESTON

MORRIS ISLAND

JAMES ISLAND

NORTH

THE HUNLEY IN PORT

I

The Little Sub That Could
. . . and Did

February 1864

A SAND CRAB SCURRIED ALONG THE BEACH AND DARTED into a hole. A man dressed in the officer's uniform of the Confederate States glanced at the crab briefly, then rose and brushed off the damp sand that clung to the knees of his uniform. His hair was the color of fallen autumn leaves, the eyes a light blue, set in a boyish face framed by large ears. He checked the needle of a handheld compass and jotted the readings on a scrap of paper.

"They've anchored for the night," said a sandy-haired man standing next to him.

Lieutenant George Dixon neatly folded the paper and slipped it into his pants pocket. "I do believe you are right, Mr. Wicks."

They both stared over the sea at a ship that rose and dropped on the late afternoon swells. From 4½ miles away, the vessel seemed like a small, dark toy rocking against a curtain of Wedgwood blue. The sails on her yards were furled, and a wisp of smoke curled from her stack, indicating that her furnaces were being kept stoked and fired so she could move quickly should her lookouts spot a blockade runner trying to sneak into Charleston Harbor.

"What ship do you make her out to be, sir?" asked Wicks.

"The *Housatonic,*" answered Dixon. "A spanking brand-new Yankee sloop-of-war, fresh out of a Union shipyard. A fast ship, equal or superior to any commerce runner I know."

"Not for long," Wicks said solemnly.

Dixon smiled and nodded. "God willing, tonight's the night."

An hour after sunset, the nine-man crew of the Confederate States submarine *Horace L. Hunley* walked onto the wooden dock in the channel behind Sullivan's Island. A pelican atop one of the pilings stared at them through a beady eye before stretching its wings and soaring across the back bay. The iron hump of the submarine with her two hatch towers and a twenty-foot pipe that extended from her bow was all that was visible above the water. She looked like some prehistoric beast asleep in a Mesozoic pond.

Two crewmen attached the torpedo to the end of the iron pipe and then checked the line attached to a reel set to pull the detonating trigger. A heavy barb, attached to a copper canister containing a hundred pounds of black powder, was inserted over the end of the pipe like a thimble on a finger. In theory, after the barb was embedded beneath an enemy hull, *Hunley* would back off at least 150 yards before the line reached the end of the reel and detonated the charge. But the mechanism had yet to be fully tested.

Canteens of water, a small container of food, and a lantern with a blue lens were passed to those already inside the submarine. This was a night mission that would take from sunset to sunrise. The crew members of *Hunley* were conditioned to enduring damp cold, a claustrophobic existence, and physical exertion that left them with aching muscles and in a stage of near total exhaustion.

The physical toll on the men during the past weeks had been immense. Five nights a week they went out in futile attempts to sink enemy warships, often barely escaping capture by Union picket boats or being carried out to sea by hostile currents. The opportunities for dying far exceeded those for living. After cheating death on so many occasions, the crew began to look upon themselves as immortal. They took pride in being on the cutting edge of technology, of being a part of the first submarine they knew would some night sink an enemy ship.

Seaman Frederick Collins walked back to the dock from Breach Inlet, the channel that split Isle of Palms from Sullivan's Island. He had thrown a cypress twig into the current and watched as it was carried quickly out to sea. He approached Dixon and saluted.

"The tide has turned and is running strong, sir."

Dixon returned the salute. "Thank you, Mr. Collins. Please take your place on board."

Silently, Collins followed his shipmates into the narrow twin hatches that rose above the iron spine of *Hunley*. They took their individual seats and placed their callused hands on the metal sheaths surrounding the crank handles. Only after Seaman Wicks entered and took his seat next to the rear ballast tank did Dixon snake through the forward hatch. He came to a standing position behind the boat's steering wheel, mercury diving indicator, and compass.

"Everyone accounted for?" asked Dixon.

"All in place," reported Wicks from the stern.

Dixon made a motion with his hand to the sentries standing on the dock. "Stand by to cast off." Then he motioned to Wicks behind him. Both men threw off the hemp lines looped around the hatch towers. The sentries pulled in the lines and pushed the submarine away from the dock with their feet. *Hunley* swayed in the water until Dixon gave the command to move forward. Then the eight men behind him began turning the crank that was connected to the propeller at the stern, and *Hunley* moved slowly toward the end of Sullivan's Island, where she joined the tidal current sweeping through Breach Inlet into the sea beyond.

For weeks they had propelled themselves toward the Union fleet, only to be turned back by bad luck. More than once they had approached so close to enemy picket boats that when Dixon raised the hatch for fresh air they could hear the Yankee sailors singing and talking in the darkness. Now, once again, they lit candles to illuminate their coffinlike container and set them in holders bolted to the iron wall.

Months of training had been endured without complaint. Now Dixon's crew was honed tough and tenacious, bound tight by shared hardship and from staring death in the eye night after night. Tonight was to be their night.

The moon was a crescent and the sea calm. Maintaining a slow rhythm as they cranked the propeller, and taking advantage of the outgoing tide, they moved along at nearly four knots for the first mile. Blessedly, the cold interior soon turned warm from their body heat, and the walls dripped with condensation from their breathing. Dixon, able to keep the forward hatch open because of the smooth sea, stared over the top as he steered the sub toward the lights of *Housatonic*.

"A great pity we can't carry a keg of beer with us instead of a paltry canteen of water," muttered Collins.

"Good thinking," replied Private Augustus Miller, a recent volunteer from a South Carolina artillery company, who had joined the crew along with Corporal Charles Carlson. Except for Dixon, they were the only nonsailors manning the submarine.

"The shaft feels stiff," said Seaman Arnold Becker to Wicks.

Without answering, Wicks reached into a metal pail of animal fat and greased the shaft where it entered the stuffing boxes that held leakage to a bare minimum. Becker's complaint was routine. He was the only one who ever whined about a sticking propeller shaft.

Time crawled as the men pushed and pulled on their crank handles. They began working in twenty-minute shifts, four men on, four men off, to conserve their strength for the final surge against their enemy and then the long haul back to

Breach Inlet. Helped by the current, they propelled the craft through the glass-smooth sea at an easy 2½ knots.

Dixon kept the front hatch open and navigated mostly by sight. The dim moonlight enabled him to read the sea for a hundred yards in front of the bow, giving him ample time to close his hatch cover should he perceive an approaching wave high enough to wash over his exposed position. The dark hull of *Housatonic* grew larger with agonizing slowness. Battery power was in its infancy, and it was at moments like this that Dixon wished he could have engineered a mechanical propulsion system that would work underwater without the need for air.

From his cramped vantage point he began to make out a few men walking the decks of the Union sloop-of-war. Lookouts, he assumed, watching for a Confederate attack out of the night with one of their infernal underwater machines. He dropped down and closed the hatch. Then he turned to his crew, moving like phantoms in the flickering flames of the candles.

"We're only three hundred yards away. Rest a minute, then every man work the crank."

"A ship," murmured Seaman Joseph Ridgeway. "Are we really going to attack a Yankee ship?"

They all saw Dixon's teeth as his lips parted in a smile. "We'll not go home empty-handed this night."

"Glory to the Confederacy," said Seaman Collins.

"Glory to all of us," added Wicks. "We put that blasted Yankee on the bottom and we'll all share in the prize money."

"I make it about five thousand apiece," said Ridgeway.

"Don't spend it too soon," cautioned Dixon. "We have yet to earn it." He carefully wiped the three tiny glass viewing ports in the hatch tower that had become clouded with moisture from the humidity created by the breathing and sweating of the men inside. Through the forward port he studied *Housatonic*.

The ship was anchored with her bow pointing west by northwest toward Fort Sumter. Dixon observed little movement on the deck. *Hunley* was slowly approaching on an angle astern and slightly off the starboard quarter of the Union warship. There was no sign the sub had been observed.

When he spotted the floating buoys that supported the outer net around the ship, Dixon made a crucial decision. He voiced an order over his shoulder. "Mr. Wicks, fill your ballast tank to the quarter mark."

Everyone went silent and stared at each other questioningly. They all expected the lieutenant to ask for two-thirds ballast, enough to slide *Hunley* under the surface and out of sight of the lookouts on board *Housatonic*.

"Beggin' your pardon, sir," said Wicks. "We'll not be attacking underwater?"

"We've come too far to miss her in water blacker than ink, Mr. Wicks. Besides, she has a protective net sunk along her hull. We'll go in over the net with only our hatch towers awash and place the charge just below their waterline. If we miss this opportunity, they won't give us a chance for a second one."

In less than a minute the correct amount of water was pumped into the forward and aft ballast tanks; the sub sank beneath the surface until only a narrow band of upper hull and both hatch towers were exposed. There was no thought of turning away, no hesitation. The men inside *Hunley* experienced no fear, nor were they stoic about their fate. They persevered and pushed themselves beyond the depth of endurance. They probably did not realize that undying glory was in their grasp.

"Now!" Dixon said more loudly than he intended. "Crank hard, crank like hell. We're attacking."

The men turned the crank with every ounce of muscle in their arms and shoulders until the propeller beat the water to froth. Standing in the forward hatch tower, squinting through the darkness until the enemy warship completely filled the three-inch-diameter viewing port, Dixon pushed hard on the rudder wheel and swung the submarine in a wide arc toward *Housatonic*'s starboard side. He used her mizzenmast as a guide and steered toward the black hull directly below it.

* * *

Walking the deck of his command, U.S.S. *Housatonic,* for a final inspection before turning in for the night, Captain Charles Pickering stopped and gazed over the black water outside of Charleston at the lights of the steam sloop *Canandaigua.* Larger and more heavily armed than Pickering's ship, *Canandaigua* was stationed one mile further to sea as part of the stranglehold to intercept commercial ships attempting to supply the Confederacy. Pickering turned and gazed with contentment across the length of his own ship. She was prepared for any threat, above water or below.

One of four new screw sloops fresh out of the shipyards of Boston, *Housatonic* mounted thirteen guns, one of them a big rifled hundred-pounder. She displaced 1,240 tons and measured 205 feet in length. Her beam was 38 feet and her draft, 16 feet, 7 inches. This night only 12 feet separated her keel from the soft silt of the seabed.

Pickering had been alerted to the dangers of a possible attack by the Confederate torpedo boat. The entire Union fleet knew about the threat, courtesy of spies and deserters who had described her. As a precaution, Pickering ordered his crew to drop around the ship nets weighted by shot to act as a shield. He thought, mistakenly as it turned out, that the nets could snag the underwater craft if it crept close to his ship. Additional lookouts were posted and howitzers on the deck were aimed not at land but at the water below. Engineers were ordered to have twenty-five pounds of steam on the boilers at all times. The engines were also set in reverse to allow the ship to slip her anchor and back away in a hurry without entangling herself in the chain.

Satisfied, Captain Pickering retired to his ornate, cedar-trimmed cabin, lit his fuel lamp, and began studying charts of the South Carolina coastline. His executive officer, Frank Higginson, was the watch commander. A good man, Pickering thought. Nothing would escape his attention.

Lieutenant Higginson spoke briefly to watch officer John Crosby, who stood on the bridge peering through binoculars for telltale sparks from the stack of a blockade runner.

"I didn't think it got this cold down south," said Higginson, his hands jammed deep in the pocket of his coat.

Crosby lowered the glasses and shrugged. "Before the war, my brother married a girl from Georgia. She claimed that it often snowed in Atlanta."

After the brief conversation, Higginson dropped below-decks for an inspection of the engine room. He had no sooner approached Assistant Engineer Cyrus Houlihan than he heard a commotion topside.

At about 8:45 P.M., Lieutenant Crosby saw something in the water that he thought at first was a porpoise. He hailed the nearest lookout, who was stationed in the rigging above him. "Do you see anything in the water about a hundred yards off the starboard quarter?"

"No, sir, only a small ripple on the water."

"Look again!" Crosby shouted. "I see something coming toward us very fast."

"I see it now," replied the lookout. "It has two knobs showing on the surface."

Crosby prodded awake a young drummer boy. "Beat to quarters." Then he gave orders to slip the anchor chain and rang the engine room to back the ship. His orders were carried out in less than twenty seconds. The propeller was already turning when Higginson rushed back on deck. "Is it a blockade runner?" he asked Crosby.

The watch officer shook his head and pointed over the side. "There it is. It looks like that damned torpedo boat."

"I've got it," acknowledged Higginson. "It has the appearance of a plank with sharp ends. Look there, a glimmer of light is coming through the top."

Captain Pickering raced from his quarters, carrying a double-barreled shotgun. He inquired about the cause of the alarm. On being shown the closing torpedo boat, he repeated Crosby's orders to slip anchor and back astern. To Pickering, the torpedo boat was shaped like a large upside-down whale boat with two projections a third of the way from each end. Then he leveled his shotgun and began blasting at the strange craft in the water, shouting as he pulled the trigger, "Go astern faster!"

Higginson grabbed a rifle from a lookout and also opened

fire. He was soon joined by others, including Ensign Charles Craven, who squeezed off two shots from his revolver. The attacking craft was now so close that Craven had to lean over the side to fire a third shot.

Craven saw that small-arms fire was useless, and he ran to the nearest thirty-two-pound gun and attempted to train it on the object in the water, now backing away from *Housatonic*. He was about to pull the lanyard when the deck suddenly rose beneath his feet.

The instant the barb on the end of the long spar that held the canister containing the hundred pounds of black powder rammed through the copper sheathing of the hull, Dixon cried out, "Reverse the crank, quickly!"

The men inside the submarine furiously reversed the direction of their cranking, and the little craft slowly backed away from her adversary. As the gap widened, Dixon could look up through the view port and see men shooting over the railing of *Housatonic*. He heard the small-arms fire harmlessly striking *Hunley* and ricocheting off into the water. He was certain the barb containing the charge had penetrated and gripped the hull. Now they had to get clear and detonate the charge.

Then Dixon spied a gun being trained on *Hunley,* the thirty-two-pounder manned by Ensign Craven. The submarine was now fifty yards away, far short of the required distance to safely survive the explosion. Driven by desperation, Dixon realized they were within seconds of being shot out of the water. He saw no choice but to gamble and hope the odds ran in his favor. He intended to crack the hatch cover, snake out an arm, grip the detonation line with his hand, and trigger the explosion himself.

Before he could act, a shot from Ensign Craven's revolver struck the reel and wedged it against the spindle. The line tightened, stretched, and then activated the detonator.

The barb on the end of *Hunley*'s spar entered *Housatonic*'s hull, where it rounded inward near the rudder and propeller. Detonation erupted deep under the ship, with the main force absorbed by the stern section of the hull. There was no explosive thunder, no column of water, smoke, or flame. To those on board the Union vessel the convulsion came more like a collision with another ship. One of them said that the explosion sounded like the distant firing of a howitzer, followed by a ground tremor. Another reported fragments of the ship soaring in the night air.

Water burst into *Housatonic* through a huge opening, crushing timbers and smashing through bulkheads. The engine raced as the propeller shaft was shattered apart. Most of the starboard part of the ship aft of the mizzenmast was blown off. The ship began to sink immediately by the stern. Like a dying animal, it gave a lurch to port and settled to the bottom as the black water drew a death shroud over the hull. Less than five minutes after the explosion, nothing remained above the surface of *Housatonic* except her masts and rigging.

During the sudden frenzy, Acting Master Joseph Congdon shouted for the launches to be cleared away. Only two out of the six boats hanging in their davits were lowered free of the sinking ship. They swiftly began picking up the men who were carried overboard as the officers drove the rest of the crew into the rigging to save themselves, since very few knew how to swim.

Badly bruised, Captain Pickering shouted from the rigging to the men in the boats. "Row for the *Canandaigua,*" he ordered, "and request assistance!"

Not until the following day would a muster reveal that five of *Housatonic*'s crew were missing after the disaster and presumed drowned.

The shock wave from the explosion affected the men inside *Hunley* far worse than it did the crew of *Housatonic*. The concussion knocked the wind out of them and threw them against the crank and walls of the submarine. Dixon was momentarily stunned and watched numbly as an explosion-driven wave surged over *Hunley,* twisting her sideways and pitching her up and down like a raft through rapids. Until now, he had no way of knowing the effects that an underwater explosion might have on a submarine from a short distance. No tests, that he was aware of, had ever been performed simulating such an occasion.

Seaman Wicks was pitched into Arnold Becker, the man nearest him on the crank, and bloodied his nose. In the middle of the submarine, Seaman Simpkins's head jerked back against the inside of the hull, then forward against the crank handle, rendering him immediately unconscious. Frederick Collins smashed his chin, while the man next to him, Corporal Charles Carlson, wrenched his back.

Artilleryman Augustus Miller fell against the crank on the rebound as well, snapping a front tooth cleanly in half. "Damn!" he muttered through bleeding lips. "My tooth is missing. Help me find my tooth."

Everyone suffered from a ringing of the ears, and nearly all suffered bruises. There was no panic or chaos inside the submarine. Most simply sat in a state of shock for a few moments before the triumph of their feat began to sink in. Dixon shook the cobwebs from his dazed mind and peered through a view port. Already the tide had carried *Hunley* another fifty yards to the southeast away from the sinking ship, but he could see that *Housatonic* was settling fast.

"Is anyone badly injured?" he called out.

"Simpkins was knocked senseless," reported Wicks.

"I think I broke my nose," said Collins.

"I'm missing a tooth," grunted Miller.

"What happened, lieutenant?" asked Wicks anxiously. "Did we get her?"

"Take a look through the rear view ports," replied Dixon, excitement replacing numbing shock. "We sank the damned Yankee."

The tension was suddenly released. Almost as if they were transformed into another life, each man shook off his lethargy and began cheering. After incredible adversity, they had put their lives on the line and won. *Hunley* had vindicated herself. She had finally accomplished what she had been designed to do.

"We're not out of the woods yet," cautioned Dixon. "Take up the crank. I want to put another three hundred yards between us and *Housatonic* before the Union fleet is alerted to her sinking."

Their mood one of elation, seven of the crew propelled the craft as if their pain and fatigue did not exist. Simpkins began to come around, but he was too dazed to take up cranking duties. Dixon spun the wheel and steered a course eastward a quarter of a mile before he turned the bow toward Breach Inlet. Once he felt they were a safe distance away, he ordered his crew to stop and rest.

"Three of you work in shifts to keep us in position until the tide turns, and we can head back to port. I'll crank for Simpkins until he comes back on keel."

"Beggin' the lieutenant's pardon," said Wicks. "But instead of going back to Battery Marshall, I say we head into Charleston and tell old General Beauregard what we done, personal like."

"I agree," Dixon said, smiling. "But that would mean going through half the Union fleet. Best we return through Breach Inlet and continue to Charleston through the back bay."

Taking turns rotating the propeller just enough to keep *Hunley* from being carried further out to sea until the tide turned, the men passed out the canteens of water and relaxed with a meal of turnips and dried beef. Dixon and Wicks opened their hatch covers to let in fresh air.

Then Dixon stood, raised his arm through the hatch tower, and waved a blue light, the signal for sentries at Battery Marshall to light a bonfire as a beacon to guide *Hunley* home.

At 9:20 P.M., on board the Union warship *Canandaigua,* Captain Joseph Green was called on deck by his watch officer, who reported a boat pulling alongside. Green immediately made his way to the railing and shouted over the side. "What boat are you?"

"From the *Housatonic,*" answered Seaman Robert Fleming. "We were sunk by a Rebel torpedo craft. What's left of our crew is clinging to the rigging."

Having heard no sound from an explosion, Green and his officers were surprised at the news. The captain immediately hoisted distress signals and sent up three rockets to alert the rest of the fleet. Then *Canandaigua* slipped her anchor chain and came directly to *Housatonic*'s assistance. On the way, they picked up the second boat, with the unfortunate Captain Pickering on board.

They arrived at the sunken ship at 9:35 P.M., lowered their boats, and began picking up the men clinging to the rigging. None of the officers and crew of *Canandaigua* reported anything unusual or out of the ordinary during their run to rescue the survivors of *Housatonic*.

Too late Dixon felt a vibration in the water through the iron sides of *Hunley*. Too late he discovered the lights of the ship coming to rescue *Housatonic*'s survivors. Too late the hatch covers were slammed shut as he ordered the submarine to dive. Too late he shouted a warning. Eight men desperately attacked the crank in a vain attempt to move *Hunley* out of the path of *Canandaigua*. Time had run out for the men inside the submarine.

Dixon stood frozen as he stared through the view port at the bow of the Union warship looming up in the dark. The shock of the impact rolled *Hunley* over on her side and pushed her deep into the sea. Iron plates separated and water burst inside, filling the interior within seconds.

No one can be sure of the final images that passed through the minds of the doomed crew of *Hunley* as she slipped beneath the waves for the final time. Dixon's last thoughts were probably of his sweetheart, Queenie Bennett, waiting for him in Alabama. James Wicks may have visualized his wife and four daughters before blackness swept over him.

Hunley's final score of her own dead now stood at 22.

In time, the bones of Dixon and his crew would be preserved by the silt that slowly filtered inside the submarine and filled her interior. A hundred and thirty-one years would pass before anyone learned where or why they died.

* * *

The story of the little undersea craft that entered the history books as the first submarine to sink a warship, a feat that would not happen again until the *U-21* torpedoed the British cruiser H.M.S. *Pathfinder* in World War I, began in New Orleans in early 1861.

Her grandfather and predecessor was called the *Pioneer.* A brainchild of machinist James McClintock and built three years before *Hunley,* she was a cigar-shaped craft with conical ends, thirty feet long and four feet in diameter. Gaining a seventy-year jump on Howard Hughes's racing aircraft, *Pioneer* used countersunk rivets to join quarter-inch iron plate to her interior framework, which reduced friction as she moved under the water. Reports say she worked surprisingly well when operated by her three-man crew, who actually blew up a schooner on Lake Pontchartrain during a test run.

Two of *Pioneer*'s financial backers, Horace L. Hunley and Baxter Watson, became very excited at the prospects of turning her into a privateer, so they took out the necessary letters of marque for a privateer. Unfortunately, Union Admiral David Farragut had different ideas. He ran his fleet past the forts on the lower Mississippi River and captured New Orleans before *Pioneer* was completed.

Hunley ordered the *Pioneer* scuttled to keep her from falling into Yankee hands. Many years later, a submarine reputed to be the McClintock craft was recovered in a canal and now sits in Jackson Square. However, the size and shape do not match contemporary eyewitness accounts of the *Pioneer.* Researchers also claim that Hunley and McClintock's submarine was raised and auctioned off for scrap several years after the war.

Hunley, McClintock, and Watson escaped to Mobile, Alabama, and quickly began assembling a second submarine in a machine shop owned by Thomas W. Park and Thomas B. Lyons. They were ably assisted by two engineering officers from the 21st Alabama Regiment, Lieutenants William Alexander and George E. Dixon.

Referred to as simply *Pioneer II* and occasionally called the *American Diver,* the new craft was larger and more efficiently designed to travel underwater than her predecessor. She performed well and handled without undue effort. Her trials went smoothly, but when she set out on her first mission to sink a blockading Union ship, a sudden squall blew in from the sea. While being towed across Mobile Bay by a tugboat, the waves carried over *Pioneer II*'s open hatches. Bailing proved hopeless, and her crew abandoned the sub before she slipped beneath the sea off Fort Morgan.

With more guts than foresight, Hunley scraped up the funding to begin a third submarine. McClintock acted as advisor on this project while Lieutenant Alexander did the design work and directed construction. She began life with what is thought to be an old locomotive boiler that was sliced horizontally and heightened by a one-foot strip of iron riveted between the halves. Solid iron wedge-shaped bow and stern castings were added, while bulkheads were placed three feet inside the hull to form water ballast tanks.

The craft that became famous as the *Hunley* torpedo boat was amazingly advanced for her time. Her hull configuration was very similar to the much later *Nautilus* nuclear sub designs. She had diving planes attached on each side of the hull, manual pumps to increase or decrease water ballast, a single propeller and rudder protruding from the center of the stern, again much like a modern nuclear submarine. Iron weights on the keel could be dropped with the twist of a wrench to decrease ballast during emergencies. Two small raised openings with viewing ports served as entry and exit hatch towers. They were barely wide enough for a man to squeak through if he held his arms over his head. There was even a rudimentary snorkel system, called an air box, with pipes that could swing vertical, their ends above the water surface. It was almost as if Henry Ford had built a 1929 Model A sedan on his first attempt at a horseless carriage. *Hunley*'s only shortcoming was her primitive propulsion system. Electrical battery power and diesel engines were far over the horizon. She had to rely on eight strong men to turn the crank that rotated her propeller.

Hunley's overall length ran about thirty-five feet, while

her hull rose five feet in height with a four-foot beam. The rudder was steered by a wheel and operated by the captain, who stood and navigated through the view ports in the forward hatch tower. She carried a twenty-foot iron pipe as a spar from her bow. Slipped over the end like a sleeve was a saw-toothed barb attached to a round copper canister, containing a charge of black powder. The idea was for the crew to crank the propeller as fast as they could and drive the barb into the target's hull. Then as she backed away, the spar would slip from the barb and canister while a firing lanyard was paid from a reel beside the forward hatch. At 150 yards, the line would trigger the firing mechanism, detonating the charge, with *Hunley* a safe distance away.

She was described in the flowery journalistic prose of the era as an "infernal contraption," more appropriately, the "peripatetic [or itinerant] coffin." To newspapers in the North, after news of her construction was leaked by spies, she was considered "the South's secret weapon."

The choppy waters of Mobile Bay proved too rough for the submarine, and Union ships remained too distant to reach in a single night's attempt, so Hunley and his associates began to forget any hopes of lucrative privateering. Then an offer they couldn't refuse came in.

General Pierre Beauregard, commanding the Charleston, South Carolina, defenses, requested the submarine be transported to his district to eliminate the Union fleet blockading the harbor. Horace Hunley and his co-builders jumped at the opportunity, especially since a wealthy merchant and owner of several blockade runners, John Fraser, offered a prize of $100,000 to any vessel that could destroy the Union admiral's flagship, the *New Ironsides,* or $50,000 for every monitor or other armed warship sent to the bottom.

The sub was soon hoisted onto two railroad flatcars, tied down, and sent across the forested Southern countryside to the hotbed of secession. She must have presented quite a sight to the gawking residents of the cities and towns along the way. *Hunley* was no giant cork, and the flatcars groaned under her iron mass. Estimates have placed her gross weight anywhere between four and ten tons.

Horace Hunley placed McClintock in command of the sub. The operation got off to a less than auspicious start. McClintock and his civilian crew tried several times to leave the harbor and attack the Union fleet, but failed owing to mechanical problems and rough seas.

The military were not impressed. When they strongly suggested sending along a naval officer as an observer, McClintock turned them down cold. Not a wise move. *Hunley* was promptly commandeered in the name of the Confederacy, McClintock was given his walking papers, and a crew of navy men from the harbor ironclad fleet, under the command of Lieutenant John Payne, came aboard to try their luck.

They drew a losing hand.

A short time later, through inexperience, Payne caused the boat to dive while he was caught in a rope snarled in the hatch cover. The open hatches tilted underwater, and the submarine sank. Payne leaped free, shouting for his men to abandon ship. That was easy for him to say. He was already standing half out of the forward hatch tower. The poor souls in the interior behind him stood a better chance of swimming the English Channel handcuffed than escaping the iron coffin.

Lieutenant Charles Hasker, who was standing in the aft hatch tower manning the ballast pump, was carried to the bottom when the suction of the water pulled the cover closed, trapping his leg and breaking the bone. As the sub filled with water, the inside pressure equalized and Hasker pulled his fractured leg free. He stroked for the surface forty-two feet away, miraculously reaching air and sun without drowning or suffering an embolism. After the Civil War, Hasker liked to boast that he was the only man to go down on the *Hunley* and survive.

Five men drowned. *Hunley* was on the scoreboard with her first victims.

She was raised, her dead removed, and the interior dried out. Horace Hunley volunteered the services of the team who created her, including Thomas Park, in whose shop the craft had been constructed, and Lieutenant Dixon. Beauregard accepted. Hunley and his people arrived and promptly put the submarine back in diving order.

Practice maneuvers began in the Ashley and Cooper rivers and proved quite impressive. On a number of occasions, *Hunley* and her crew slipped underwater a hundred yards away from an anchored ship and popped up the same distance away on the other side within ten or fifteen minutes.

On October 15, 1863, the sun was covered by a thick morning haze. Dixon, who normally commanded the sub, was not present that day, and Hunley took the helm for a practice dive. For some unknown reason the boat was also short by one other member of her crew, who now totaled eight.

The men stepped off the wharf onto the small planks leading to *Hunley*'s open hatch towers. They squeezed through the tight openings and took their places at the propeller crank, sitting in staggered rows and crowding the narrow confines. Then Thomas Park entered through the aft hatch and sealed it while Hunley did the same forward.

Hunley steered for the *Indian Chief,* a receiving ship used by the Confederate Navy to support the harbor mine operations. The sub's commander had two options for underwater running. He could flood the ballast tanks until the hatch towers were barely above water, and then take her down by tilting the diving planes, thereby controlling the angle for desired depth. His second choice, and the easiest for his human propulsion system, was to flood the tanks until he achieved neutral buoyancy at the correct depth, the same basic method used on all modern submarines. Trim was stabilized by Park, who worked the valves and pump for the aft ballast tank. When Hunley was ready to come up, he and Park pumped the water ballast from the tanks in unison, and the sub rose to the surface. Providing all went smoothly.

But this day something went terribly wrong.

Witnesses recall watching the sub dive beneath the surface, and then waiting in vain for it to reappear. After a few hours it became apparent that Horace Hunley, along with his crew inside the "infernal contraption," was lost.

It was another case of human error. Hunley had miscalculated his angle of descent and allowed the forward ballast tank to overflow. The sub lost trim and rammed its nose deep into the bottom mud, her stern raised slightly toward the surface, 145 feet away. Now, one of the engineering defects came into play. The bulkheads for the ballast tanks did not extend to the top of the hull roof, and the forward tank began to overflow, the water pouring into the main compartment.

Frantically, Hunley slammed the pump handle back and forth, ordering Park to blow the aft tank in a desperate effort to increase the buoyancy. Park kept his head and the stern lifted until it rose at the steep angle of thirty degrees. Hunley, unfortunately, panicked and forgot to close his valve, and despite his efforts at the pump the water continued to pour in.

He shouted for the crew to drop the iron ballast plates attached to the keel. Working off balance, they struggled to turn the rusting bolts but only succeeded in twisting them halfway before the relentless flow of water crept over their heads. In a last-ditch attempt to save themselves, the men made an effort to escape through the hatches and swim to the surface. The covers would not budge, sealed tight by the water pressure. When their bodies were recovered, most still clutched candles in their hands.

The score was now *Hunley* 13, the Confederacy 0.

The story traveled around the city that "the *Hunley* would sink at a moment's notice and sometimes without it." The Confederate Navy took the stance "I told you so," and washed their hands of the submarine. Despite his reservations, Beauregard ordered the *Hunley* to be salvaged. Divers led by Captain Angus Smith were engaged to bring up the sub for the second time. Hunley was found with his head raised in the forward hatch tower, one arm lifted as though pushing against the cover. Thomas Park was found in the same position in the aft hatch tower. Both had suffocated. The other six men had drowned.

Those who saw the blackened and distorted faces on the bodies never forgot the ghastly sight. The blood and gore of the battlefield was a horror they could accept, even understand. But death in an iron box under the sea filled them with a loathing far worse than any nightmare.

The funeral took place the following Sunday. The body of Hunley was escorted to Magnolia Cemetery in Charleston by two companies of soldiers and a band. After a solemn ceremony, he was laid to rest, followed by his ill-fated crew the following day.

The sub was propped on a wharf until Beauregard could figure out what to do with her. A Southern artist, Conrad Wise Chapman, wandered by, sketched the torpedo boat, and later painted a small picture of her that now hangs in the Confederate Museum at Richmond. Primitive in her construction though surprisingly modern in shape, she sits like the proverbial fish out of water, her torpedo spar aimed forlornly across the water at the enemy fleet.

Hunley was damned as a Jonah, and the majority of those who voiced criticism demanded that now her crew was recovered she should be dumped back on the bottom and left there. Beauregard called a halt to any further underwater operations, seeing no reason to throw more lives away on a "contraption that had yet to leave the harbor." There were only two who argued with his decision.

Lieutenants George Dixon and William Alexander, who helped construct *Pioneer II,* upon hearing of the tragedy hurried to Charleston from Mobile. Both refused to accept defeat.

Together, they persuaded a reluctant Beauregard that it was a terrible waste to forget the heroic efforts of the dead and ignore the potential threat of the submarine to the blockading Union fleet. Less than enthusiastic, Beauregard finally gave in, but only on the condition that any attacks on the enemy be made with the sub afloat, not submerged.

The two enterprising young engineering officers quickly overhauled the boat and, what is most incredible, assembled a new crew from a host of volunteers before the ground settled over Hunley and his comrades' graves. Perhaps the tantalizing offer, still in effect, of $100,000 for sinking the *New Ironsides* fogged over the ever-hovering threat of a horrible death. It has never been known for certain if the reward was in gold or Confederate currency.

The boat was officially renamed the *Horace L. Hunley,* with Lieutenant Dixon as its commander. It now came under the wing of the army, with the navy acting as support. Mooring the boat in the backwater channel behind Battery Marshall on Sullivan's Island, Dixon and Alexander set up quarters at Mount Pleasant and launched what has to be the world's first submarine school. The crew were instructed in the basics of underwater operation by diagrams traced in wet beach sand. They were also ordered to do nineteenth-century calisthenics. If only we had videos of that. Afternoons were spent in practice dives and long-distance runs. In the last light of day, the two young officers would lie on the beach and take compass sightings of the Union ships riding at anchor. When they agreed that sub and crew were in a state of readiness, they began to make nightly runs against the enemy fleet, leaving on the ebb and returning with the incoming tide.

Admiral John Dahlgren, Union commander of the South Atlantic Blockading Fleet, was kept well informed of the *Hunley*'s progress by Confederate deserters. He instructed his ship captains to keep a sharp eye while they were anchored at night. Floating booms with dangling chains were placed around the ships as a primitive form of antitorpedo netting. Bright calcium lights were primed and ready to flare, and manned picket boats constantly moved around the mooring sites. Dahlgren also ordered his ironclad monitors to anchor in shallow water so there could be no room for *Hunley* to maneuver from below.

Night after night, the ungainly submarine and her hardened crew churned into the sea off Charleston to sink a Yankee ship. And each time they returned empty-handed, racing the dawn to avoid discovery, beaten by choppy water, adverse currents, and high winds, or by arms too weary to turn the propeller crank another stroke.

Watercolor of the Long Island steamboat Lexington *soon after launching by Bard.*

Lithograph of the burning of the Lexington *by Currier.*

Drilling in Galveston, Texas, parking lot for the Zavala.

Author's model of Republic of Texas Navy warship Zavala.

U.S.S.
Cumberland
at the
Portsmouth
Navy Yard
about 1860.

5

6

U.S.S. Cumberland *after being rammed by*
C.S.S. Virginia (Merrimack).

7

Famed Confederate raider C.S.S. Florida.

8

Author with artifacts recovered from U.S.S. Cumberland
and C.S.S. Florida.

9

Author's model of Confederate ironclad C.S.S. Arkansas.

10

Battle between Union ironclad U.S.S. Carondelet *and* C.S.S. Arkansas.

Famous River War ironclad U.S.S. Carondelet.

Historic Confederate submarine Horace L. Hunley, *on the dock in Charleston, 1863.*

13

Union sloop-of-war U.S.S. Housatonic *sunk by the Confederate submarine* Hunley, *February 17, 1864.*

14

Confederate submarine C.S.S. Hunley *torpedoing Union warship U.S.S.* Housatonic.

15

Esteemed inventor Dr. Harold Edgerton with author during the first search for the Hunley, *1980.*

16

Peter Throckmorton, America's dean of marine archaeology, with author during the Hunley *search.*

17

Bill Shea demonstrating exciting search techniques with magnetometer.

Cussler watching Cal, the city maintenance man, excavate the Confederate Blockade Runner Stonewall Jackson, *on the beach at Isle of Palms, South Carolina.*

18

19

Left to right: Walt Schob, author, and Bill Shea
marking search grids for Hunley.

20

The first men to touch the Hunley *in 131 years.*
Left to right: Wes Hall, Ralph Wilbanks, and
Harry Pecorelli III.

Sign set up by Craig Dirgo and Dirk Cussler during the discovery announcement.

21

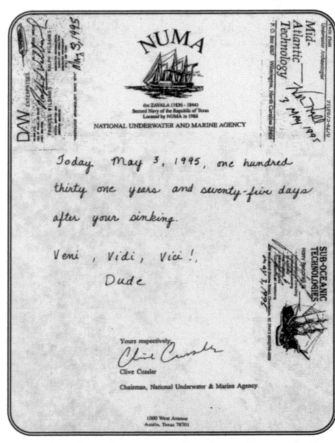

22

Just so there is no mistake as to who made the discovery. Waterproof certification placed inside forward hatch of the Hunley.

23

*A Baldwin 4-6-0 of the same type as the locomotive
lost in Kiowa Creek.*

24

*The first wolfpack. U-12, U-20, and U-21 were all found
by NUMA, 1984.*

25

British scout cruiser H.M.S. Pathfinder. *First ship sunk by a U-boat.*

26

Sinking of Pathfinder *by U-21, September 5, 1914.*

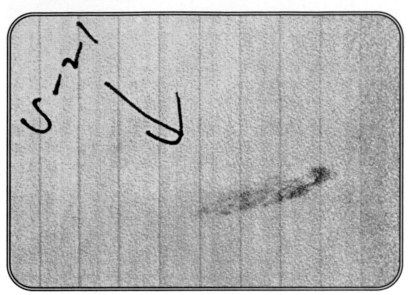

27

Side scan sonar recording of U-21 *in the North Sea, depth 190 feet.*

28

Belgian troop transport Léopoldville, *torpedoed Christmas Eve, 1944, off Cherbourg.*

Cussler with the prettiest girl in Bridlington, England.

Captain Jimmy Flett of the Arvor III.

31

The motley NUMA crew after their potato attack on a French missile frigate. Left to right: John the first mate, Dirk Cussler, Derek Goodwin, Jimmy Flett, author, Colin the cook, Wayne Gronquist, and Bill Shea.

32

Author being honored by Bob Hesse at the 66th Infantry Division reunion of the Panther Veteran Organization.

Winter brought cold, miserable weather, and the *Hunley*'s forays became even more difficult. More than once contrary currents almost swept them out to sea. On other occasions they were still within range of Union guns when the sun rose. An exhausted Dixon decided to give his crew a rest while conducting further underwater experiments in the calm waters behind Sullivan's Island. One such experiment that intrigued him was an endurance dive.

If they were apprehended by a picket boat or were under fire by a blockading vessel, there would be no escape except by diving and waiting it out on the bottom. Their lives might depend on knowing how long they could stay down in order to throw the Union picket boats off their trail.

After agreeing on a coordinated plan, Dixon and Alexander waved to the soldiers lining the dock at Battery Marshall. Then they closed and bolted the forward and aft hatch covers. Then they checked the time on their watches. The ballast tanks were flooded and the sub slowly settled into the mud of the back channel. To simulate actual running conditions, the men slowly rotated the propeller, each steeling himself not to be the first to shout, "Up!"

Twenty-five minutes later, the candles refused to burn. Each second passed by like an eternity. The dampness from their breathing raised the humidity inside to an intolerable level. Blackness lay like a smothering blanket. The usual joking conversation died into silence, broken only by an occasional "How is it?" followed by "All right" that passed between Dixon and Alexander.

The interior became stifling from the used-up air mixed with the smell of sweat. Never in history had humans remained submerged underwater so long. And still none begged for deliverance.

They far exceeded any limit expected of them. At last, as if preordained, all nine men gasped in chorus, "Up!"

Quickly, Dixon pumped out the water ballast forward. But Alexander's aft pump was not operating. With incredible coolness, he analyzed the problem. Working by feel, he unscrewed the cap on the pump, twisted out the valve, and pulled out a wad of seaweed that had plugged the inlet.

By now, the bow had ascended while the stern remained firmly mired in the mud. The others fought against creeping panic as grim visions of Hunley and Park and their crew's final moments materialized in their minds. Death stared them square in the eye, and yet none blinked.

Unconsciousness was edging into Alexander's brain as he reassembled the pump and frantically worked the lever. For an agonizing moment the bottom mud refused to release its grip. Then suddenly the stern broke free and the *Hunley* leveled out just as the hatch towers broke the surface. The covers were unbolted and thrown back. To a man, the crew sagged in exhaustion and immense relief as they inhaled the cool, brisk air.

The sun was shining when they began the test, and now it was dark. Only one solitary soldier remained on the dock. The rest had dispersed, certain the *Hunley* was up to her old tricks. He whooped in happy realization at her sudden resurrection when Alexander yelled for him to take a mooring line.

A match was struck and timepieces were checked. They had remained underwater for two hours and thirty-five minutes. An astonishing feat when considering the small cubic displacement of the sub's interior. The *Hunley* was truly a pathfinder in the submarine conflicts that were to come in the future.

Beauregard was most impressed with the performance and ordered that the submarine and her crew be given whatever assistance the army and navy could provide. With renewed support, Dixon took the craft out whenever weather permitted, taking ever greater risks in futile attempts to reach an approachable target.

Then unexpectedly, in early February of 1864, Alexander was ordered to go from Charleston to Mobile to engineer and construct a breech-loading repeating gun. In his own words, he said, "This was a terrible blow both to Dixon and myself after we had gone through so much together."

His requests to remain with the *Hunley* were rejected. The needs of the service dictated that Alexander go where his talents were most essential. He was replaced by a volunteer from an artillery unit stationed at one of the city's many forts.

Dixon carried on alone until he was lost that fateful night of February 17, 1864.

II

The Toughest Find of All

July 1980

THROUGH THE CENTURIES, SAILORS HAVE BEEN HAUNTED by superstitions concerning their lives at sea. A woman on a ship was once considered unlucky. Ships with male instead of female names met unfortunate fates. No sailor would kill an albatross, a no-no long before the Ancient Mariner came along. In light of modern technology and progressive thinking, most sailors' superstitions have been thrown overboard and forgotten. One tradition, however, still has its share of firm believers. They contend that it's unlucky for a ship to sail from port on a Friday. Right up until the turn of the century, insurance companies charged an extra premium for any ship that cast off for a voyage across the sea on a Friday.

In 1894, a Scots merchant and shipowner in Liverpool became incensed at having to compensate his captains and crews for laying over until Saturday. Nor was he excited by the prospect of paying outrageous premiums to greedy insurance company owners. He decided to explode the old wives' tale once and for all time.

He ordered a ship built. The keel was laid on Friday. The vessel was launched on Friday and christened the *Friday* on

194

Friday. A captain was even found whose name was Friday. Then, after loading an expensive cargo on board and refusing to insure it, the Scots merchant waved farewell as the good ship *Friday,* with Captain Friday at the helm, sailed off on Friday bound for New York.

The good ship *Friday* and her intrepid crew were never seen or heard from again.

There are unlucky ships and there are unlucky ships, but the Confederate submarine *Hunley* has to hold some kind of record. Three times she sank, two times she was raised. Over twenty men died within her iron walls. Nine still lie entombed there.

For someone like me, addicted to mysteries of the sea, *Hunley* cast a spell that I found about as irresistible as a starving cat staring at an overweight rodent exercising on a treadmill.

Through the decades after she triumphed and vanished into oblivion, many tried to find the little sub that could, and all failed. Claims were made of discovery, but none were substantiated. No photo or proof was ever produced. All that was known for certain was that she was never seen again.

Theories abounded on the fate of the vessel. They were so numerous you had to pick a number before advancing a new one. Was she destroyed in the explosion or sucked into the hole she made in the *Housatonic,* as several researchers touted? Did her crew suffer from the effects of concussion and drift out to sea unconscious or dead before the sub sank? Could the blast have loosened her plates and rivets, causing her to sink before completing the return voyage to Breach Inlet? Suppose her crew, jubilant from the triumph, headed into Charleston Harbor to tell the populace and the city's commander, General Pierre Beauregard, in person, and were run down by one of many Confederate harbor transports? What if she made it all the way home and then sank at her dock?

Here was a mystery with a thousand clues but no conclusive leads.

I never accepted her fate as united with *Housatonic.* The post–Civil War salvor, Benjamin Mallifert, was no slouch.

He extensively salvaged the Union sloop-of-war and emphatically wrote in his diaries that he found no trace of *Hunley.* Lieutenant Churchill, in the salvage schooner *G. W. Blunt,* dragged the bottom five hundred yards around the *Housatonic,* finding nothing of the torpedo boat.

After the war, diver Angus Smith and his brother searched five acres around the wreck, hoping to cash in on P. T. Barnum's $100,000 reward for the famous sub. In a letter dated 1876, Smith said that he had sat on the fish torpedo boat that was lying alongside the *Housatonic,* and could raise her at any time. But like so many who followed with their claims of discovery, Smith never produced a shred of evidence.

In 1908, diver William Virden was awarded a contract by the Army Corps of Engineers to lower the wreck because it had become a menace to navigation. After raising four tons of old iron and blasting the remains of *Housatonic* to smithereens, he received $3,240 and stated that he saw no signs of the submarine.

The case for the sub's escape after blowing a hole in the stern of her enemy was established when researcher Bob Fleming pried open the wax seal and laid his eyes on 115 pages of handwritten testimony from the naval court of inquiry proceedings after the sinking. Resting in the archives at Suitland, Maryland, and unopened for 120 years, the testimony by *Housatonic* crewmen reported that the torpedo boat had pulled back close to fifty yards before the explosion. One ship's crewman, Seaman Fleming (no relation to our researcher), reported that after the ship sank under him, he climbed to the rigging ahead of the rising water. Under further questioning he stated: "When the *Canandaigua* [the ship that came to the survivors' rescue] got astern, and was lying athwart [neither perpendicular nor parallel but on an angle] of the *Housatonic,* about four ship lengths off, while I was in the fore rigging, I saw a blue light on the water just ahead of the *Canandaigua,* and on the starboard quarter of the *Housatonic.*"

This was enough for me to believe the *Hunley* had left

the site of the sinking. It was also a billboard advertising the resting place and fate of the submarine, but I failed to grasp the significance.

There was also the report by Colonel O. M. Dantzler, commanding Battery Marshall off Breach Inlet, where the *Hunley*'s dock was located: "I have the honor to report that the torpedo boat stationed at this post went out on the night of the 17th instant and has not returned. The signals agreed upon to be given in case the boat wished a light to be exposed at this post as a guide for its return were observed and answered. An earlier report would have been made of this matter, but the Officer of the Day for yesterday was under the impression that the boat had returned, and so informed me. As soon as I became apprised of the fact, I sent a telegram to Captain Nance, assistant adjutant-general, notifying him of it."

There were those who were skeptical of this report, especially about the part where the *Hunley*'s lights were "observed and answered." They thought perhaps Colonel Dantzler was lax, had ignored the failure of the submarine to return, and was covering his tail by blaming his officer of the day. I disagreed and initially bought the report as truth, and so I originally laid out our search grid close to shore, figuring a blue light held on the surface of the water could not be seen much over a mile. Relying on Colonel Dantzler was a miscalculation I later regretted.

I began preparations for my first attempt at finding the *Hunley* by applying for a permit from the University of South Carolina's Institute of Archaeology and Anthropology (SCIAA). Alan Albright, the institute's lead archaeologist, was most cooperative, despite a few reservations about some upstart outfit that claimed to be a nonprofit foundation that did not seek treasure.

Dubious of someone who claimed he wanted no artifacts for profit, Albright stared at me with the look of a fox scenting a wolf on a changing breeze. "If you find the *Hunley,* what then?"

I smiled cagily and answered, "That's your problem."

* * *

The NUMA team began to arrive in Charleston and drove across the bay to the Isle of Palms, where my advance man, Walt Schob, had arranged for everyone to stay in a rundown old motel whose little stucco bungalows looked as if they might have served as a meeting and storage facility for Prohibition bootleggers. Bill Shea thought perhaps Puff the Magic Dragon had crawled there and died after frolicking in the autumn mist. I'd rarely seen separate bedrooms with a common bathroom in the middle. It made for some wild and crazy confrontations.

We certainly had a diverse crew. Doc Harold Edgerton appeared with his side scan sonar and subbottom penetrator, as he called it. Peter Throckmorton, who launched ancient shipwreck archaeology in the Mediterranean, came. Dan Koski-Karell, the archaeologist our state permit was issued to, also came. Bill Shea, Dirk Cussler, Walt Schob, Wayne Gronquist, and Admiral Bill Thompson, the driving force behind the Navy Memorial in Washington, D.C., all showed. Dana Larson was as always on hand to lend support, and our resident psychic from Duke University, Karen Getsla, appeared to head up our magic department.

Adding to the gala festivities, everyone's wife and girl-friend also showed up, the girlfriends of the single guys, that is. I can't recall if they were invited, but they all came anyway. Miraculously, everyone got along and had a jolly time.

The only ticklish moment came when Throckmorton announced that he was going to prepare a community supper, serving his renowned sautéed shrimp with special sauce, stolen from a discriminating goatherd in Turkey. He took over the motel kitchen and recruited the wives and girl-friends, driving and ordering them about as if he were Captain Bligh commanding a seagoing cooking school. His demands did not go down well with the ladies. While Peter poured his soul into his exotic sauce for the shrimp, his kitchen help quietly mutinied behind his back.

One of the ladies found an old pair of castaway socks in a trash can behind the motel. As Peter's gourmet shrimp sauce was simmering on the stove, the socks were added and stirred into the pot. The ladies of the kitchen demonstrated great discipline by not saying a word, but simply setting the bowl with the sauce on the buffet table with the rest of the entrées. I believe Walt Schob and Bill Shea were the first ones through the line, and as they lifted the ladle to spread the sauce on their shrimp and rice, their expressions of anticipation slowly transformed to looks of bewilderment. Without a word, they skipped the sauce and moved on down the line. The performance was repeated by all the men, not sure whether the socks were for seasoning or a joke. The ladies, of course, fought so hard to keep from coming unglued with laughter their eyes flowed with tears.

At last the moment the whole world was waiting for. Throcko started through the food line. When he came to the sauce and ladled up a sock, he froze in stunned awe. It was as if he underwent a total personality change. He stood there looking like a man whose wife just ran off with an itinerant raccoon breeder. Then he slowly picked up the pot by both handles, went to the door, and threw sauce, socks, and pot into an oleander bush that had expired by the time we closed down the expedition and headed home.

The escapades on shore were only matched by those at sea. One that averted tragedy occurred two days later. The crew of the Zodiac inflatable boat that I had chartered to run search lanes close to shore consisted of Bill Shea, who scanned the proton magnetometer, Dan Koski-Karell, directing the navigation, and my son, Dirk, who steered and operated the boat's outboard motor.

In those years the most accurate navigation system for running tight thirty-meter lanes was the Motorola Mini Ranger. We found that, rather than mounting the equipment in an already crowded boat, it was more efficient to direct the search from a van on shore via radio. Each morning, the search team would proceed through Breach Inlet, the same channel used by *Hunley* 120 years previously, and then take up a base position as instructed by the Mini Ranger operators.

This morning as Shea, Koski-Karell, and Cussler motored through the inlet, they noticed people on shore shouting and waving frantically at the water ahead of their Zodiac. Only then did the NUMA team spot three tiny heads in the water being swept out to sea by the strong ebb-tide current. Cussler steered the boat toward the bobbing heads. As he pulled alongside, Shea and Koski-Karell jumped overboard, grabbed three little boys, none of whom were over nine years old, and hoisted them into the boat.

It was a near thing. Another minute or two and the boys would have drowned. As it was, they were in the initial stages of shock and beginning to turn blue. It was nothing short of a miracle that the only boat within miles that could navigate the shallow but treacherous waters of the inlet happened to be at the right place at the right time.

Returning to the beach, the rescuers were met by the hysterical mother and aunt of the boys, who immediately hustled them into a car and drove off, no thank you, no words of appreciation, not even a wave of acknowledgment.

When we returned the following year, I met up with the local sheriff and asked if he ever heard anything about the three boys who were snatched from the water by our team. He said he wasn't sure, but he thought one of them might have drowned. I straightened him out by happily reporting that all three were pulled from the water alive and kicking.

I used to wonder why fate whispered in my ear to go and find *Hunley*. Perhaps there was more to the message than merely finding a shipwreck. Because our NUMA crew was there that day, three children have grown to adults and perhaps, just perhaps, they walk the beach with their children and tell them how Daddy would have drowned if not for three strangers in a rubber boat.

While the Zodiac began searching for *Hunley* along the shore, working out toward the open sea, our second boat surveyed the site of *Housatonic*. Probes pretty well established the outline of the remaining hull and one boiler. There was no indication of the submarine.

No cartoon series could have done this part of the expedition justice. The boat was an old dilapidated twenty-seven-foot cabin cruiser called the *Coastal Explorer* long past its prime. The boat had two engines, and one of them was always dying from some mechanical malady. And though she broke down every afternoon like clockwork, repairs were made and she somehow always brought us home. Well, almost. Once, as we headed for home after a day of surveying, both engines coughed and ran out of fuel a hundred yards from the dock. Fortunately, the boys in the Zodiac happened along at the same time and towed us in.

A voyage in the *Coastal Explorer* always reminded me of a trip to downtown Oz.

The boat was owned and captained by a truly nice guy, whose name was Robert Johnson. We affectionately referred to him as Skipper Bob. His two crewmen, who were students at the famous Charleston Citadel, were a pair of real characters. These guys made Gilligan look like a paragon of efficiency. What they lacked in finesse they more than made up with humor. When things got tedious, they would march around the boat to a drumbeat. I'd never seen anyone beat a drum with a flyswatter before. Their true names are forgotten, which is probably best. We called them Heckle and Jeckle.

One day the sea was a bit choppy and the door to the cabin kept swinging open and then banging shut. The latch was either nonexistent or broken.

"Fix that damned door!" ordered Skipper Bob.

Heckle and Jeckle sprang into action. As Doc Edgerton and I watched in fascination, Heckle grabbed a huge sledgehammer as Jeckle snatched up a nail the size of a railroad spike. Then, in one deft motion, they drove the spike through the bottom of the door and into the wooden deck.

"The door will swing no more," Heckle announced triumphantly.

Skipper Bob nodded with satisfaction, seemingly immune to the damage to his boat.

"You've got to admit," Doc said to me with his celebrated grin, "there's a method to their madness."

"Maybe," sez I, shaking my head in wonder. "But I doubt if they'll be asked to write a handy hints column for the *Ladies' Home Journal.*"

Working with Doc Edgerton was a joy. He would sit in a

lawn chair staring at the recorder of his subbottom penetrator, rocking in motion with the boat. Just at the point where we all swore he was about to fall over, the boat would roll in the opposite direction, and he'd sway back in unison.

The *Coastal Explorer* follies continued without letup.

The crew were especially fascinated by Karen Getsla as she sat on the bow and tried to tune in on *Hunley*'s location. Seemingly going into a trance and holding up her hands as if they were antennas, she could envision the bits and pieces of scenes during the sinking. But she could not pin down a precise site.

I'm convinced psychics can see things in their minds that go far beyond anything I can imagine. The problem for psychics with locating a sunken ship is that there are no landmarks on open water. No nearby railroad, water tanks, telephone poles, or rivers to mark a position. Still, they're fun to work with, and I never hesitate to give them a chance to try their powers.

On the next voyage of our intrepid boat, Wayne Gronquist's girlfriend, Debbie, a gorgeous creature who stood at least five feet ten, came along for the ride. I've always welcomed women on our search boats. But I'm always apprehensive in light of the fact that we seldom have bathroom facilities and females are not noted for iron bladders. I get this from my wife, who makes me stop at every other gas station when we're on the road.

As soon as we left the harbor and circled around a two-mile rock jetty into the open sea, Debbie stripped down to her bikini and stretched out on the roof of the forward cabin directly in front of the windshield, soaking up the sun and displaying her pulchritude to bulging eyes inside the cabin.

Heckle and Jeckle stared enthralled. It was as if they were witnessing the second coming of the Messiah. Even Doc looked impressed.

Skipper Bob peered at the expanse of smooth feminine flesh that filled his entire windshield, turned to me, and muttered vaguely. "I can't see around her."

I shrugged. "Steer with your compass and do the best you can."

It goes without saying that we didn't accomplish much that day.

Even the final voyage before we rang down the curtain on that year's expedition did not go without incident. On the way in, Skipper Bob decided to save three miles and twenty minutes attempting a short cut by crossing over the rock jetty at high tide. There are times it's better to be safe than sorry. This was one of them.

With a dull thud *Coastal Explorer* bounced onto the rocks of the jetty and came to an abrupt halt.

I dropped into the water and dove under the hull. The keel appeared to be hung up between two rocks. I found that by standing on a rock and putting my shoulder against the bow I could actually move the boat a few inches as the crest of each wave passed under. While I was engaged in saving *Coastal Explorer* for another day, I heard a splash behind me and felt the presence of someone who had joined in the effort. I turned, and there was Doc in his shorts pushing for all he was worth.

A newspaper reporter, who had come on board for the day and was apparently a good Catholic, thought the boat was doomed when Doc and I went over the side. To him, we were abandoning a doomed ship. He began running his rosary beads through his fingers so fast smoke came out of them.

Then I looked up. The fearless crew were all leaning over the railing and idly watching while drinking cans of Pepsi. Doc was seventy-seven, I was only fifty, and none of the high and dry observers had yet to see twenty-five, yet they all stood by while two old farts grunted and eventually heaved the boat into deep water.

Coastal Explorer had been holed, and by the time we reached the dock there was nearly two feet of water in the engine compartment and main cabin.

The following year when we returned for another try at finding *Hunley,* I was saddened to see the remains of the faithful boat all chopped into pieces, lying forlornly in the marsh behind Sullivan's Island.

Despite a short run, the NUMA follies managed to eliminate a two-mile-long grid, beginning at Breach Inlet and extending a half mile out to sea. We were now reasonably sure that the elusive little submarine had not gone down close to shore or in the surf but must be lying further out toward *Housatonic.*

I've always affectionately recalled this expedition as the Great Trauma of '80.

III

Once More with Feeling

June 1981

MOST OF THE OLD GANG CAME BACK FOR ANOTHER TRY THE
following summer. This time Walt put us in a big, comfortable house on the beach at Isle of Palms. He even obtained
the services of a cook. She turned out sumptuous meals,
usually drowning in grease. She went through Crisco faster
than a whale through plankton. Her only quirk was that she
refused to make grits, a dish I've always enjoyed. But since
I was the only one partial to grits, the rest of the team
couldn't have cared less.

I love that old Southern down-home cooking. Give me
red-eye gravy and biscuits, grits with butter, and chicory in
my coffee, and I'm ready to snatch up a sword and lead
Pickett's charge up Cemetery Ridge.

Obtaining the permit this time was merely a formality.
Alan Albright generously offered a top-of-the-line archaeological dive team and first-rate outboard boat. The total crew
ballooned to seventeen people with the arrival of half a
dozen young volunteers: Coast Guardsman Tim Firmey; two
students from the North Carolina Institute of Archaeology,
Bob Browning and Wilson West; my son-in-law, Bob Toft;

my son, Dirk; and a local young man, David Farah, who proved most helpful and whose parents threw a wonderful barbecue for the search team. This time we were also joined by Ralph Wilbanks and Rodney Warren from the university. Bill O'Donnell and Dave Graham of Motorola flew in to operate the Mini Ranger positioning system.

This expedition went as smoothly as a fashion model's shaven leg. The equipment ticked away without missing a beat, the weather cooperated with smooth seas, and the only injuries, luckily, were sunburn, seasickness, and hangovers. Running thirty-meter lanes, we searched a total of sixteen square miles, taking up where we left off the year before, searching out and beyond *Housatonic.* Success was mingled with failure. Although we did not find *Hunley,* we discovered five Confederate blockade runners and three Union ironclads.

Walt Schob handled the university boat and tracked the grid lines, while Bill Shea, fighting *mal de mer* every foot of the way, operated his homemade proton magnetometer. During communications over the portable radio, Walt referred to the outboard as the *Steak Boat.* His reason for calling it that came from not wanting it known he was associated with state property. There are some things that just can't be explained articulately.

Dirk and Dave Graham sat in a Budget rental van, parked in the backyard of a house next to Breach Inlet, and operated the Mini Ranger. When the boys on shore got bored keeping the *Steak Boat* on track, they engaged in elaborate fly-killing contests, keeping score by scotch-taping their victims to the wall of the van.

The lady who owned the house was most accommodating. One afternoon, she invited the crew in for cocktails. She was a very gracious host until 6:30 rolled around. Then we were informed that we had to leave because she was having another party for her friends and neighbors and she didn't think we had anything in common. I guess there are some idiosyncrasies about Southern hospitality that those of us from the North and out West will never quite fathom.

For the dive and chase boat, we chartered a dependable

vessel owned by Harold Stauber, a guy with the patience of a tree trunk, who knew the waters around Charleston like his own living room. With this boat, named *Sweet Sue,* our team followed up the targets picked up by the *Steak Boat,* dove on them, and identified them as either old shrimp-boat wrecks or sunken barges. Most anomalies proved to be junk tossed off ships. Over a span of three hundred years enough debris has accumulated on the bottom in and around Charleston Harbor to keep a scrap dealer in business for three generations.

During slow days when *Steak Boat* failed to run across any anomalies that remotely suggested a submarine, my team on *Sweet Sue* searched for other historic Civil War shipwrecks. The previous month I had stumbled on an interesting piece of data. While comparing old nautical charts with new ones, I noticed longitude meridians prior to the twentieth century ran approximately four hundred yards farther west than later projections. What caught my eye was that the 52nd meridian seemed much closer to Fort Sumter on an 1870 chart than on a 1980 chart. Testing this revelation, we discovered several wrecks four hundred yards west of where they were marked on contemporary charts.

The first ship we located was *Keokuk,* a dual-turreted citadel ironclad that went down after being struck ninety-two times by Confederate cannon fire. She lies off the old abandoned Morris Island lighthouse under four feet of silt. The Union monitor *Weehawken* came next, a famous warship sunk in heavy weather, the only ironclad that actually defeated another during the war. We found her buried eight feet under the seabed.

Most people think that shipwrecks sit proud on the bottom. A few lie exposed, but the majority that went down close to land settled in the soft silt and were slowly buried by wave action over the years. One surprising discovery was *Patapsco,* a Union monitor that struck a Confederate mine in 1865 and sank off Fort Moultrie, taking sixty-two members of the crew with her. Because she sits in the channel, which is scoured by currents, we dove and found her sitting upright on the bottom. Though she was extensively salvaged after the war, the U.S. Navy still considers her a burial site. So we looked but didn't touch.

Whenever we found a wreck, Ralph Wilbanks would entertain *Sweet Sue*'s crew by dancing a country jig. Solidly built and no lightweight, Ralph made the whole boat shudder when he began stomping. There is nothing like brisk and boisterous freewheeling humor and frivolity to lighten up monotony.

Probably the luckiest find I ever made was a Confederate blockade runner. One day, when the sea was too rough to run the grid lanes, I thought we could use the lost time to look for the blockade runner *Stonewall Jackson,* lost during an attempt to run into Charleston in the spring of 1863. She was shot up by blockading warships of the Union fleet, ran aground on the Isle of Palms, and was destroyed along with her cargo of artillery pieces and forty thousand shoes. Over the years, she became deeply buried under the sand by wave action.

An 1864 chart of the waters outside Charleston Harbor showed the general location where she had come ashore and burned. When laying a transparency of the '64 chart over a modern one, I could see that the beach now stretched a good quarter of a mile farther out to sea than it did during the Civil War. Allowing for the four-hundred-yard difference in longitude, I laid out a rectangular search grid for the team to walk that encompassed one mile parallel to the beach by a quarter of a mile either side of the surf line. This was possible because the water was shallow for a considerable distance.

An area this size is easy to cover while sitting in a moving boat, but walking up and down a hot, sandy beach with a metal detector is a tiring and time-consuming process. On land, your forward movement is about one-half mph while swinging the detector from side to side as you work a swath, but from a boat you can cruise along at eight knots.

Several members of the NUMA team and I assembled on the beach and marked out the lanes we intended to walk with our magnetometers. I carried the Schonstedt gradiometer and set its recorder down on the sand. Then I hooked up the batteries and tried to calibrate the settings while studying the readings on the dial and listening to the squawk of the speaker. If set correctly, the gradiometer emits a low buzzing sound that increases to a screech when its sensor comes near the presence of iron. Strangely, the readings kept flying off scale and the speaker screamed. I became irritated when I couldn't get the instrument to settle down. What was wrong with this thing? I wondered. Rechecking the battery connections and fiddling with the adjustment knobs failed to remedy the situation.

And then it hit me. Not only had I walked out onto the beach and laid the gradiometer squarely on top of the wreck of the *Stonewall Jackson,* I was reading the metal mass of its buried engine and boilers. Discoveries like this only happen with the regularity of being struck on the head with a meteor. And yet no other recorded shipwreck lay within a good half mile.

While waiting for a maintenance man from the Isle of Palms street department, a congenial guy whose name was Cal, to appear with a backhoe, Bob Browning, Wilson West, and Dirk Cussler eased stainless-steel probes through the sand and struck a large piece of metal. Interestingly, the impact of the probes set up a vibration under our bare feet. Everyone became excited at the prospect that they were rapping on the ship's boilers. As soon as word spread along the beach, a large crowd gathered to watch the excavation.

The backhoe dug an eight-foot trench but struck only salt water. Then Cal suggested that he run to the city maintenance shop and bring back a portable water pump and a length of plastic pipe. The idea was to shoot water through the pipe and sink it in the sand, much as kids do when tunneling in the dirt with a nozzle on the end of a garden hose.

Cal quickly returned and ten minutes later we began to strike the past. At ten feet, coal and beautiful pieces of mahogany came bubbling up. Since the probes indicated the presence of a boiler, the coal seemed to confirm it. We dredged up no shoes but we felt reasonably assured that we were standing on the remains of *Stonewall Jackson.* The wood served to add credence to the discovery. Someday, I hope they excavate and see how much of her is preserved beneath the sand. In light of the cost and a growing lack of interest in our history by the young people of our nation, it's a pity that such an event may never happen. Our NUMA team, all history buffs, felt they had had a productive day at the beach and went home happy. Hence the motto of NUMA: "Do it big, do it right, give it class, and make 'em laugh."

One episode occurred during the expedition that still haunts a few of us.

Late one afternoon, we accidentally ran over a large metallic anomaly while returning to the dock in *Sweet Sue.* The magnetometer's recorder had been left on, and one of the dive team happened to glance at it when the stylus zigzagged across the graph in the blink of an eye. An anomaly with a large iron mass from the look of it. We immediately turned back to the site and ran a grid pattern until we picked it up again. Then we threw in a buoy and anchored.

The student archaeologists, Bob Browning and Wilson West, along with Coast Guardsman Tim Firmey, dove in and began probing the site. Within minutes, West came to the surface and announced, "We've got an object over thirty feet long by about four feet wide. Don't quote me, but the ends appear to be tapered."

Anticipation set eight hearts pounding. The time was nearly six o'clock, but we had a good two hours of daylight left. So we raced to the dock, lifted a suction dredge onto the boat and hightailed it back to our buoy. We passed *Steak Boat,* which had knocked off and was returning for the day. Schob and Shea stared at us as we waved, at a loss as to why we were heading out so late in the evening.

With Ralph Wilbanks and Rodney Warren in the water operating the dredge, the rest of us sat and waited expectantly. Sharks often appear during a dredging operation, attracted by the sea life caught up in the induction hose. One did come snooping while the divers were down, and we threw cans of Pepsi and shouted at it till it swam off in search of easier pickings. It was nearly dark when the divers surfaced and we called it quits. Ralph drew a sketch of what he and Rodney found after digging a two-foot hole.

It appeared to be a quarter-inch piece of iron standing at an angle and attached to a metal plate that disappeared in the silt. Since they saw no rivets holding the object in place, it looked as if the object were welded to the plate. Knowing that metal welding was as yet unknown in the 1860s, we assumed that what we found was a sunken Coast Guard buoy, approximately the same size and mass as *Hunley*.

Time had run out. We had covered a great deal of territory and discovered over seven shipwrecks, but the search for *Hunley* came up as empty as a hermit's address book. She still refused to be found. Or had the sub played a cruel trick on us?

IV

If at First You Don't Succeed

July 1994

I CAN'T REALLY EXPLAIN WHY IT TOOK ME THIRTEEN YEARS to give the sub another go. Perhaps I'd developed a mental block or just wasn't in the mood. For various reasons some shipwrecks can never be located. I did not believe this to be the case with *Hunley*. Many were those who said it wasn't there simply because it had been salvaged by someone who left no record. I could not accept that. It had to be out there off Charleston somewhere, and this time I was not going to cry quits.

It was déjà vu all over again. Walt came early and arranged for boats and lodging. Bill Shea came in with his television camera and shot video of the expedition. We enjoyed watching the results, especially the scenes where Bill ran on camera, repositioned his subjects, and then dashed off again without turning off the Record button.

Conversations were held with new people at the South Carolina Institute of Archaeology. Instead of giving a permit, they asked if we could make it a joint venture. Old softie that I am, I agreed. Not a wise move on my part as it turned out.

212

Because Hurricane Hugo had flattened our old motel and the big house on the beach (not so much as a stick of wood remained of either one), Walt Schob set us up in the local Holiday Inn. We were moving up in the world. The fact that my book royalties had increased significantly over the ensuing years didn't hurt either.

I've frequently complained about returning to certain towns or cities for another attempt at finding a shipwreck, but I was always happy to come back to Charleston. There are few cities finer in Caroliner and most other states. The people are cordial and as affable as old friends, the city is picturesque, and what is especially appealing to someone like me with sensitive taste buds and a warehouse for a stomach, they have great restaurants. Despite its being the middle of summer, we were greeted with mild and balmy weather.

I was indeed fortunate that Walt had hired the services of Ralph Wilbanks, who had left the university and now headed his own underwater survey company, Diversified Wilbanks. Ralph is as steady and enduring as the faces on Mount Rushmore. Humorous, with a sly smile fixed beneath a Pancho Villa mustache, he worked tirelessly day after day, fighting choppy water to keep the search boat on track, with never a discouraging word.

His favorite comment when he was staring at the magnetometer recording graph while high swells tossed the boat like a cork in a blender was "Boy, we're maggin' now!"

His partner, who watched over the detection gear, was Wes Hall, archaeologist and owner of Mid-Atlantic Technology. He and Ralph often worked together on underwater survey jobs. He is as handsome as they come, and women believe he could double for Mel Gibson. Wes is quiet and unyielding, the kind of guy who could walk through a hurricane, a forest fire, and an earthquake while maintaining his set little grin, then step up to a bar, order a beer, and ask the bartender where the action is.

Their endurance was little short of incredible. The hours spent running search lanes seemed a lifetime, but they never wavered. At 8 A.M., Ralph and Wes were waiting at the dock. Their day did not end until they returned to the dock, refueled the boat, and pulled it up the ramp onto its trailer. They seldom saw home before eight o'clock in the evening. No matter how rotten the weather or how rough the sea, they hung tough hour after hour.

The name of Ralph's boat was *Diversity,* and the only times he looked a bit irritated was when everyone insisted on calling it *Perversity,* especially over the radio for all to hear. Naughty minds are difficult to control.

Visitors who came on board thinking they would find the search filled with thrills inevitably asked to be taken back to the dock after two or three hours. If they didn't become seasick, they were dying from tedium. Shattering novice visions of excitement and adventure became a daily routine. The hunt for shipwrecks takes dedication and perseverance. Leisure time comes only when you step onto a nice steady dock.

On this expedition the South Carolina Institute of Archaeology and Anthropology supplied the dive boat, using sport divers who paid for the privilege of hopefully finding and diving on *Hunley.* This part of the operation became very reminiscent of the follies on board *Coastal Explorer* fourteen years earlier. They lost the buoys our boat dropped over their dive sites for them, once claiming they were carried off by dolphins. Finding and probing the targets was also a hit or miss proposition. The university's chief project investigator, as he was called, was fond of announcing that every anomaly they dove on and probed had the same dimensions and configuration as *Hunley.* He was particularly enamored of one such target that turned out to be an old steam engine. On one occasion, a sport diver had a problem on the bottom and came within an inch of drowning. He might have if not for Harry Pecorelli III, a fine diver and archaeologist, who made the rescue.

Craig Dirgo and Dirk Cussler, however, did their best to provide entertainment during the long days on the water. Craig is a big man both in size and weight, who ran the NUMA office for several years. When standing next to each other, with Dirk scaling six feet four and thin as a garden hose, they could have presented a reasonable facsimile of Laurel and Hardy. One played off the other. I couldn't help wondering if Heckle and Jeckle had been reincarnated.

They were given a small fifteen-foot outboard boat and sent out with a gradiometer to run lanes in shallow areas. The boat looked as if it was used in the invasion of Normandy: tired, worn, and rundown. Starting the motor was a major event. At least three times their call for help came over the radio of *Diversity.* Then we'd have to break off our search lane and perform a rescue operation. We'd always find them with a dead motor, drifting out into the ocean toward Portugal.

Finally giving up on their lemon, Dirk and Craig came on board *Diversity,* where they entertained the crew by performing their rendition of *Treasure Island,* with Craig taking the role of the pirate, Long John Silver. There were laughs, but the reviews were mixed.

Craig's contribution to our communication network came when we were contacted by Walt Schob on the dive boat. Walt radioed that Craig's voice was breaking up over his receiver. So Craig picked up a bullhorn, set the speaker against the transmitter, turned up the volume, and hailed the dive boat. All of us laughed till it hurt when Walt's voice came back: "Hear you loud and clear now. Atmospheric conditions must have improved."

There wasn't much I could contribute on board during the long hours, except making an occasional decision concerning where to search next. I spent the time dozing, listening to big-band music over my Walkman, and flying kites. I've often thought of trolling for fish since we only travel at about six to eight knots, but could never muster enough interest.

One evening while we were cruising up to the fuel dock after a day's search, a fellow shouted across the water, "Are you Clive Cussler?"

Egotistically flattered at being recognized by my striking features, I asked, "How did you know?"

"By the orange dial on your dive watch," he replied. "Like the one Dirk Pitt wears in your books."

I looked down at my big twenty-seven-year-old Doxa dive watch and sagged in disillusionment. He had guessed it was me by my wristwatch, not by my devilish good looks. There is nothing like a dose of reality to bring one down off his pedestal. Actually, my biggest disappointment was yet to come, and it had nothing to do with ego.

After eliminating another ten square miles and identifying several buried anomalies as old sunken trash, our third attempt at finding *Hunley* slowly wound down and was written off as another failure. To me, this was a hard setback. Certainly there was no regret in making the effort, but the futility of knowing we were looking in the wrong place hurt.

What piece of evidence had I overlooked? What signs pointing to the final resting place of the sub was I ignoring? Had I misinterpreted the research?

Earlier, I had relied on Colonel Dantzler's report and concentrated the search between Breach Inlet and *Housatonic*. But *Hunley* was not there. The only straw left to grasp was in expanding the borders of the search grids.

Determined to find *Hunley* and her crew before my final deathbed gasp, I made a decision that assured success. I contracted with Ralph Wilbanks and Wes Hall to keep the search alive during their free time. They agreed, and I returned home to Colorado to write another book and pay for all the madness.

Ralph and Wes went out rain or shine and searched the grids I faxed them through the fall and winter of '94 and into the spring of '95. Then on May 4, I received a phone call from Ralph at six in the morning.

Still half asleep, I heard him say, "Well, I guess I'm going to send you my final bill."

"Are you giving up?" I asked in a sudden wave of disappointment.

"No," Ralph said calmly, "we found it."

I can't remember my immediate reply, but I think it was something stupid like "Are you sure?"

"It's a done deal," said Ralph. "Wes and I and Harry Pecorelli dug through the silt and came in contact with the forward hatch tower. Then we uncovered the snorkel box and the port dive fin."

"Before we unveil the discovery," I said, "we must have absolute proof. People have been claiming they found *Hunley* since 1867, but none of them ever produced a shred of proof. We've got to have photos."

"We can do better than that. Wes, Harry, and I will go back and shoot video."

I held my breath and asked, "Where did you find her?"

"About a thousand yards east and slightly south of the *Housatonic*."

"Then it survived the explosion, but had yet to begin its return voyage to Breach Inlet."

"Looks that way," said Ralph.

"Isn't that about where we dove in '81? On that object we thought was a Coast Guard buoy?"

"I've had nightmares over that for fourteen years," Ralph sighed. "But I'm not going to let myself believe we misidentified it."

"My fault for not insisting you uncover more of it."

The answer had been lurking in the dust of time. I had previously ignored Seaman Fleming's sighting of the blue light while awaiting rescue in the rigging, because I saw no reason for *Hunley* to hang around the area for nearly an hour, risking capture before the Union warship *Canandaigua* arrived to rescue *Housatonic*'s survivors. The problem lay in my miscalculation of the time high tide turned to ebb and the water began sweeping toward the shore. I put it too early. For some inexplicable reason I assumed the tide reversed soon after the sinking, not two hours later.

Too tired to crank their propeller against the adverse current, *Hunley*'s crew must have moved away from *Housatonic* and waited until the tide worked to their advantage and carried them home.

But that didn't answer why she sank and disappeared. Again, Fleming produced the key when he stated that he saw the blue light just ahead of *Canandaigua*. That suggests that *Hunley's* crew had perhaps thrown open the hatch covers to soak in the fresh night air while waiting for the tide to turn. As *Canandaigua* steamed past toward *Housatonic,* her wash rolled into the exposed openings and swamped the submarine. Or, perhaps, as the closed hatch covers indicate, the Union warship unknowingly rammed *Hunley,* and sent her to the bottom.

Someday soon, when the submarine is raised, we'll have the final solution.

The team's historic discovery had taken place on the afternoon of May 3, 1995. Ralph had tried to call me that evening, but I wasn't home. After hearing the wonderful news, I wandered around in a daze for three days before the significance of our achievement truly sank in.

The find came one afternoon when Ralph had a hunch. After eliminating one of my grids, he decided to return to the *Housatonic* site and work farther east. After an hour, the magnetometer recorded a target that was appropriate for *Hunley*'s metallic mass. Harry Pecorelli had accompanied Wes and Ralph that day, and he went down first to probe the target. Harry moved the silt until he touched a large iron object. He came up and notified Ralph and Wes that what little he saw didn't appear to be a sub, but he recommended further investigation.

Wes Hall dove and enlarged the hole in the silt until it was about twenty-five inches wide by twenty-four inches deep. He identified what proved to be the knuckle on the hinge of a hatch cover. Returning to the surface, he announced, "It's the *Hunley.* We've come down on one of the hatch covers."

Ralph immediately swam down and enlarged the hole until the hatch tower was eighty percent uncovered. He noticed that one of the little quartz viewing ports was missing, so he eased his hand inside and discovered that the interior of the submarine was filled with silt, a factor that may well have preserved the remains of the crew.

Satisfied that they had indeed found *Hunley,* they returned to port, drove to the museum in Charleston, and stood gazing at the sub's replica. "Do you realize," said Ralph, "that we're the only three people in the world that know what parts of the replica are incorrect."

Then they bought a bottle of champagne, went out to Magnolia Cemetery, and celebrated with the ghost of Horace Hunley.

Shortly after the *Diversity* team returned from videotaping the buried submarine, my son, Dirk; Craig Dirgo; Walt Schob; and I flew in to make the formal announcement at a news conference. First we all gathered on Ralph's boat the day before to go out and see *Hunley* for ourselves. But Mother Nature must have been suffering premenstrual syndrome. What she giveth she taketh away. We were beaten out by heavy weather and high seas. There was no diving that day.

I'll just have to wait until the day *Hunley* is raised before I can see the results from years of effort and $130,000, the approximate cost of all the research and four surveys. My only memento is Ralph's buoy that marked the wreck during the video shooting.

We held a press conference to announce the discovery on May 11 beside the replica of the *Hunley* in front of the museum in Charleston. Videotapes were provided for television stations, and photos were given out to the press.

Then the excretion struck the oscillator.

A great fight erupted over ownership. The State of Alabama, where *Hunley* was built, wanted it. South Carolina claimed it belonged to them for future display in Charleston. Even descendants of the original salvor of *Housatonic* filed a claim. The Federal Government said no way, since all abandoned Confederate property fell under the jurisdiction of the General Services Administration.

The vultures came to roost like gargoyles brooding over a derelict cathedral. Wilbanks, Hall, and I all caught hell because we held back on giving out coordinates to the location until we were reasonably assured the submarine would be recovered and preserved in a proper and scientific manner.

The state institute of archaeology demanded we turn the

site over to them for verification. What was there to verify? I was actually sitting on the fence until the director of the institute said a buoy should be placed over the wreck as a warning to vandals. My feeling was that a buoy was no different from a neon sign that proclaimed, THIEVES, COME ONE, COME ALL. Not a bad call as it turned out after rumors floated around reporting that collectors of Civil War artifacts had offered $50,000 for a hatch cover and $100,000 for the sub's propeller.

NUMA made no claim. I only wished to go home and begin research on the next wreck I hoped to find. Yet I was accused of desecrating the grave of Confederate war heroes, raping the wreck, ransoming the sovereign state of South Carolina, and scheming to carry off *Hunley* and set it in my front yard in Colorado. The Sons of the Confederate Veterans wanted to burn my books. I was called a glory-hunting charlatan, a con man, a scavenger, and a Benedict Arnold for betraying the noble profession of marine archaeology. Rodney Dangerfield gets more respect than me.

For a while I was afraid they were going to take away my bicycle.

Fortunately, saner minds prevailed, who were fully aware of what the NUMA team had truly accomplished. My combined expeditions had spent a total of 105 days running 1,196 miles of survey lines over rolling seas in search of the submarine with no thought of financial gain or veneration by the masses. We looked upon the project as a challenge, and our only profit was the satisfaction of achieving a long-sought goal and preserving our maritime heritage.

The good people at the General Services Administration eventually turned title of the submarine over to the U.S. Navy and their Historical and Archaeological Department, led by Dr. William Dudley and Dr. Robert Neyland, who are dedicated to seeing *Hunley* raised and conserved by the most skilled and experienced professionals in the business, using the latest technology to do the job right.

South Carolina State Senator Glenn McConnell formed a commission to work with the navy in the recovery and eventual display in Charleston after it was agreed to turn over the historic vessel to the state in perpetuity. Since then, scientists from the National Park Service's Submerged Cultural Resources Center, who had surveyed the battleship *Arizona* and the ships sunk after a nuclear blast at the Bikini Atoll, have uncovered about fifty percent of the Hunley to determine its condition. They found that the submarine was more advanced and sophisticated than previously thought. Their consensus is that she is sound and can be moved following proper archaeological guidelines.

With the proper funding a program can now be created to give the *Hunley's* crew a proper entombment with honors and enshrine the submarine as it looked during her voyage into history. We hope that by the time you read this, the hull will have been lifted from the silt in which it has lain for over a hundred and thirty years and be resting in a preservation facility in Charleston. From there, it is only a matter of time before *Hunley* will go on display to be viewed by future generations for centuries to come.

Perhaps Ralph Wilbanks's greatest contribution, besides his discovery of *Hunley,* was his cocktail creation, which he shared with everyone on the team. Goslings Black Seal Rum mixed with South Carolina Blenheim Bottling Company's fiery ginger ale and an entire sliced lime. There is absolutely no drink like it. Three glasses and you're ready to walk along the beach and kick sand on Hulk Hogan.

I could have used a shot during a television news show when the interviewer asked me, "Mr. Cussler, considering your long years of effort and the nitpicking flak that has surrounded your find, do you actually believe the staggering amount of money you spent was worth it?"

"Worth it?" I snapped. "Hell, yes, it was worth it! There are some things you can't measure in time and money. The search for *Hunley* was one of them. If we hadn't discovered the only intact warship from the Civil War, I'd still be poring over charts and writing checks while Ralph and Wes were out on the water hunting for it."

Sometimes, but not always, it pays to be a tenacious optimist.

Part

7

The Lost
Locomotive of
Kiowa Creek

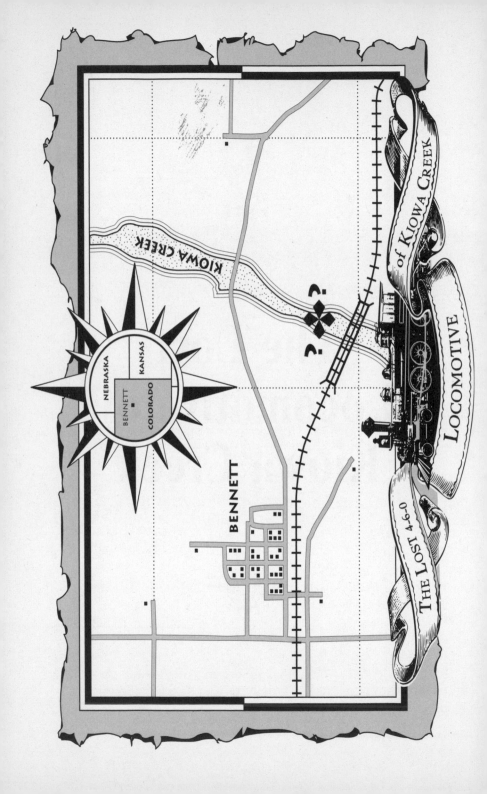

I

Journey to Nowhere

May 1878

THE BUSTLE OF ACTIVITY IN THE RAIL YARD OF THE KANSAS Pacific Railroad in Denver, Colorado, gave no indication that a disaster was impending. Colorado had become a state two years earlier, and Denver was rapidly growing in regional importance. Trains from the East, bearing the fruits of eastern industry, rolled into the yard several times a day. There they were unloaded, and some, for the trip to California, reloaded onto trains with extra locomotives for the climb over the Rocky Mountains. This evening, except for a downpour from a storm that never seemed to pass, it was business as usual.

The heavy rain had been falling hard for days, and half the city became flooded when Cherry Creek and the Platte River overflowed. The record-setting deluge was unusual for May, but Colorado's climate was notorious for changing from sunny warmth to three feet of snow within twenty-four hours. The only thing that could be safely said about the Rocky Mountain state's weather was its guarantee of unpredictability.

Walking from his home on 32nd Street, Kansas Pacific

Railroad engineer John Bacon crossed the bridge over the South Platte River. The river was swollen and muddy from the rains.

The battered remains of a large freight wagon were wedged against the bridge pilings by the current. It had flipped sideways and its wood-spoked wheels were spinning crazily, like a badly injured animal lying on the ground kicking its legs. It almost seemed fitting, Bacon thought to himself. Freight wagons were fast becoming antiques. Steam-powered locomotives had rapidly made horse-drawn freight wagons and passenger stagecoaches yesterday's transportation. Bacon sniffed the damp evening air. A strong breeze bore the smell of fresh mud and coal smoke from the rail yard. Continuing across the bridge, he walked down a dirty alley, then stepped over four sets of track rails toward the dispatch office.

He scuffed the mud from his boots on a burlap sack and stepped inside. The floor was wood-planked and still new enough to retain the scent of pine sap. A potbellied stove with a blue-enameled coffeepot stood in the far corner. Nodding at the stout Friar Tuck–built man alongside a standing desk, Bacon made his way to the pot. Reaching for a metal cup hanging on a nail, he wiped away a coating of dust with a handkerchief, then filled it with steaming coffee.

The stout man, dispatcher Chester Tubbs, was marking a railroad scheduling chart, using a straight-edge ruler and a pencil. Tubbs was nearing his fifty-fourth year and had worked for the railroad for over thirty of them. "Wet enough for you, John?" Tubbs said without looking up.

"Come August, we'll be glad we had this downpour," Bacon replied. "The farmers out on the eastern plains don't mind it at all."

Tubbs shifted from one leg to the other, held up his chart, and pointed with the pencil. "You'll be running *Train No. 8* to Kansas City."

"What's the cargo?" Bacon inquired.

"Scrap railroad iron."

"What engine did you assign me?"

"No. 51."

"Baldwin 4-6-0," Bacon said easily. "Good engine with plenty of traction."

"Even so, you'll have to keep up a good head of steam with this load," said Tubbs.

"How many cars?"

"Twenty-five and a caboose," replied Tubbs.

Bacon mentally estimated the approximate weight of twenty-five freight cars loaded with heavy scrap rail iron pulled by a locomotive driving over wet rails. "It's a downgrade from here to Kansas. I should have no trouble keeping your schedule."

"Just so long as the storm doesn't follow you across the plains."

"Did you crew me with my brother-in-law, Frank Seldon?" Bacon asked.

Tubbs nodded. "I also scheduled your poker pal George Piatt as your brakeman."

"You're a good man," Bacon said cheerfully.

"Have to keep the engineers happy," Tubbs replied, smiling.

"When my crew arrives, tell them I'll be on *No. 51*," Bacon said, finishing his coffee and hanging the cup back on the nail.

Leaving the dispatch office, Bacon walked along the track leading to *Engine #51*. He found it standing cold and silent on a siding, coupled to its coal tender. He paused and glanced toward the southeast. Far over the plains toward Elbert County, shafts of lightning exploded against black skies. Thunder quickly followed and rumbled ominously. It was turning into a very nasty night indeed.

Frank Seldon and George Piatt walked the tracks from the dispatch office together. A brass lantern flickered inside the cab of *Engine #51,* and a wisp of smoke curled from the locomotive's tall diamond-topped smokestack. As the men climbed the ladder to the cab, they heard the heavy boiler door being slammed.

"The engineer doing a fireman's work?" Seldon said to Bacon with a grin.

"Somebody's got to put fire in the beast so we can make our schedule," Bacon said to his brother-in-law half in jest. "Is Piatt with you?"

The answer came with the sound of a pair of size-thirteen boots clumping onto the cab's iron floor as George Piatt climbed inside. Piatt was muscular but badly overweight in the wrong places. His arms were the size of most men's legs, thick and bulky. Each of the cars in the train had a manual brake, and Piatt's job was to engage the brakes when necessary. The brake wheels did not turn easily, but Piatt's great strength gave him a distinct advantage.

"Evening," said Piatt in a chipper tone.

"Evening, George," greeted Bacon. "How was your day off?"

"Mary made me take her to the Sloan's Lake ballroom."

Bacon smiled. "Somehow, I can't imagine you waltzing on a ballroom floor."

Piatt ignored the ribbing. "Tubbs said the train is coupled and sitting on track twelve. If you and Frank bring *No. 51* around when you've got steam, I'll be waiting to hook you up."

"We'll be there soon as we can," said Bacon as Seldon grabbed a shovel and began banking the fire inside the furnace.

Fifteen minutes later, Bacon slowly pulled the throttle arm, which was hooked to a rod traveling to the steam dome atop the boiler, where the throttle valves were located. Then he pulled the Johnson bar to send the locomotive into reverse. Seldon jumped down, trotted ahead, and switched the rails so the engine could back onto track twelve and meet Piatt, who stood motioning at the front coupling on the lead freight car. Bacon lightly stroked the throttle arm, easing the coupling behind the coal tender into the one on the car.

"Pins in place!" Piatt shouted from behind the tender.

Bacon gently eased the throttle arm open. With a series of loud clunking sounds, the couplings took up the slack. Then he gave a sudden pull on the throttle, sending a burst of steam to the piston and spinning the big drive wheels to heave forward the great weight behind *Engine #51*. Chugging slowly at first, *Train #8* to Kansas City crept from the railroad yard in Denver. Passing parallel to Larimer Street, the train began to gather speed.

The Baldwin-built Mogul class 4-6-0 locomotive was the workhorse of the nation's railroads. With four wheels on a pivoting truck at the front and six 54-inch-drive wheels, she was considered a monster for her time, able to pull a long string of heavily laden freight cars up long grades without great strain. Only three years old, *Engine #51* was one of only three heavy haulers in the Kansas Pacific Railroad's rolling stock. Though she was normally scheduled to pull trains over the mountains, this trip called for her immense power to transport the ponderous load of scrap iron to the smelters in the East.

Black paint covered most of her metal, now glistening under a film of water. Thin hand-painted red striping outlined the rims of her wheels, the cab's window frames, and hand railings above the drive wheels. The cowcatcher, never designed to catch wandering open-range steers but to scoop their dead carcasses off to the side, jutted ahead of the engine just above the rails. Forward of the tall smokestack with its diamond top sat a great headlight, whose kerosene lamp and mirrored reflectors cast a wide beam into the dark night.

After jerking the chain to the steam whistle and pulling the cord to the bell, Bacon braved the rain and leaned out the side window as the engine passed over Steele Street and the outskirts of the city toward the great flatlands stretching from the Rockies to the Mississippi River. *Train #8* was now steaming on her monotonous eastward run across a landscape devoid of trees and shrubs. No one on board had a premonition that this would be their last run together.

Fifty miles down track a wall of surging water smashed into Bridge 607.80. The flood arrived with a surge not borne by anger or revenge, but simply enormous momentum assisted by gravity. Slamming into the bridge supports, wooden pilings driven eight feet deep into the streambed, the churning water snapped them into huge slivers and washed them away. Swept downstream by the unholy force of the raging stream, the pilings were tossed crazily about like straws in a hurricane. The iron rails atop the bridge swayed without their supports but remained suspended, creating an illusion of safe passage.

Jesse Dillup was lying in a scooped-out hole alongside the swollen stream below the Kansas Pacific tracks and underneath a grove of cottonwoods. A tattered wool blanket, now soaked by the drenching rain, was clutched around his shoulders. His few meager belongings were bundled in a haversack at his feet. He sneezed and rose from his muddy shelter.

Dillup was on his way from Texas to California, catching rides in empty freight cars. There was work in California, or so he heard. His journey was built on the hope his luck would finally change. He had recently gambled away what little he had amassed in his life and was nearly broke as he made his way west. A small supply of food, what few personal effects he carried in his tote, and four dollars in coin were all he possessed.

The hole, its bottom now a deep puddle, was no longer habitable, and the river was rising toward his shelter at an alarming rate, so he decided to wander further west in hope of finding a more comfortable place on higher ground to spend the ungodly night. Climbing quickly up the grade to the ballast stones under the ties and rails, he paused when he reached the tracks and out of habit peered back through the rain for an approaching train. Instead of the light from a locomotive he saw the shattered remains of Bridge 607.80 under a series of flashes from lightning bolts. The iron rails hung suspended in the air above the torrent of rushing water. As he watched, the huge trunk of a cottonwood tree smashed into the eastern base of the bridge and ripped loose the last of the supports. The wooden skeleton that gave the bridge its strength was now completely gone.

Dillup raced along the track toward the nearby town of Kiowa Crossing, intent on warning the stationmaster. Slipping on the wet ties, he fell and gashed his knee on a spike.

Wrapping a rag from his pocket around the wound, he continued stumbling west over the track.

A trail of cinders, sparks, and thick smoke spewed from the stack of *Engine #51* as it raced eastward toward the bridge. Frank Seldon kept the furnace blazing and the boiler at full steam while Bacon kept a close eye on the gauges. The rain had diminished a bit, slightly increasing his range of vision under the headlight. He pulled the throttle another notch as he sent the locomotive thundering over the wet rails.

Toward the center of the train, George Piatt moved from car to car, checking the brake settings and making sure the backup ratchets functioned properly.

Oblivious of the danger that was rapidly approaching, the men on board *Train #8* had only seven minutes to live.

Safe from the storm inside the station house at Kiowa Crossing less than a mile from the bridge over the creek, Abner Capp was dealing a round of cards on a table, playing four hands by himself. He paused and nibbled on a sliced turkey sandwich his wife had packed for his late-evening meal. The big Seth Thomas clock on one wall read two minutes to midnight.

The interior of the small wooden station house was comfortably warm. Capp shuddered at the thought of stepping outside in the damp gloom. Still, the schedule of trains was specific and he had to be standing by the tracks as *Train #8* traveled through in case any mail or company instructions were extended off the train by a conductor with a stick and caught in a small handheld net by the stationmaster. Capp wasn't aware that this night *Train #8* was not carrying a conductor.

He was slipping on his overcoat when Jesse Dillup burst through the door, looking like a drowned rat.

"The bridge is out!" Dillup gasped.

Capp stared at the bedraggled traveler. Dillup's hair hung in wet ringlets and was plastered against a face badly in need of a shave. His clothes were tattered and old, and his pants were torn and bloody where he had cut his knee.

"Have you been drinking?" Capp asked directly.

"No, by God!" Dillup snapped. "I'm telling you the bridge east of here has been washed out by floodwaters. The rails hang over the track with nothing under them. The supports are gone."

Two short miles to the west, the shrill steam whistle of *Engine #51* broke the splattering sound of rain on the station roof. Time was running out.

Less than four minutes' running time from the little town of Kiowa Crossing, the freight train raced east toward the bridge that no longer existed. Seldon sat back in his small metal seat, resting after stoking the furnace into an inferno. Bacon partially tilted his face around the window frame and peered through one eye, trying to pierce the watery darkness ahead.

Seven cars back, George Piatt adjusted a dragging brake, and then began to make his way forward to the locomotive for a few moments of warmth and a short chat with Bacon and Seldon.

Twenty-five flatcars, each loaded with twenty thousand pounds of scrap iron, gathered momentum on the slight downgrade that ran east toward the Colorado-Kansas border.

Capp tossed a spare raincoat to Dillup and handed him a brass lantern with a red glass lens. Then he motioned toward the bridge. "You go east toward the bridge and hang this light on the post alongside the tracks."

"Sure you don't want me to head west to warn the train?" asked Dillup.

"I'll take care of that chore. Since you've got an injured leg, I'll make faster time than you." Capp threw open the door to a chill gust of wind and rain. "Go now!" Then he jumped onto the track and began his futile attempt to wave down the train.

The sound of the rapidly approaching locomotive reached the men running in opposite directions down the track. Capp moved faster than Dillup, but he had further to go. He did not reach the eastern light warning pole before the train was upon him. He waved the red lantern frantically high over his head, praying the engineer would see it.

But at that instant, Bacon had turned his attention from the track ahead to check on the gauges. Capp and his frenzied signal were unseen. His panic mushrooming, Capp hurled the lantern against the side of the cab. But he misjudged the speed of *Train #8* and threw too late. The lantern smashed against the wall of the coal tender behind the locomotive cab and went unnoticed.

Dillup limped down the tracks as fast as his injured leg could take him. Reaching the signal pole, he climbed the ladder and hooked the lantern in place high above the track. Then he lowered himself to the ground beside the pole just as the light from the Baldwin locomotive transfixed his body in its glare.

John Bacon spotted Dillup and the red lantern. He responded immediately, jerking the steam-whistle cord twice in rapid succession. Still not knowing the reason for the stop signal, he fervently hoped George Piatt was in position to engage the brakes. He shoved the throttle closed and pulled the Johnson bar in almost the same movement. Then he yanked open the throttle again, sending the big drive wheels rotating madly in reverse.

"They gave us a red light outside of Kiowa Crossing," he shouted to Seldon.

"The Kiowa Creek bridge must be washed out!" Seldon shot back.

"Has to be. I can't think of another reason to flag down a freight train on a night like this."

Piatt was only two cars back when he heard the twin screams of the whistle. Without hesitation, he spun the wheel on the freight car that locked the front brakes. Then he leaped across the scrap rails stacked on the flatcar and raced to the rear brake before engaging it as well. Then it was on to the next car, where he repeated the procedure.

The crew had reacted amazingly fast, but the train's momentum was just too great.

Capp hurried down the tracks, chasing the red light on

the back of the caboose. He ran recklessly over the rail ties. As if in a nightmare, he felt his heart thumping against his rib cage.

Two hundred yards ahead of Capp, the wind draft whipped Dillup's raincoat as the train roared past. He suddenly realized there was no way the train could stop in time. He had done all he could do, but it was not enough.

"I think we're okay," said Bacon, seeing the locomotive's light beam reflect on the rails ahead.

"Looks like the bridge still stands," said Seldon unknowingly, as he leaned out the opposite window of the cab.

With the brakes of three cars locked by Piatt, whistle screeching, drive wheels spinning in reverse, *Train #8* was slowing as it traveled down the raised track bed coming out of Kiowa Crossing, but was far from stopping as it rolled across the unsupported rails. The train's great momentum carried it nearly midway across the mad sweep of floodwater before the twin strands of iron broke and contorted under the weight of a hundred tons of heavy metal. Twisting like a dying serpent, the locomotive and eighteen of the twenty-five cars rolled into the raging water, where they were flipped end over end by the irresistible flood into one entangled mass of wreckage. Debris and rails were ripped off the flatbed cars and shoved downstream as if shot from a cannon.

Bacon, Seldon, and Piatt died almost instantly, their bodies pummeled and swept downstream.

From his position on the tracks above Kiowa Creek, Jesse Dillup stood in mute horror as he watched the big headlight of *Engine #51* plunge beneath the water, still glowing for a few seconds until the front lens was smashed and the swirling water extinguished it. Seven of the flatcars and the caboose remained on the tracks as a grim reminder of the tragedy. Dillup sagged to a sitting position, rain spattering in his face, in shock and unable to stand.

Abner Capp came running up. He stopped beside Dillup and gazed through unbelieving eyes at the black swirling water and the wreckage. An icy nausea coursed through his body as he saw the great empty gap in the middle of the bridge. "Did you see anybody?" he asked Dillup.

The down-and-out traveler shook his head. "Not a soul. They must all be drowned."

"The locomotive?"

"Went straight in with its headlight still shining."

"Whereabouts?"

Dillup pointed north of where the bridge once stood. "Almost to the center of the stream, over near that grove of cottonwoods."

Capp nodded solemnly, the shock of the disaster sinking into his soul. "I'm going back to the station house and telegraph the company."

"What can I do?" asked Dillup.

"Nothing," Capp answered. "You best come home with me. The missus will put a good warm meal in your stomach and you can stay over until the storm lets up."

Together, the stunned men turned their backs on the disaster and walked slowly through the rainy night back to Kiowa Crossing.

After the sorry news was telegraphed by Capp to the Kansas Pacific offices in Denver, a train was dispatched with investigators and men to search for the bodies. The morning sun rose into a sky clear of rain clouds when the train braked to a stop just short of the washout. Fifty men stood silent for several minutes as they surveyed the destruction.

Overnight, as if the flood had been an apparition, the murderous waters subsided until they were flowing calmly no more than four feet deep. The force of the flood surge was evident by the uprooted cottonwood trees half buried in the creekbed. Sand and mud had been deposited and formed at the high-water mark like small levees. All that was left of the bridge span was one or two rails that protruded from the water. They had been twisted and corkscrewed by the weight of the locomotive as it spiraled into the rampage.

The thick wooden pilings and their trusses that once formed the bridge supports were nowhere to be seen. They had been washed far downstream, when the torrent was at its highest peak. Across the void, hanging between the remaining trusses, empty rails trailed east toward Kansas.

Seven of the cars that had fallen into the creek were still partially visible fifty feet north of the former bridge. Bits and pieces of their beds and trucks protruded from the mud and quicksand. *Engine #51,* its tender, and the remaining eleven cars had completely disappeared.

After studying the situation for an hour, the Kansas Pacific superintendent, Colonel C. W. Fisher, put his hand on Capp's shoulder and pointed downstream. "Did you arrange for local help in hunting for the bodies of our men?"

Capp nodded. "Twelve ranch hands are ready to leave at your command."

"Tell them they can begin the search," Fisher said quietly. Then he turned to the locomotive engineer, who had driven the train from Denver. "Go with Mr. Capp to the station house, and telegraph my office in Denver. Tell them I want a pile driver and a railcar mounted with a crane to set new pilings and lay rails. Add to that a bunk car to house and feed our crews. I want the necessary equipment pronto to run a temporary spur across the creekbed and get traffic moving again. This railroad is the lifeline to the West. It must be reopened quickly."

Working around the clock, Fisher's track crews had the temporary spur open for traffic less than fifty hours later. For weeks afterward, passengers on the Kansas Pacific could view the wreckage of *Train #8* as they passed.

Frank Seldon's body was the first to be found.

Local ranchers Sam Williams and John Mitchell were riding the west bank along the flood's high-water mark when Williams pointed to a piece of debris sticking from a mound of sand.

"Looks like part of the locomotive's cab," he said.

Dropping from their saddles, the two men tied their horses to a fallen log and approached the mound. Mitchell kicked away the damp sand around the mound with his boot. "A piece of the cab all right." Then he nodded at an object a few feet away. "That looks like the remains of the smoke-stack."

Williams pulled away a pile of tree limbs embedded in the mound by the flood current. "I've got what looks like a hat," he said as he dug deeper.

Mitchell joined him. "You might have something—" His voice abruptly died as his hand touched something soft and pliable. "Oh, God! I think we've got a body."

They were one and a half miles downstream from where Bridge 607.80 once crossed Kiowa Creek. Frank Seldon had traveled the shortest distance of the three.

Later that same day, a second group of ranchers found George Piatt. His big body was badly beaten by his death ride. He was recovered three miles downstream.

Six days after the wreck, Engineer John Bacon was finally located. He had been carried seven miles below the shattered bridge. His body was stuck in the limbs of a cottonwood tree twelve feet high. The distance from the ground had kept the coyotes away, but the birds had visited and pecked. Bacon's face was unmercifully disfigured, and he would be buried in a closed casket.

In honor of the dead, a thirty-day period of mourning was declared by the Railroad Engineers' Union. Bacon and Seldon had been married to sisters with the maiden name of Bennett. The town of Kiowa Crossing was renamed Bennett in honor of the widowed sisters.

With the spur complete across the creekbed that was now almost dry, the railroad company decided it was time to locate the missing locomotive and salvage the cars. Recovery efforts were concentrated around the few cars that were still visible a short distance from the washed-out bridge. Cribbing was driven into the sand to prevent the soft walls from collapsing. Then salvage men began excavating. A small donkey steam engine was hooked to a pump that was kept running twenty-four hours a day to keep the expanding hole clear of seeping groundwater.

The work was difficult. The load of scrap rail iron carried on the cars had been wrapped around the wreckage like frozen spaghetti by the incredible force of the flood. Each rail had to be cut free before the cars could be lifted back onto the track for removal to a repair shop.

The Kansas Pacific official in charge of the salvage operation was N. H. Nicholson. He was tall and a bit of a dandy. A thick, carefully waxed mustache graced a handsome face that was tanned a deep brown from a life spent outdoors. Sipping from a tin dipper of water, he brushed his mustache dry with the back of his hand.

"August first, and still no sign of the locomotive," he said to Johnnie Schaffer, a local ranch hand hired to assist the railroad.

"Maybe when that air pump comes we can burrow down and strike her," said Schaffer.

"It should be here Wednesday."

"We can sure use it." Schaffer nodded in a direction beyond Nicholson's shoulder. "Here comes Mollie with lunch."

Every man stopped what he was doing as a twelve-year-old girl approached. Katherine Mack, called Mollie by everyone in town, was followed closely by her pet deer as she walked the tracks east from Kiowa Crossing. Her arms were loaded with baskets and tin pails. Her mother had been contracted by Nicholson to feed the salvage crew their noontime meal. As Mollie stopped and set down her burden, her pet deer hung back a distance.

"That deer just doesn't seem to like us," Nicholson said to Mollie, smiling broadly.

"Maybe he's afraid we'll eat 'im," Schaffer joked.

"He only likes me," said Mollie, making a face at Schaffer. "My mother packed beefsteak, bread, potatoes, and cake today."

Nicholson motioned to Henry Nordloh, who was only a year older than Mollie.

Henry was big for his age, and his father had hired Henry and his brother Gus to work the donkey engine during their summer vacation.

Henry bashfully tipped his hat. "Afternoon, Mollie."

Mollie smiled a shy smile. "Mr. Nordloh." After passing

out the food to the men, Mollie saved the last basket for Henry and spread a napkin on a fallen tree trunk. As he began to eat, she sat alongside and stared at the huge hole, which looked like a moon crater.

"How's the progress today?"

"We'll have the last car out of the ground by the end of the week," answered Henry as he chewed a piece of beefsteak. "We dug up the coal tender, but we still can't find the engine. Mr. Nicholson is bringing in pumps to blow air down a pipe. He thinks that if he makes enough holes, one will hit the engine."

"You might have to help your father with the harvest before then."

"He said Gus and I can work to earn money until school starts," he said with boyish confidence.

Both children grew up, grew old, and swore to their dying day that *Engine #51* was never located and dug up. They passed on an account of their ties to the missing locomotive to their children. Yes, Henry and Mollie became childhood sweethearts and were married in 1885 and produced a family of six lovely girls and two fine boys.

The probable theory at the time was that the engine was swept miles downstream and buried in quicksand so deep it could never be found, much less recovered.

Newspaper Item in the *Rocky Mountain News:*

May 22, 1880. Denver people all remember the accident on the Kansas Pacific two years ago last night in which Engineer John Bacon and Fireman Frank Seldon were killed. At that time the Kiowa Bridge was carried away by a flood, and when the train plunged into the torrent the engine was never seen again, although every effort has been made to find it. It is supposed to have sunk in the quicksand, as the tender was found ten feet below the bend in the creek.

Out of this disaster grew a suit for damages. The suit of Mrs. Bacon was decided yesterday. The verdict: "We, the jury, find for the plaintiff and assess the damage at $5,000. John Best, foreman." A similar suit by Mrs. Seldon resulted in the same verdict. Attorneys for the railroad, Usher and Teller, will fight these cases to the bitter end.

Over the next hundred years, newspapers and railroad journals still reported *Engine #51* as missing. Haunting stories were told of a mysterious light resembling the one on a locomotive that crossed halfway over the new bridge at Kiowa Creek before suddenly blinking out. A few of the local ranchers swore they saw ghostly images of the crew wandering the creekbed.

If *Engine #51* was never found, where was it?

II

One That Got Away

May 1989

WHAT DOES A TRAIN WRECK ON THE FLATLANDS OF COLO-rado have to do with shipwrecks? Except for a comparable process combining research with on-site investigation, absolutely nothing. Let's just say I had a soft spot in my heart for old *Engine #51*. I owed her a debt of gratitude.

In the May 21, 1978, Sunday Empire section of the *Denver Post,* Elizabeth Sagstetter wrote an article. The title was "The Locomotive That Never Returned." It was the first time I learned of the tragedy. At the time, I was intrigued, not so much with launching a search for the elusive engine but about working its disappearance into a concept for an adventure novel starring my hero, Dirk Pitt. Two years later, I wrote THE END on the final page of the manuscript and sent it to my literary agent, Peter Lampack. The story of a train that was thought to have gone off a bridge over the Hudson River but was later found sealed in an abandoned tunnel was published in 1981 under the title *Night Probe.* Thanks to the lost locomotive of Kiowa Creek, *Night Probe* was one of my better plots.

My son, Dirk, and I made the sixty-mile drive from Denver to Kiowa Creek on a couple of occasions. We walked grids with the Schonstedt gradiometer under and around the modern steel-girder bridge (built in 1935) that spans the creek over the exact spot as the one that was washed away in 1878. Except for a few small contacts, we turned up no readings that remotely suggested a large iron mass under the ground. I then put the mystery aside and went on to other projects. The story of the lost locomotive languished in my NUMA files for almost ten years before my fascination with its disappearance surfaced again, and I decided to give it another try. I was prodded by any number of friends and neighbors who thought I should look for a lost object in Colorado, especially since it was in my own backyard.

By 1988 Craig Dirgo had come aboard NUMA and was working out of a small office in Arvada, Colorado, fielding correspondence and arranging the logistics for our summer shipwreck expeditions. Craig, a fun guy who is built like a college football linebacker, also became caught up in the mystery and asked if he could pursue it. After having failed to locate the locomotive in my high-probability area, I was not optimistic. But having an antipathy to giving up a project without results, I gave Craig my blessing.

I thought it strange that during the 111 years since the old *#51* had vanished in the creek, so few people had bothered to hunt for her. One was Denver grocery-store owner Wolfe Londoner. Shortly after the salvage crew threw in the towel that summer, Londoner heavily charged a crowbar with electricity and turned it into a magnet. After tramping up and down the creekbed, he hit a hot spot that violently agitated the crowbar before it plunged into the sand, dragging Londoner with it, all to the delight and astonishment of several onlookers. Londoner was pulled free, exhausted and soaked. He proclaimed that he had found the lost engine and demanded a reward. Colonel Fisher, representing the railroad's new owner, Jay Gould, turned him down cold—an unusual denial that much later fit the ultimate solution to the enigma.

The only other recorded search was by Professor P. A. Rodgers of the geophysics department of the Colorado

School of Mines. In May of 1953 he and several of his students conducted a systematic search with military-type mine detectors. An area 150 by 400 feet was explored with no results.

Craig contacted the director of the little museum in Strasburg, Colorado, only a few miles from Bennett and the Kiowa Creek bridge. Emma Michell, the director, turned out to be a real sweetheart of a lady, whose family had resided in the county for several generations. A writer as well as a historian and museum curator, she had penned a book called *Our Side of the Mountain,* a fascinating narrative of the pioneers who settled Adams County. An incredible number of their descendants still lived in the area.

Emma mentioned she knew a brother and sister whose parents witnessed the events after the bridge washout and asked if we would like to interview them. We immediately agreed, and a meeting was set up. The following day, Craig and I drove to Bennett and were introduced to the siblings.

Charles and Henrietta Nordloh were remarkable people. Chuck was ninety-two and Henrietta ninety-five, and they were as bright and sharp as someone half their age. Their mother was, of course, Mollie Mack, the girl with the pet deer, and their father was Henry Nordloh, the donkey-engine operator.

Chuck Nordloh displayed a devilish sense of humor. When Craig asked him if he had lived around Bennett his entire life, Nordloh winked and said, "Not yet."

When searching for something that is lost, it is always a good idea to spend time questioning the elderly who lived the events or were much closer to the actual time than we are. Most of them recall the past with amazing clarity. More than once a chance remark by an old-timer has put NUMA on the right track to a discovery. Charles and Henrietta could not provide any fresh revelations, but I can't remember a more pleasant conversation. They told the stories their mother and father had passed on to them in vivid detail.

The Nordlohs' ranch was the closest to where the railroad crossed over Kiowa Creek, and they both distinctly recollected their parents saying that, although the crew searched the entire summer, no trace of the engine was found. At some point the cost of the salvage operation would exceed the value of the battered locomotive, so the Kansas Pacific logically ceased work. If they looked through the summer of 1878 with no luck, it stood to reason *Engine #51* was still buried in the creek.

Driving back to Denver later in the afternoon, Craig looked pensive. "A big iron mass like that should be detected by a good mag within one, maybe two hours."

"It's not near the bridge," I said. "Trust me, Dirk and I have already eliminated the easy part."

"Then it should be a piece of cake to find it further downstream."

"Cussler's search guide rule number twenty-two," I said. "If it was easy to find, someone would have got there first."

The next step in locating the engine was to organize a more extensive search. Craig threw himself into the logistics and groundwork. He met with residents of Bennett, who generously offered their community center so searchers would have a place to warm up and use the bathrooms. They also offered the use of their city backhoe if NUMA paid for the gas and any needed repairs.

By December, plans were finalized and the expedition began coming together. Over lunch one day, I asked Craig, "How many calls have you received from people offering their services?"

"Close to a hundred," Craig answered.

"There's no way that many are going to show up and tramp around frozen ground in the dead of January. We'll be lucky if we get ten."

"You're probably right," said Craig. "It'll be colder than a Popsicle in a Good Humor truck out there on the plains. Why did you pick January the twelfth anyway?"

"Fig Newtons."

He stared at me. "What do cookies have to do with anything?"

"Barbara brought home a sack an hour before I set a date."

"So?"

"Didn't you know that excessive indulgence in Fig Newtons leads to hallucinations?"

Craig looked as if he were afloat in a sea of doubt. "Amazing. People will freeze to death in Kiowa Creek because you got stoned on stupid cookies."

Actually, I lied. I hate Fig Newtons. It was a sack of chocolate-chip cookies. Besides, who would believe me if I admitted I picked January 12 as the date for the search because the *Farmer's Almanac* predicted a sunny day?

Earlier, Craig called and casually mentioned that the director of the Colorado Historical Museum had offered to run a small blurb in their monthly journal. Craig thought it was a good way to ask for volunteers. Thinking we'd receive maybe three or four responses from people with the proper equipment, I told him to give it a try.

Craig wrote a small one-column piece on the upcoming locomotive hunt and ended the article by saying, "If anyone who owns a metal detector would like to come on out to Kiowa Creek, he or she would be welcome." This announcement was picked up by the *Rocky Mountain News* and the *Denver Post* newspapers. Then the local TV stations got in on the act, followed by a story over the wire services across the country. It quickly became what is referred to as a media event.

George Schott, a sergeant in the Air Force, came on board and proved invaluable. Harold Perkins of Bennett offered to operate the backhoe. Claudia Mueller took on the job of assembling maps and instructions and mailing them out to volunteers who called on the phone. The project began to take on a life of its own.

One afternoon, Craig showed up at my house. "I wanted to touch base with you," he said wearily, "but my telephone wouldn't quit ringing long enough for me to dial out."

"You could have gone home and called from there," I suggested brightly.

He shrugged sheepishly. "I gave the reporters my home number. Can I hide out here for a while?"

Where was this all leading? I wondered.

On the morning of the search, even with the mercury barely touching 10 degrees above zero, volunteers appeared like an army of ants. Over four hundred people converged under the Kiowa Creek bridge. If the Union Pacific Railroad had learned that a horde of people were stomping around their real estate and climbing over their track right-of-way, their corporate attorneys would have gone into cardiac arrest.

Search fever had spread like an epidemic. Whole families drove out to Bennett, kids bundled up in snowsuits. One couple still stands out in my mind. A man and woman in their late sixties, and obviously married, stepped from their Mercedes-Benz sedan ready to dig. She was wearing a mink coat and hat. He wore an expensive cashmere topcoat with silk scarf and leather gloves. They were both carrying brand-new shovels purchased only minutes before from the Bennett hardware store.

George Schott borrowed a huge tent from the Air Force, and by the time I arrived he and Craig, along with several other rugged individuals, had it erected, a generator with a heater operating, and coffee brewing. Teams were formed by several diggers around whoever owned a magnetometer or metal detector. Don Boothby, a geophysicist, brought a ground-penetrating radar unit to the site, a valuable asset in imaging any contacts by the detectors. Craig had even arranged for a ham radio club to provide communications with each search team leader, who had a radio operator assigned to him. A remote camera was also set up that beamed images to the command tent so that Jim Grady and Marie Mayer, resident archaeologists, could view and identify any objects or artifacts dug up by the searchers.

An inspired demonstration of efficiency, more than impressive enough to make the United States Special Forces green with envy. All that were missing were the dancers for the Hawaiian number.

Craig assembled everyone by shouting through a bullhorn. They all stood around in good spirits despite the frigid weather that brought steam issuing from every mouth and nose. Starting under the current bridge, I lined up the teams behind the people carrying the metal detectors, spacing the operators ten feet apart, with me and the Schonstedt gradiometer at the center. The idea was to sweep down the now dry streambed, covering every square inch.

I might as well have tried to herd cats.

After walking about twenty paces, I turned and looked around. My little army had dissolved and scattered in every direction of the compass, each intent on following his or her own instincts. I tried to instill a shred of order, but it proved impossible. These people were out for fun and not about to listen to some weirdo book author tell them where to look. The only teams that worked with any effectiveness were the two I sent three miles downriver to work back toward the bridge. They eliminated a considerable amount of creekbed before the day was out.

I particularly asked them to check out a sharp bend in the creek. It often happens that a large buried object will alter the natural flow of a river or stream. This has happened quite often with a flow as strong as the Mississippi. The bend ultimately proved to be a buried cottonwood tree.

By early afternoon, several promising targets were located and exposed by the backhoe. Most were bits and pieces of debris from the wrecked cars and bridge. I was amused to watch the search teams drop everything and come running whenever the backhoe began to dig. Not wanting to miss out on anything is a human reaction that goes back to our ancestors in the trees.

Craig called me aside and voiced his concern that we were not covering the grids properly. "I can't control them," he lamented.

"Next time, we bring flamethrowers and incinerate anyone who doesn't search where he's told," said I sarcastically.

"There must be a better way."

"I agree. Good flamethrowers are expensive."

"No," Craig said, exasperated. "The teams need more instruction."

"Look, my friend," I said seriously, "there is only so much ground we can cover. The creek is barely fifty yards wide in most areas. As screwed up as the search has become, the entire creek from bank to bank and three miles downstream has been covered, some of it five times, because the teams keep crisscrossing each other's paths."

"What if we've missed it?"

"There is always that possibility, no matter how slim. Me? I'm beginning to think the damned thing isn't here."

I no sooner said it than a great cry went up in a field west of the creek and just north of the bridge. The Brauer brothers, Mike and Scott, had located a promising anomaly. Craig and I swept the gradiometer past the spot. The reading was good but very concentrated. Not what I'd hoped unless the locomotive was buried thirty feet deep. Fortunately, we had a method for seeing under the earth.

Don Boothby ran his ground-penetrating radar over and around the anomaly. In radar-interpretation schools, they're now displaying the recording of the object we found to show students what an abandoned oil-drilling pipe looks like. The image was picture perfect.

At four o'clock, I brought everybody in and called it a day. I was met with a sea of discouraged faces when I told them there was little reason to continue. Pieces of the puzzle weren't coming together. More research was called for before another attempt should be made. I thanked everyone for a magnificent effort. They in turn applauded Craig and me for providing the opportunity to tackle something that gave them pleasure and that they could always talk about. They were proud, it seems, to have been involved with the search for old *Engine #51*. To them, it was an adventure.

Driving back through Denver to my house on Lookout Mountain in the evening gloom of that cold Sunday in January, I mentally sifted through all the data for any clue I might have missed. After dinner, I read and reread every paper in my research file, racked by my inadequacies in not solving the mystery.

Perhaps, just perhaps, as I told Craig, the damned thing wasn't there.

Bob Richardson, who runs the Colorado Railroad Museum in Golden, Colorado, maintained that the locomotive had been recovered. He cited an article published in 1953, stating the locomotive used that fateful evening was #51, and that particular engine was listed as being rebuilt in 1881 with the number then changed to #1026.

I found problems with the article for a couple of reasons. One, no other source can be uncovered that supports the 1953 article's statements. To take a report as gospel you need more than one reference. And two, why did the railroad take nearly three years to put the locomotive back in service when it could have just as easily been repaired and on track in a matter of a few months?

I had all but given up finding an answer when by a lucky coincidence I was asked to do a radio interview while attending a conference of mystery writers in Omaha, Nebraska.

During the phone-in part of the show, a caller inquired about NUMA's search for the lost locomotive of Kiowa Creek. When asked the reason for his interest, he said he worked in the archives of the Union Pacific offices there in Omaha. I obtained his address and phone number and we began to communicate.

During his spare time, he dug through the old legal records of the Kansas Pacific from the time of the wreck until the company merged with the Union Pacific. After three months, he struck paydirt.

The story he ferreted out was one that is not uncommon in the present day and age. It seems that N. H. Nicholson, in charge of the original salvage operation, had indeed found the locomotive with probes sunk in the sand by his air pump. Without revealing his discovery to the salvage crew or local ranchers, he notified company officials in Kansas City. The now long-defunct Kansas Pacific Railroad then immediately filed an insurance claim of $20,000 for the purported loss of the locomotive, and collected.

A few weeks later, in the dead of night, a special train with Nicholson in charge arrived at Kiowa Creek. They dug up the locomotive, lifted it onto the track with a giant railroad crane, and towed it to the company maintenance shops in Kansas City. There it was rebuilt, its exterior appearance altered slightly; it was given a new number and put back into service. The operation went so smoothly that none of the ranchers in the area were ever aware of the recovery. Records did not indicate whether the locomotive was renumbered #1026, as Bob Richardson suggested. That part of the story may never be known.

I owe a debt of gratitude to the hundreds of people who gave the search their best shot. Although we didn't find the engine, we did solve what appeared to be a 120-year-old insurance scam by a railroad that no longer exists.

But did we?

Despite the records in the archives, there are many who refuse to believe the locomotive was found. The local ranchers insist that it still lies buried beneath the sands of Kiowa Creek. It's whispered that around midnight, when no trains are due to pass, the plaintive wail of a steam whistle can be heard approaching in the distance. Then comes the clank of a bell and the roar of steam exhaust. If conditions are just right and there is a rain falling, a light is seen coming down the grade from the west toward the creek. Upon reaching the bridge, the beam suddenly blinks out and the sounds of a locomotive melt into the night.

As long as she is remembered, the spirit of old *Engine #51* will never die.

Part 8

H.M.S. *Pathfinder,* *U-21*, and *U-20*

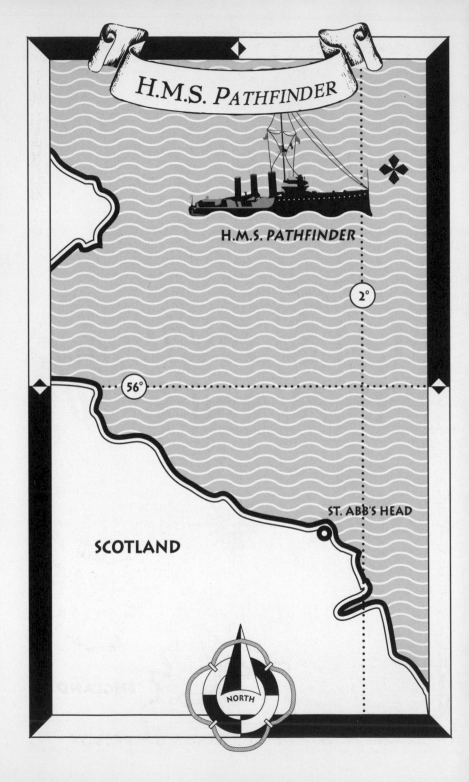

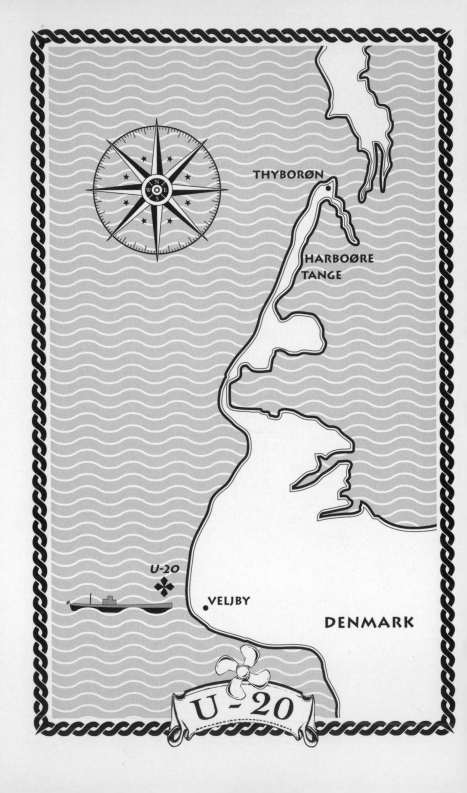

THYBORØN

HARBOØRE
TANGE

U-20

VELJBY

DENMARK

U-20

I

Death from the Depths

September 5, 1914

"ALL HORIZONS CLEAR," THE LOOKOUT, PERCHED ON A small extension on the conning tower, announced to his commander.

Thirty miles off Saint Abb's Head, Scotland, the sea was flat, with only a mild chop. Cruising at twelve knots in waters that seldom knew fair weather, the *U-21* pounded through water as green as a field of unpicked corn. The spray of cold water, splashing across the decks of *U-21*, made a sound similar to the squishing of soggy shoes. The time was 3:40 in the afternoon. The air was clear and pure, with a light breeze, a brilliant fall afternoon.

As the submarine slipped like a steel wraith through the tossing seas, the sculptured lines of its gracefully tapered outer hull gave the boat stability in rough seas. Her outer hull, however, was a façade. Her visible exterior was simply a streamlined skin, flooding when the boat was underwater. The unique design provided a faster speed while the submarine was cruising on the surface.

Her operating machinery was comfortably mounted within a separate tubular steel pressure hull, where the crew lived and worked. American- and British-built submarines of the First World War were shaped like cigars, and they wallowed in rough water like stricken whales. Not the German *Unterseeboote*. Their special dual-hull arrangement gave them a fast cruising speed both above and below the surface. For 1914 it was considered a brilliant design.

"Horizons still clear," the lookout reported.

Extending through each side of the outer hull were twin shafts mounting fore and aft diving planes. These were the wings on which the sub traveled up and down in the depths. When the order was given to dive, the ballast tanks were flooded from the surrounding seawater until the prescribed depth was reached and neutral buoyancy achieved. Picture a child placing his hand out the window of a moving car. By merely angling his fingertips, his hands will fly up and down from the resistance of the air current. The principle is the same with submarine diving planes.

Twin tubes that fired long twenty-three-foot-six-inch torpedoes flared from the stern section of the hull alongside the dual bronze propellers and rudder. A second pair of tubes sat low on the bow below the anchors, which were held by rigid supports that prevented their movement when the boat was under way. Below the deck line, the U-boat was as graceful as a needlefish; above, she was as ugly as a warthog.

The flat upper deck consisted of twin levels, covered with black rubberized paint that provided traction for foot traffic. Four-foot-high metal railings lined the areas of the deck where the crew most often found themselves when under way. Elsewhere on the deck, the crew had to be careful and tied themselves to lifelines to prevent being washed into the sea. Even when riding the surface of calm water, the deck was nearly awash.

Twelve feet tall, the conning tower rose like an upside-down anvil, sharply angled on each side and rounded toward the center. A two-inch deck gun was mounted halfway toward the stern. The U-boat's four diesel engines, two each connected to a propeller shaft, could push her through the water at fifteen knots on the surface and nearly nine knots when submerged. Like her sister submarines, *U-21* was painted light gray to blend with sea and sky.

"Twenty more minutes for batteries to reach full charge," the engineering officer shouted through the speaking tube to Korvettenkapitän Otto Hersing, commander of *U-21,* who stood above in the conning tower. Hersing was a distinguished-looking man with sad brown eyes. His black hair was cropped short and combed flat. Tall and slender, with hawklike features, he was considered quite attractive by women.

He glanced briefly at the dim coastline in the distance, then turned his attention to a marine chart. After only a week at sea, the paper was beginning to deteriorate from the relentless damp of the sea. Hersing was engaged in playing a dangerous game of hide and seek with the British fleet. The ships of the Royal Navy that passed through the Firth of Forth were out on patrol, searching for German warships above and below the water. To his frustration, *U-21* kept missing them.

One month and one day had passed since the guns of August launched the war that engulfed nearly every country in Europe, and the *U-21* had yet to fire a torpedo. Since the Confederate *Hunley* had sunk *Housatonic* during the American Civil War, no ship had been destroyed by a submarine. Hersing would have given a year's pay if *U-21* could have had the honor of the first kill among the thirty U-boats Germany fielded at the beginning of the conflict.

Breathing in the sea air and salt spray kicked up by the bow behind the conning tower's weather screen, Hersing took every opportunity to leave the close confines of the pressure hull with its smell of dampness, diesel fumes, and sweat. Condensation was so bad that the crew had to sleep with oilskins covering their faces and rubber sheets pulled over their bodies. The ventilating system did a reasonable job of cleansing the atmosphere, but the fetid air lingered as if embedded in the steel bulkheads.

"We'll remain surfaced after we're fully charged," Hersing shouted into the speaking tube to the engine room.

He was in no rush to seal the hatches again. Better to

allow the crew to relish the fresh air while they could. Besides, with the U-boat's low silhouette, he could see an enemy ship long before it spotted *U-21*.

He arched his back and stretched, staring at the sky free of clouds, and thought momentarily of his village in Germany, wondering if he would live to walk its narrow streets again. Reluctantly, he turned his attention back to the business at hand, raised a pair of binoculars to his eyes, and scanned the sea for signs of the enemy, a hunter waiting in ambush with no prey in sight.

Where were the British hiding? Hersing wondered. The largest fleet in the world couldn't stay lost forever.

Unlike Hersing, who savored conning his vessel in the open air, British Royal Navy Captain Martin Leake stood in the comfort of H.M.S. *Pathfinder*'s wheelhouse and sipped tea from a china cup. His light cruiser had spent the first few weeks of the war on routine patrol duty, finding no sign of the enemy. He felt little fear of enemy submarines. His ship had twice the speed of those underwater coffins. To most British naval officers, they were underhanded, unfair, and un-English. Already two U-boats had been lost, the *U-15* rammed and sunk by the cruiser *Birmingham* and the *U-13* presumed to have struck a mine.

Leake was proud of his sleek warship. She was fast and she was deadly. He believed he could dodge any U-boat by the skillful exercise of speed and maneuver. His orders were simple. He and *Pathfinder* were to patrol the North Sea off the Scottish coast and sink any German in sight.

Constructed ten years before and rated at 2,940 tons, *Pathfinder* had recently been refitted by the British Navy at a cost of nearly half a million pounds. Built at the yards of Cammel Laird, the fast scout cruiser was 370 feet in length with a 27-foot beam. She mounted ten 12-pound guns and eight 3-pound light-duty cannon. The stem that graced the bow was a businesslike straight up and down. None of that rakish clipper-ship bow for her.

Amidships, the sidewalls of the hull were cut down so the stern deck was much lower to the water than the bow.

Rising above the high forward quarter, the wheelhouse stood awkwardly on a maze of stilts. A tall mast rose immediately behind, sporting a radio antenna and a lone crow's nest. Still farther aft, triple smokestacks that vented the coal-burning furnaces towered above the deck. Five lifeboats, two motor launches, and the captain's gig hung in their davits above decks amidships.

After the refit, Leake was pleased her updated systems seemed to be operating properly, but the newly installed furnaces were throwing out more smoke than he would have liked. Still, the crew performed their duties skillfully and the ship responded to the helm like a horse bred to chase hounds.

Everything aboard *Pathfinder* was going well, almost too well. Daily dispatches from the Admiralty Office warned ships of their fleet to stay vigilant. But five weeks of tedious patrol duty dulled any real sense of jeopardy. The dreaded underwater ghosts were out there somewhere, haunting the sea. But this early in the war there were few trained eyes that could spot telltale signs of a periscope.

Leake placed the cup back on the saucer. *Pathfinder* was up to the job, he thought. She could handle almost any opponent except a battle cruiser. He considered turning over the helm to his first officer and retreating to his cabin for a few moments of solitude. But he did not feel tired and decided to turn in later.

It was a decision that would save his life.

Hersing climbed down the steel-runged ladder from the conning tower into the control room, a jungle of instruments, gauges, wiring, and pipes that ran along the curved walls like hardened snakes. Electric lightbulbs, contained in metal cages to prevent shattering if the crew was tossed about during a depth-charge attack, cast a weird yellow glow. The lights seemed to be spaced haphazardly, creating areas of twilight in the far corners of the boat.

Forward of the control room was a tiny galley. Twin hot plates and a fifty-quart stew pot cooked the food both the officers and crew shared. For a boat that carried forty-two men and several officers there were only two heads, one often used as a food locker at the start of a voyage. The heads could not operate below eighty feet. And even if the boat was on the surface, the series of levers used to flush the little commode were so complex that one wrong twist and the contents of the toilet bowl blew back in the user's face.

Germany's U-boats were never designed for comfort. They were designed to kill, and they were as cold and heartless as a tax collector's soul.

Hersing sat down at a tiny table reserved for him and his first officer, and ate a meal of potato soup and sausage, washed down with a cup of cocoa. As he finished, one of the *U-21*'s crew popped his head in the cramped galley.

"Sir, the first officer requests your presence topside."

Hersing rose, jamming his officer's cap on his head at a rakish angle. Climbing the ladder from the control room, he returned to the conning tower.

"What have you got?" he asked without preamble.

First Officer Erich Heibert handed Hersing his binoculars and pointed toward the northwest. "There, to the northwest, a column of smoke."

Hersing peered at the dark smudge on the horizon. He later described the "thick, black promising smoke as an obscure smear gradually growing into the outline of a ship." Patiently, he waited until it became more distinct. "She appears to be a British light cruiser. Scout class. Alert the crew and give the order to dive."

With a sound like the clanging of a fire bell, the *U-21*'s dive alarm rang loudly inside the tight confines of the submarine. The crew scurried quickly to their duty stations, ducking heads while snaking through the cramped hatchways. The conning-tower hatch was dogged shut, valves were turned to flood the ballast tanks, and *U-21* slowly slipped beneath the restless waters of the North Sea.

"Adjust diving planes for periscope depth," Hersing ordered.

* * *

Steaming in her patrol pattern off the coast of Scotland, *Pathfinder* sailed on unaware of the threat. The trail of thick black smoke still bothered Leake, but there was little he could do about it until his ship returned to port.

"Watch report," Leake ordered.

"Watch reports all clear," came the reply of his first officer.

"Time?"

"Sixteen forty hours, sir."

Leake gazed at the great column of smoke that merged from *Pathfinder*'s three big stacks, curling high in the sky without benefit of a brisk wind. "We're throwing out a rather large amount of smoke," he said. "We might as well advertise our position to every German ship within fifty miles. Ring down to the engine room and ask if they can't reduce it somewhat."

Belowdecks, Sub-Lieutenant Edward Sonnenschein was checking the position of the watertight doors, making notations on a clipboard. Born in England, Sonnenschein had a distinctly German name, yet he was British through and through.

"Powder magazine door secure," reported a seaman.

"Door secure," Sonnenschein acknowledged.

On it went until all doors were inspected and certified in good working order. Then Sonnenschein slid the checklist into the document slot outside the captain's cabin and reported to the bridge.

"All doors are secured, sir," he said to Leake. "The report is in your slot."

"Very good." Leake spoke without turning his attention from the sea ahead. His thoughts were more on German surface ships than U-boats.

Pathfinder sailed on.

At a keel depth of sixty feet beneath the waves the only sound that came from *U-21* was her electric motors, which purred like an army of cats. Fifteen minutes before five o'clock in the afternoon, *U-21* began her attack approach.

Hersing reversed his peaked cap with the brim to the rear and pressed his eye against the focal adjustment of the two-inch-diameter periscope. After no more than ten seconds, he leaned away.

"Down periscope," he ordered. "Come to heading two-nine-zero."

"Two-nine-zero," his helmsman repeated.

"If the Britisher maintains his present course," Hersing said to his crew in the control room, "we should be within strike range in another fifteen minutes."

Like a tiger slinking toward its quarry, *U-21* methodically closed in for the kill. Hersing raised the periscope again, relocated the target, and made his course corrections to launch a torpedo. The British cruiser steamed into view almost dead ahead. No more than half a mile separated the two vessels.

"Tube one, stand ready," said Hersing. Patience was a requirement for German U-boat commanders. He waited for the range to close as calmly as if he were waiting for a taxi.

First Officer Heibert, standing forward in the weapons room, unscrewed the cover from the firing mechanism and stood poised to carry out the command he knew would be issued shortly.

The U-boat and the cruiser were only fifteen hundred yards apart when Hersing shouted in the same breath, "Away torpedo! Periscope in!"

The torpedo leaped from the bow of *U-21*. Like a spear thrown from a mythical god's hand, the deadly tube streaked toward *Pathfinder.* Hersing waited anxiously for the sound of a muffled explosion and the following concussion. He was as ignorant as Lieutenant Dixon fifty years before about the effects of underwater explosions. He tapped one foot nervously on the cold steel deck.

Thirty seconds ticked away. Then a full minute. A miss, Hersing thought. Considered the best scorer in practice with torpedoes in the U-boat flotilla, he could not believe his calculations were not correct. A minute and fifteen seconds. Too long for a run of only fifteen hundred yards.

* * *

"Torpedo!" the lookout high in *Pathfinder*'s crow's nest cried. "Starboard aft!"

Captain Leake reacted instantly. "Full speed, hard to starboard."

Pathfinder rolled on her starboard beam, stern deck nearly awash, as her big propellers bit into the water and turned it white, her powerful engines racing to escape certain doom. In a desperate gamble, Leake attempted to throw the torpedo off course with *Pathfinder*'s prop wash.

Set on a collision course, the torpedo narrowed the gap. Fifty yards, thirty, ten. Watching from the wheelhouse, Leake felt as if time had stopped and gone on hold. Then it was abruptly released.

The torpedo's warhead slammed into *Pathfinder* under the forward funnel, fracturing the steel plating and piercing one of the boilers. Superheated shrapnel punctured the bulkheads surrounding the powder magazine and ignited a massive explosion that ripped out the guts of the ship.

The concussion was far more severe than Hersing had conceived. An immense surge of water pressure pounded the hull of *U-21*. Several crew members were knocked off their feet and injured as they fell against any steel object that got in their way. The lights blinked out and came on again as the battery connections were shaken loose.

"Up periscope." Hersing leaned against the eyepiece and was pleased at what he saw across the water.

The British cruiser was clearly in its death throes. As Hersing watched, another explosion rocked the already shattered vessel as the forward ammunition locker detonated. Pieces of the wheelhouse burst through the air and splashed the water like a heavy rain. She plunged bow-first, stern lifting until it was straight in the air, propellers still spinning and seemingly clawing at the sky. Hersing scanned the water for lifeboats. He saw one half swamped, but no evidence of survivors.

Standing firmly at the periscope, he watched the unfolding spectacle in growing astonishment. Another explosion rocked the ship as a boiler burst from the sudden contact with cold seawater. Hersing stared as if hypnotized as *Pathfinder* slid beneath the waves and was gone as if she had never existed.

"Down periscope," Hersing muttered quietly, in awe. "Come around to zero-three-zero."

Running silently underwater, *U-21* distanced herself from her first victim and turned away in search of another.

All but a handful of men from *Pathfinder* were denied the opportunity to abandon ship. None were given time to launch lifeboats, most of which were destroyed before the ship sank. None were given time to scramble from the bowels of the ship. "If you were not on the open deck when the torpedo struck, you were dead," Lieutenant Sonnenschein recalled. He had emptied the bridge locker of all the life belts before jumping into the water. He tied them around a cluster of men left struggling amid the floating debris. He felt sickened at seeing so pitifully few.

Captain Leake, though badly wounded, was alive. As *Pathfinder* lurched from the initial torpedo strike, he was thrown through the wheelhouse door, seconds before the structure was blown out of existence. The chief surgeon was also wounded but conscious. He had been on deck smoking a cigarette.

"I say," he muttered through teeth clenched with pain. "Could someone help keep me afloat? I seem to have broken both my arms."

"Physician, heal thyself," Sonnenschein said with a tight grin. He swam to the chief surgeon and lashed him to a plank that once had been part of a motor launch. Then Sonnenschein towed him toward the only lifeboat and two rafts that somehow survived intact.

The water in the North Sea felt bitter cold to the men struggling to live. They paddled or gripped flotsam to stay afloat, struggling to reach the boat and rafts, then waiting for a rescue they were sure would come too late. They knew death from hypothermia was only a matter of time, and they began to lose faith and talk of death.

Sonnenschein would have none of it. "Damn your hide!" he shouted. "Don't give up. Help is on the way."

A sailor spat a mouthful of salt water through his teeth. "It's no use, lieutenant. I doubt Sparks got off an SOS."

"Keep the men close together," Leake said weakly to Sonnenschein. "Don't let them drift off."

Sonnenschein began to recite Rudyard Kipling's poem "If." "If you can keep your head when all about you are losing theirs and blaming it on you . . ."

Slowly, one by one, the survivors began to rally as Sonnenschein made them repeat the poem over and over again.

Pathfinder had gone down in four minutes. A vast majority of her crew went with her. The lucky ones in the water were rescued shortly after the sinking. The explosion was seen from land and reported. A British destroyer in the neighborhood was diverted almost immediately and pulled the survivors out of the water a short time later.

Out of a complement of nearly 350, only 11 survived. The second ship ever sunk by a submarine, and the first in a long line sunk by German U-boats, *Pathfinder* carried a far greater loss of life than *Housatonic*.

Otto Hersing and his *U-21* made history by becoming the first submarine to sink a ship *and escape.* Together, they went on to great glory and gained other firsts.

After rendezvousing with a tanker off the coast of Spain, *U-21* became the first submarine to be refueled at sea. She was the first to sail into the Mediterranean, where she sank two battleships off Gallipoli. Her score also included over twenty merchant vessels that she sent to the bottom.

There were other U-boat commanders who sank more ships than Hersing, but none matched his tonnage. He went after the warships, often passing up several merchant vessels to send his small supply of torpedoes into a destroyer or cruiser.

Of Germany's first hundred submarines, only a small handful survived the war. *U-21* was one of them. After the Armistice, on November 20, 1918, Hersing was ordered to surrender his boat to the British Navy at Harwich, England, where it was to be impounded and scrapped. On the voyage from Kiel, Germany, he reported to his British escort that his boat had sprung a leak. Too late to prevent the scuttling, British seamen could only pick up the German survivors.

Defiant to the end, Otto Hersing had sent his beloved *U-21* to the bottom of the North Sea rather than turn her over to the enemy.

Several years after the war, famed explorer and correspondent Lowell Thomas visited Hersing in his village just thirty miles from the North Sea. The legendary U-boat commander, now a gentleman farmer, lived in a small cottage surrounded by fruit trees and gardens. After he was pulled from the North Sea and sent back to Germany, the British belatedly put a price on his head, but he managed to elude arrest until feelings of hatred had died away.

When Thomas asked the former scourge of Allied shipping how he kept busy, Hersing replied, "I grow fine potatoes."

II

Down in Eighteen Minutes

May 7, 1915

LIKE A WANDERING SPECTER, *U-20* MATERIALIZED OUT OF the fog in the Irish Sea, and slipped alongside a small square-masted schooner before it was noticed. "Man the gun," Kapitanleutnant Walter Schwieger ordered quietly.

Beneath his boyish good looks, blond hair, and fair skin, an undercurrent of ruthlessness ran through Schwieger's veins. Sending a ship to the bottom with noncombatants on board did not interrupt his sleep. On an earlier voyage, he had crept up on a well-marked hospital ship and sent a torpedo after her. Fortunately it missed, or his future reputation as a ghoul would have been even further enhanced.

The gun crew quickly rammed a two-inch shell into the breech of their weapon and aimed it at the schooner. Schwieger reached for a megaphone and shouted across the foggy surface of the water. "What ship are you?" he asked, noting the British cross of St. George flying from the halyards.

"Earl of Latham," the surprised captain answered, staring wide-eyed at the menacing submarine.

"Prepare to be boarded," Schwieger instructed him.

The five-man crew of the small schooner assembled on deck as the submarine's inflatable boat rowed across, and Schwieger's first officer, Raimund Weisbach, climbed on board. "Where is your manifest?" Weisbach asked the captain.

The captain silently walked below and returned, holding out a single sheet, which listed the schooner's cargo. "Mostly potatoes and bacon, en route from Limerick to Liverpool. Nothing worth concerning yourself about."

"Food for your troops," guessed a shrewd Weisbach. "Make to your boats. We are sinking this vessel."

As the crew of *Earl of Latham* lowered their boats and pulled for the shore, only three miles distant, Weisbach returned to *U-20* and reported to Schwieger. "Potatoes and bacon. Since we still have plenty of potatoes, I suggest we help ourselves to the bacon."

Schwieger smiled. "Please do so, Leutnant. But be quick about it. We can't risk being found by a British warship."

"Shall we scuttle or burn her?"

"I think it faster if we use grenades and the deck gun. She certainly isn't worth wasting a torpedo on."

After fifty pounds of bacon had been carried on board and lowered into the hull, the submarine's crew lobbed grenades into the hatches of *Earl of Latham*. Then the deck gun opened up, blasting three holes below the waterline. The crew of the schooner looked back and watched sadly as their ship rolled on her beam ends, sails hanging limp from the yards, and plunged below the waves.

Two hours later, *U-20* sighted a steamer, fired a torpedo at her, and missed. The ship steamed on, her crew blissfully unaware of how close they had come to being blown up. Then Schwieger spotted the Norwegian flag flying from the ship's mast and called off the attack.

So far, the voyage of *U-20* was coming up hollow. They needed a real target. Something worth using their last torpedoes on. Then Schwieger got lucky. In quick succession, he torpedoed the passenger liner *Candidate* and the freighter *Centurion*. Miraculously, all passengers and crews of both ships were saved.

Schwieger was down to his last torpedo. He decided to linger for another day in hopes of adding to his score before turning about and heading for home port in Germany to refuel and refit.

Fog lay thick across the sea as *Lusitania,* on her voyage from New York, neared the rugged southern coast of Ireland. Captain William Thomas Turner prowled the bridge of his ship, staring into the dense mist, listening for an echo from his foghorn that signaled the presence of another vessel. Watching from the bridge window, he saw the crewmen on the forward deck appear and disappear like phantom apparitions as they went about their duties.

Never stepping more than a few paces away from the helmsman, Turner stayed close in case he had to shout the order "Full astern" if another ship suddenly appeared from the curtain of gray. He gazed into it as if attempting to see through to the other side.

"Keep a sharp eye to avert a collision," said Turner to the officers peering through the wheelhouse window. "We're not the only ship in the Irish Sea."

"Better another ship than a German U-boat," muttered the junior third officer, Albert Bestic, under his breath.

Turner overheard and replied caustically, "No submarine can find us in this soup, Mr. Bestic. Any blind man can tell you that."

"Sorry, sir, I was only thinking out loud about reports of German torpedoings."

"All this talk of submarines and torpedoing," Turner snorted. "No submarine I ever heard of can make twenty-seven knots."

Bestic wasn't about to continue his argument with the *Lusitania*'s master. It was an argument he could not win, especially if he wanted a good efficiency report on his record with Cunard Lines. But it was no secret among the crew that because of a shortage of stokers, many of whom had been inducted into the Royal Navy for the duration of the war, and the high price for coal caused by scant supplies,

Lusitania was running at less than two-thirds her normal speed. With six of her twenty-five boilers unlit, *Lusitania* was making only eighteen knots. On a good day, if all her furnaces were properly fired, her engines could generate seventy thousand horsepower, which swirled her four great bronze propellers, thrusting her through the sea at thirty knots, enough speed to outrun any torpedo fired at her.

A seaman approached Turner and handed him a radio message that read, "Steer midchannel course. Submarines off Fastnet." Fastnet Rock, off the southern tip of Ireland, was a prominent landmark for mariners. This message had been repeated throughout the night.

Turner seemed unimpressed. He jammed the message into his coat pocket and said nothing. Will Turner was a tough old salt. He had gone to sea as a deck boy on sailing ships, and over the course of thirty-seven years had worked up to master of Cunard Lines' biggest and most prestigious ships. A strange old duck, as one officer remembered him, Turner never liked to mingle with the passengers. "A lot of bloody monkeys," he once called them. Shipwrecked on one occasion, he was later commissioned a commander in the Royal Navy by King George himself.

The messages came fast and furious the rest of the morning: "The British Admiralty recommends using a zigzag course when approaching areas of danger," followed by "Submarine active in southern part of Irish Channel . . ." Still another warning: "Submarine five miles south of Cape Clear proceeding west when sighted at 10 A.M."

Crumpling the paper, Turner tossed the latest warning in a receptacle. "Damned management," he grunted. "If the main office would allow me to fire all the boilers, we could simply outrun the damn U-boats and their torpedoes."

Why Turner, an experienced mariner with almost four decades as a trusted ship's master with Cunard, ignored the warnings and failed to act on their instructions is still a mystery today. It was almost as if he tried to put *Lusitania* directly in the path of Walter Schwieger and his *Unterseeboot, U-20,* sister submarine to Otto Hersing's *U-21.*

In less than an hour the two men and their commands would meet in a way neither expected.

In one of the luxurious first-class staterooms of *Lusitania,* Charles Frohman, the famed theatrical producer, lounged in an ornate flocked chair. Dressed in silk pajamas and robe, he paused from reading a manuscript by a composer of musical plays, and wiped his reading glasses with a handkerchief.

"How do you find it?" asked his valet, William Stainton.

"With the right musical numbers, it has possibilities."

Unlike most servants, Stainton enjoyed his employer's company. Over the years he had worked for the producer the men had become close. Frohman treated his valet more as an assistant than a servant. Instead of speaking only when spoken to, Stainton never hesitated to question his employer to determine his needs.

"Will you be taking lunch in the dining room, or shall I have food brought to the suite?" valet Stainton asked.

"I'll be dining with friends in the saloon," answered Frohman as he began dressing in the freshly pressed blue suit Stainton had laid out on the bed for him.

Stainton poured several pills onto a silver tray and set them alongside a glass of tomato juice. The producer suffered from arthritis that affected his leg joints. "I had the ship's doctor prepare some pills that will ease the pain in your knees."

"Is it that obvious, William?" Frohman said as he swallowed the pills.

"I couldn't help noticing you limp when you awoke and walked to the bathroom," Stainton said with concern as he handed Frohman a cane.

"You can remain here if you like."

"If it is all right, sir," said Stainton as he opened the door leading to the deck, "I would like to accompany you to the dining room and make sure you are seated properly."

"As you wish," Frohman said, smiling as he made his way down the passageway before stepping into the heavy mist outside the suite, his cane tapping lightly on the polished teak deck.

Wealthy socialite Alfred Vanderbilt entered the dining room and made his way to the table near the window he had requested from the purser. He was dressed in a charcoal pinstripe suit with a blue polka-dot bow tie, his head covered in a trendy tweed cap. In his pockets he carried no money or identification. He was so well known and so rich the mere mention of his name was all that was required to throw open doors and lay out red carpets.

The only object that Vanderbilt carried on his person was a pocket watch, a custom shared with most of the passengers, including the women, who generally wore smaller models around their necks. He opened the ornate solid gold timepiece and stared at the face. The hands on the Roman-numeral dial read 12:42.

His valet, Ronald Deyner, pulled the chair back, seated Vanderbilt, and then stood off to one side. "Please see if any radio messages came in for me," he asked Deyner. Then he turned. "Good morning," Vanderbilt said pleasantly, as a waiter held out the luncheon menu. He held up a hand and refused the menu. "I'll have whatever your head chef recommends."

Charles Frohman walked by Vanderbilt's table and paused. "Good afternoon, Alfred."

Vanderbilt noticed the producer's limp. "Injure one of your legs, Charles?"

"Arthritis." Frohman shrugged resignedly. "It plays hell with my joints."

"Have you tried sulfur baths?"

"And just about every other chemical bath known to man."

"Are you traveling to the Continent for business or pleasure?" asked Vanderbilt.

Frohman smiled. "My business *is* pleasure. I'm seeing what the London revues have to offer. Always on the lookout for good material and talent, you know."

"I wish you luck."

"How about you, Alfred? What are your plans?"

"I am examining some horses in London for my stables," answered Vanderbilt.

"I wish you an enjoyable trip. When you return, please have your secretary call my office and I'll send you tickets to my next production."

"I'll do that, thank you."

Frohman nodded courteously and made his way to his table in a corner, where he could observe the other diners, many of whom were celebrities of their day. There was the eccentric publisher and author of *A Message to Garcia,* Elbert Hubbard. Acclaimed playwright and novelist Justus Forman. Famed suffragette Lady Margaret Mackworth. Theodate Pope, noted architect and psychic.

Frohman and Stainton smiled at seeing the six young children of the Paul Cromptons of Philadelphia. They were boisterous and totally ignoring a frustrated nanny, who was failing miserably at making them sit quietly around a table. Mr. and Mrs. Crompton took it all in stride and seldom reprimanded them.

Frohman and most of the people seated in the dining room around him had no forewarning that this was to be their last meal on earth.

As if exiting a steam bath, *Lusitania*'s bow suddenly broke into bright sunlight. Captain Turner looked up from the logbook as the sound of the automatic foghorn ceased its monotonous blaring. Gazing astern, he saw the big funnels, their red Cunard color painted black for the war, slip from the fog like hands from gloves.

Luncheon over, passengers filed outside, some settling in deck chairs, others strolling the open decks still wet from the heavy mist. Excitement arose as they sighted the rugged coast of Ireland in the distance. Confused as to his exact position because of the dense fog, Captain Turner was surprised to find he was so close to land. He should have been at least forty miles further out in midchannel.

The chairman of Cunard, Alfred Booth, appealed personally to the Admiralty to alert the passenger liner to the loss of the *Candidate* and *Centurion* just hours earlier. But the message somehow became watered down, and Turner, as he did with the others, simply ignored it.

Lusitania sailed on, unsuspecting of her fate.

Schwieger did not have a particular course in mind. *U-20* cruised aimlessly on the surface, her commander unable to sight a victim through the fog. He waited patiently for it to clear in hope of finding an opportunity. He did not have long to wait.

Suddenly, the lookouts found themselves under blue skies and a bright sun. Running blind during the last hour had brought the submarine nearer to land. Standing below in the control room, Schwieger turned at the shout from First Officer Weisbach on watch in the conning tower.

"Ship to port."

Schwieger rushed topside and peered through his binoculars. The vessel was large, sported four big funnels, and was making good time. He guessed she was about twelve miles distant. He turned to Weisbach and sighed. "She's too far away and too fast for us. We'll never catch her."

"We're not going to try for an attack?" asked Weisbach.

"I didn't say we weren't going to try," said Schwieger. "Prepare to dive."

The dive bell clanged harshly as the crew began twisting a row of valves that flooded the ballast tanks and dropped the boat beneath the surface. Keeping a practiced eye on the polished brass depth gauge, the diving officer waited until reaching periscope depth before leveling *U-20* on an even keel.

"Come to heading zero-seven-zero," Schwieger said quietly.

"Periscope depth," reported the diving officer.

Peering through the scope, Schwieger saw that the situation was hopeless. There was no way *U-20* could maneuver into position before the big ship showed him her stern. At their maximum speed of nine knots underwater, it was an exercise in futility to think they could overtake a fast passenger liner. He gave a turn at the periscope to Weisbach, who studied the distant ship.

"At least twenty-five thousand tons," he reported. "Probably an armed liner used for troop transport."

"Can you make an identification?" asked Schwieger.

Weisbach began thumbing through a ship-recognition book. "A number of British liners have four stacks," replied Weisbach. "Judging from her superstructure, she belongs to Cunard. Could be either *Aquitania, Mauritania,* or *Lusitania.* Too many ventilators showing on her top deck for the first two. My guess is *Lusitania.*"

"A pity," said Schwieger wearily. "She would have made an easy target."

Then abruptly, as if guided by the devil, the ship made a turn to starboard.

"We've got her!" Schwieger cried suddenly. "She's come about directly toward us."

Turner recognized a lighthouse perched on a high cliff protruding from the sea and knew he was off the Old Head of Kinsale. He motioned to his first officer. "Alter course to starboard and put us on a heading for Queenstown."

Lusitania was less than twenty-five miles from a safe harbor, but now only ten miles from *U-20* and heading directly toward the submarine. No spider ever had a more cooperative victim. The web was spread and waiting.

Schwieger could not believe his luck. If the great liner kept to its new heading, he would be set up for an ideal broadside shot.

In the lives of many men some moments are etched in time. Motion and thought seem to merge, the event takes a life of its own. Schwieger watched in awe as the ship in the lens of the periscope grew until it was framed like a picture postcard.

Tension smothered the interior of the submarine. By now, the entire crew were aware that they were stalking a giant ocean liner. A mixed bag of emotions ran through their minds.

"Ready torpedo," commanded Schwieger.

Charles Voegele, *U-20*'s quartermaster, stood fixed as if in a trance. In a moment that defied discipline and tears at men's souls, he was unable to pass the order onto the forward torpedo compartment.

"Ready the torpedo," Schwieger repeated sharply.

Voegele remained motionless. "I'm sorry, sir, but I cannot bring myself to destroy a ship with innocent women and children on board. Such an act is barbaric."

To ignore a captain's order at sea during wartime was tantamount to treason. Voegele would later be sentenced to prison for his refusal to take part in the tragedy.

An ordinary seaman relayed the instruction. In the torpedo compartment, the order was carried out. Back came the acknowledgment. "Torpedo ready."

The anticipation of the next few seconds seemed to hang like mist. Schwieger was calm and relaxed. He was the only member of his crew who was pessimistic. He doubted that he could sink a vessel the size of *Lusitania* with his one and only remaining torpedo. Time and again, German torpedoes had proved insufficient, striking vessels and failing to explode. And quite often, when they did explode, the resulting damage was not enough to sink their intended victims. He had already written in his log that he thought that his torpedoes could not sink a ship whose watertight bulkheads were secured.

At 2:05 he uttered the words that would send twelve hundred men, women, and children to their deaths. "Away torpedo."

With a loud hiss of compressed air, the torpedo shot from the tube. Powered by a little four-cylinder engine turning two counterrotating propellers, it drove through the water at twenty-two knots with its depth set at nine feet. Though he had underestimated the liner's speed, Schwieger watched with great satisfaction as the churning wake beat a trail straight for the massive starboard hull of the helpless *Lusitania*.

It was a textbook bow shot from only seven hundred yards. It seemed to Schwieger as if *Lusitania* steamed right into it. The torpedo slammed into the great liner just aft of the forward mast, shredding hull plates and blowing a hole as large as a barn door. Damage was serious but not fatal. Half expecting the ship to continue as if it were merely stung, Schwieger was stunned by what he witnessed in the next few seconds.

The first explosion was followed by an even larger one that twisted the entire bow on an angle, causing the ship to heel over almost immediately on a fifteen-degree list. Thousands of tons of water poured into what had now become a gigantic cavity. Controversy would later erupt over whether *Lusitania* was holed by two torpedoes, a sympathetic explosion from the coal dust in the empty bunkers, or the detonation of 1,248 cases of three-inch shrapnel shells clandestinely carried in the forward cargo hold.

It is an enigma that continues to this day.

Turner stiffened when the lookout's dreaded cry of "Torpedo on the starboard side!" rang out. He rushed over to that side of the bridge wing just as the explosion rocked his ship. "Close the watertight doors!" he roared above the fading rumble. Disaster followed catastrophe. A second, much larger, thunderous blast entirely different from the first shook the deck under his feet. The list came so quickly he barely was able to grip a handrail to keep from spilling over the side.

Down deep, in the depths of his soul, William Turner knew his ship was doomed.

Within seconds, the tranquil scene under a peaceful sky and calm sea deteriorated into mass confusion. There was no panic, but everyone milled around the lifeboats without benefit of direction. Passengers frantically searched for loved ones or wandered about the decks as if lost. The chaos became ever worse as *Lusitania,* still under way, began her roll to starboard in unison with her plunging bow. Turner telegraphed "Full astern" to slow the progress of the ship, but problems with the turbines—one of the main steam pipes split open—prevented the order from being carried out. The helmsman spun the wheel to bring *Lusitania* around, but the rudder refused to respond. *Lusitania* continued moving ahead with just enough speed to swamp the lifeboats as they were lowered into the rushing water.

Only six lifeboats out of forty-eight carried by the ship floated away intact. Most were badly damaged or destroyed when they slid forward toward the bow, crashing through other boats and crushing any passengers who stood in the way.

Many of the crew in the engine room were either killed outright or swept upward on a torrent of water cascading through the hatches that remained open. In the radio room, second wireless operator David McCormick tapped out, "Come at once. Big list. Ten miles Old Head Kinsale." The message was heard and everything that could float rushed to the scene.

Alfred Vanderbilt remained impassive. It was not his nature to show emotion. Other than stopping a child running past, to secure his life jacket properly, he awaited death stoically like a grand lord.

Charles Frohman, it was said, quoted *Peter Pan* to frightened passengers. "Why fear death? It is the most beautiful adventure in life." Crippled by arthritis, he waited until water washed over the deck. Then he simply stepped over the side, followed by his faithful valet, Stainton, and drowned.

A bounty of one thousand pounds was offered for Alfred Vanderbilt's body. But neither he nor Frohman was found.

The Cromptons, along with their six children and nanny, were lost.

Turner was alone on the bridge, a solitary figure staring up at the decks of his ship that loomed above him. He hung there clutching a railing as the bow of *Lusitania* plunged down until it struck a granite outcropping three hundred feet below the surface. Twisting, as if rotated by some unseen hand, the great Cunard liner slowly slid under the water. Swept away by the surge created by underwater turbulence, Turner found a small wooden chair and used it for a float until he was plucked alive from the Irish Sea by a fishing trawler.

Lusitania was gone. Her death throes lasted only eighteen minutes. When the final count was tallied, 1,198 passengers and crew, out of 1,958 who had sailed from New York, were lost. Following on the heels of the *Titanic,* which took 1,500 with her in 1912, and the *Empress of Ireland* with 1,000 dead in 1914, *Lusitania*'s loss was especially staggering. Looking back, it seems incredible that so many maritime disasters with such heavy numbers of dead all occurred in the short span of three years.

It would take another thirty years before the record was broken during World War II by Russian submarines that sank the German passenger liners *Willhelm Gustloff, General Steuben,* and *Goya,* which were carrying refugees fleeing from the avenging Red Army. The combined death count from the three torpedoed liners came to 18,000.

His face clouded with disbelief that a single torpedo had caused one of the world's great ocean liners to completely disappear in just eighteen minutes, Schwieger downed his periscope and gave orders for First Officer Weisbach to set a course for Germany.

Awarded the Iron Cross for his work in the Irish Sea, Schwieger was to sink several other ships in the coming year, but then his luck slowly began to run out. The end for *U-20* came the following year in October of 1916. Because of a faulty compass, *U-20* ran aground on a shoal just off the Jutland Peninsula of Denmark during a heavy fog. Schwieger quickly sent an appeal for help to the nearest German naval base. An entire fleet of torpedo boats and destroyers responded. The Germans correctly assumed that, if the British Navy had intercepted the SOS, they would have sent every warship within a hundred miles to destroy the U-boat that sank *Lusitania.* If successful, the result would have been heralded as a great naval victory.

Tow lines were attached, and the effort to pull *U-20* off the shoal began at the first high tide. But nothing went right for Schwieger and his boat this day. The sands of the shoal, no more than a hundred yards from the beach, gripped the submarine in a tenacious grip. Ropes and chains broke several times. With each wave *U-20* sank deeper into the bottom. Schwieger decided the project was hopeless and ordered explosive charges placed in the bilges.

The crew evacuated their vessel, taking all papers and personal belongings. Except for blowing a few holes in the bottom of the hull, the following explosions had little effect on the *U-20*. Schwieger left her there with heavy heart, immune to the death and destruction they had caused together.

Given command of the *U-88,* a big new boat of the latest design, Schwieger took most of his old *U-20* crew with him. He continued to harass British shipping for another year. Then on September 17, 1917, *U-88* struck a British mine and sank with all hands. Walter Schwieger had challenged fate once too often.

U-20 sat abandoned and rusting in the sands of Jutland until 1925. Then, for some unexplained reason, the Danish Admiralty decided to destroy the infamous submarine and ordered charges of dynamite to be set around the wreck. Using nearly a ton of explosives, they blew off the upper deck and conning tower. A hail of shattered metal was thrown over a wide area. One of the men who placed the charges fell asleep in the engine room and went unmissed until after the explosion. Incredibly, he staggered out of the wreckage and swam onto the beach with only a few cuts and bruises.

During her brief life, *U-20* sank over twenty ships and caused the deaths of nearly fifteen hundred men, women, and children. Her evil deeds are engraved on the tombstones of her victims. Forever linked with *Lusitania,* she was slowly covered over by sand, her final resting place eventually forgotten.

Germany's early undersea boats had sunk an incredible 4,838 ships during World War I, 2,009 more than their descendants in World War II. In the latter war, Nazi U-boats destroyed 4.5 million tons of shipping as against 11 million in 1914–18.

The horror of the next war will not be ships sunk by torpedoes fired from submarines, but rather entire cities and nations destroyed by missiles launched from silos in their hull.

III

I'd Rather Be in Hawaii

June 1984

THERE ARE WORSE PLACES THAN THE NORTH SEA, BUT I can't think of any when you're on a sixty-four-foot boat being pounded by fifteen-foot waves. This was my third voyage into those wicked waters, and being a tad mentally deficient, I looked forward to the trip. My first two expeditions were failed attempts to find John Paul Jones's ship, *Bonhomme Richard.*

Now my objectives were even more ambitious. The six-week expedition was divided into two phases. The first three weeks were to be spent searching for H.M.S. *Pathfinder, U-20, U-21,* and several of the battle cruisers that sank during the great sea battle between the British and German fleets off Jutland, Denmark. The second phase of three weeks was dedicated to finding the World War II troop transport *Léopoldville* and the famed Confederate raider *Alabama,* which went down after a furious battle with Union frigate *Kearsarge,* off Cherbourg. Altogether, we assembled a target list of nearly thirty lost ships.

Whoever coined the phrase "biting off more than you can chew" must have had me in mind. Actually, it was more a case of trying to hit ten birds with one stone. In for a penny, in for a pound. Go for broke, think big, or go whole hog. If original sayings were worth a dime and clichés a dollar, I'd go for the big money every time.

My wisest contribution was allowing two weeks out of the six I'd scheduled to be lost due to rotten weather, problems with the boat, or our detection instruments. You can't second-guess the unknown, but you can allow yourself some leeway. When planning your project, always, always figure in nonproductive time. You'll be very disappointed if you don't.

Nearly two years of research went into the effort. Correspondence was heavy between me, Bob Fleming, and British and German naval archives. A mass of material was accumulated from English, Scottish, German, Dutch, and Danish fishermen, who knew the sea the way they knew the decks of their trawlers. A pile of nautical charts were assembled, studied, and marked. For the *Alabama,* we examined French records of the famous battle. I sat for half an hour in front of Renoir's painting "The Sinking of the Alabama" that hangs in the Philadelphia Museum of Art. Letters, diaries, and contemporary news reports were also examined.

The first setback we encountered was the conflicting position reports on World War I shipwrecks. Their last known positions as recorded by the British Admiralty and Imperial German Navy did not match the positions marked on the fishermen's charts. Nor were the fishermen's data very accurate, as we were about to find.

Take for example the wreck of *Invincible,* a British battle cruiser that was hit by a lucky shot and blown up, taking all but six of her thousand-man crew with her. In the general area where she was thought to have gone down, there were eight different position markings for an unknown ship within a three-mile radius.

How, I wondered in awe, could they misplace a 562-foot-by-78-foot, 17,250-ton battle cruiser? But they did. We stumbled on her wreck a good mile or more from the nearest estimated position. It is a fact, however, that fishermen are quite reluctant to give away locations of good fishing grounds or the snags and hangers that catch their nets. They figure if they know the exact position where fish congregate or the spot they lost a $5,000 set of nets, they're better off not enlightening their competitors. So when pumping a fisherman on a wreck site, you have to be very polite and diplomatic while wondering if you're being sold stock in a company that manufactures rumble seats and buggy whips.

My plane was late coming into London and I missed my connecting flight to Scotland, so I sat around Heathrow and read British tabloids for the latest dirt before my flight to Aberdeen was called. Arriving three hours late, I ran into a distraught Bill Shea wandering the arrival gates like a lost soul. Bill was afraid I had been abducted by alien Scotsmen and began to think perhaps he was doomed to spend eternity in the Aberdeen airport.

We hailed a cab and drove to the dock, where we found the boat I had chartered, the same one I had used to search for the *Bonhomme Richard* five years previously. Solid, tough *Arvor III* was built in Buckie, Scotland, sometime in the 1960s. Her first owner, a wealthy Frenchman, wanted a yacht that could cruise the roughest seas in the worst weather nature could throw at her. So he decided on a stout-hulled Buckie Boat used by fishermen making a hard living in the North Sea. Not many pleasure yachts are designed around a fishing trawler. *Arvor* was probably the only one of her kind.

Powered by two big diesels, she cruised at a complacent eight knots. Her main saloon and staterooms were paneled in deep red mahogany and quite large. Besides a commode, the head in the main stateroom provided a bidet. The first time I tried it, I turned the handle too far and reversed my anal canal while striking my head on the deck above.

Arvor III was ideally suited as a search and survey vessel. Solid and stable as a work platform, her living quarters were comfortable and efficient. If you walked by her on a dock, you probably wouldn't give her a second look. Not fancy, she looked quite ordinary. She was painted a no-nonsense black with white upperworks and was immaculate inside and out. I was blessed to get her, and I was doubly blessed with her remarkable crew.

In all my travels, I've found no finer people than the Scots. Despite their reputation for thriftiness, they're generous in a host of ways. Try and buy a Scot a drink. His cash is in the bartender's hand before your fingers touch your wallet. If you're cold, they'll give you the coats off their backs. Courteous, considerate, no favor goes ignored.

They're a tough and hardy people. My dad used to tell a story about the Scots when he served in the German army in World War I. Yes, my father fought with the bad guys. I also have an uncle who shot down fourteen Allied planes. Anyway, Dad used to describe the French as mediocre fighters, the British as tenacious bulldogs, the Americans as real scrappers. "But my German comrades took anything they could all dish out. It was only when we heard the bagpipes from the 'laddies from hell' that we oozed cold sweat and knew a lot of us wouldn't be going home for Christmas."

Arvor's skipper, Jimmy Flett, is a Scot any man would be proud to boast of having as a friend. Honest, with integrity nine miles long, you wouldn't give a second thought about trusting him with your life, your wife, and your bank account. Jimmy had been torpedoed twice during the war, one of the few who survived an oil-tanker explosion. Later, when he captained a coastal passenger-cargo ship, he brought her through one of the worst storms on record in the North Sea. A grateful government wanted to present him with a medal. But Jimmy refused to receive it unless his chief engineer was given one as well. Because, as Jimmy put it, "if he hadn't kept the engines running under impossible conditions, everyone on the ship would have drowned." The bureaucrats refused to give a medal to Jimmy's chief engineer, so he stuck to his guns. His only reward for saving so many lives is a photograph of the medal he never received.

Our first mate was John, who had been one of Jimmy's crew the night they fought the terrible storm. Quiet, most helpful, John was a presence seen but seldom heard. Colin

Robb, our cook from Oben on the rugged northeast coast of Scotland, never was at a loss for words. The only problem was none of us Americans could fathom his brogue. Bill Shea and I thought that after a couple of weeks we'd become accustomed to his enunciation and understand what he was saying. I'm sorry to report that when the expedition closed down six weeks later, we were still failing Scot's Brogue Translation Course 1-A. However, we did become especially adept at listening to Colin tell a joke. Unable to comprehend a single phrase, Shea and I would wait patiently until Colin paused. Then, assuming the punch line was given, we'd laugh. Amazingly, we pulled it off the entire voyage without Colin's catching on. At least we think we fooled him. Maybe we didn't. Colin never confessed.

The British trucking system being what it is, we were delayed by four days while waiting for our equipment to arrive. The side scan sonar, magnetometer, and underwater camera had been air-freighted from the States three weeks earlier and were sitting in a London warehouse. With little to do while living on the boat beside the Aberdeen dock, Shea and I wandered the town.

Going to the local movie theater was particularly interesting. After paying for our tickets, we were sent upstairs to the balcony. Neither of us had ever seen a balcony-only theater before. Leaning over the railing in the front row, we could see that the downstairs seating section hadn't been used in thirty years. The aisles and seats were buried under decades of dust. No fancy snack bar with hot buttered popcorn and jumbo Pepsis here. What we got were two girls standing on opposite sides of the balcony shining flashlights on trays of goodies strapped around their necks. I asked one of the concession girls why the main floor was deserted.

She looked up at me from the glow of her flashlight. "Why, sir, it's not safe down there."

Not safe from what? I didn't have the guts to ask why my body was more secure from harm in the balcony.

Strolling back to the boat, Bill and I came upon a crowd in front of a small building. We walked up to a bobby controlling the crowd and inquired as to the fuss. "The building you see is Aberdeen's maritime museum," he explained proudly. "The Queen Mother will arrive any minute to officially open it."

Since Bill and I figured this was as close as we were going to get to an invitation to Buckingham Palace, we stood on the curb while everybody waved little British flags and shouted, "Hooray for the Queen Mum. Hooray for the Queen Mum." A delightful old lady in her eighties at the time, she waved graciously and disappeared into the museum.

My other memorable experience in Aberdeen happened at the only phone booth on the docks. After standing in a British queue for an hour, I finally stepped inside and dialed the trucking company in London, ranting and raving over my tardy equipment. When I was informed that it was loaded on a truck whose final drop-off point was Aberdeen and was now somewhere in Wales, I became twenty degrees above steamed.

Adding to my wrath, a young fisherman, impatient to use the phone, began pounding on the door. Since I was only three minutes into my conversation, I ignored him. Then he pushed the door open and tried to pull me out. I was intent on yelling obscenities at the trucking company dispatcher and didn't turn and notice that he was thirty years younger and built much broader than me, wore all black, and had an earring in his ear—these were the days before it became a fad. I was several inches taller, but if it came to a contest in brute strength, he could have likely picked up the booth with me inside and thrown it in the harbor. Fortunately, a couple of factors worked in my favor. One, I was already madder than hell at the trucking company and didn't care if he had muscles like tree trunks, and two, I was cold sober while the obnoxious fisherman was dead drunk.

More on impulse than common sense, I placed my outspread hand in his face and gave a mighty heave. He staggered backward across a narrow alley and struck a brick wall, cracking his head. He stood there, holding up the wall with a glazed look in his eyes, just staring at me. I now recognized that this was a guy you don't tease when he's eating, so I finished my call and hastily departed.

Our equipment finally arrived, which made me happy. No more irate phone calls or nasty confrontations out of that dockside phone booth. After everything was loaded aboard and tested, we sailed out of Aberdeen and headed due south toward St. Abb's Head, eighty miles away. The day was breezy under a pewter sky of high clouds. On the way to the *Pathfinder* site, we took a short detour and spent four hours searching for the *U-12,* a German submarine rammed and sunk by H.M.S. *Ariel* in 1915. A British sonar sweep failed to find her in 1977, but we obtained a good reading for a submarine about two miles from where the Admiralty charts put her. The image showed her sitting upright with a nice shadow outlining her conning tower.

Considering the find to be a good omen, we continued to the search grid I had outlined off St. Abb's Head. I gave the latitudes and longitudes to Jimmy, who converted them on his Loran navigation chart. The sea became rough and poor Bill was barely able to function at the side scan recorder. He swallowed ten different brands of pills and plastered his entire body with Transderm Scōp patches to prevent seasickness. His nausea overcame the finest remedies on the market. I've always thought he could make a fortune hiring himself out as a guinea pig to pharmaceutical companies. If they could come up with a medication to cure Bill's motion sickness, they could rule the world without bothering to spend zillions buying Washington.

We set the side scan for one-thousand-meter lanes and began mowing the lawn in the late afternoon, running north and south with the tide, which is the only way to go. The seabed read smooth and flat, interspersed with gravelly ripples. The bottom in this area was also very clean and free of trash and debris. The hours passed. Colin fixed dinner in the galley. Bill, of course, wasn't hungry.

At 8:20 the next morning, Jimmy announced, "We just passed over a rise on the bottom."

Because his fathometer scanned directly under the hull

while the sonar sensor was dragged fifty yards astern, everyone gathered around the recorder, waiting for a peculiar object to appear. There is a hypnotic attraction in staring down on the reddish-brown smudges that slowly materialize on paper. Expectation and anticipation never seem to fade. I've seen men and women sit over a machine until their eyes turned red and swelled shut.

The image of a man-made object lying on a level bottom slowly revealed itself at the outer edge of the thousand-meter range. The object read vague, but it was there. We made another pass and switched the sonar to record a lane of only two hundred meters, obtaining a picture of a badly shattered ship, broken in three sections, lying at slightly different angles to each other. The stern section was the only part of the wreck that had distinguishing features.

We made five more passes, and on the sixth we defined a small naval gun lying beside the wreck. Next we attempted to lower our underwater video camera over the side and get a picture, but the current was so strong and the seven-foot waves tossed us around so badly the video screen revealed little more than blurred images of jagged wreckage. In retrospect, I realize we could have easily lost the camera if it had hung up on the wreck.

Identification according to archaeological standards was not positive in the sense that we didn't find a sign saying, THIS IS THE PATHFINDER. But the dimensions measured on the side scan recording closely matched those of *Pathfinder.* The discovery of a small naval cannon also adds to the evidence. And finally, there is no other shipwreck within ten square miles in any direction.

When we sent in a report of our findings to the Admiralty, they were more than pleased to update their charts with our wreck position, since it was the only one of proven accuracy. H.M.S. *Pathfinder*'s twisted and rusting remains lie lonely and forlorn under a white-capped sea thirty miles off St. Abb's Head at 56 07 21 by 02 09 15 in 155 feet of water. There are strong currents in this area, and diving is hazardous.

Now it was on to the infamous terminator of *Lusitania.*

* * *

Bill prayed for deliverance and was answered. The waters turned to glass for the voyage across the North Sea to Thyborøn, a small fishing port on the Jutland Peninsula in Denmark. On the way over we searched for several of the warships sunk during the great Jutland naval battle in 1916. After only three passes, we recorded the H.M.S. *Hawke,* a British cruiser that was torpedoed by *U-9.* She was found very close to the position reported by fishermen and Admiralty charts. One of the few times this circumstance occurred, *Hawke*'s outline was quite distinguishable and her calculated dimensions were on the money. Her hull is relatively in one piece, but her superstructure appears crumpled on one side of the wreck.

Moving on, we searched for the wrecks of H.M.S. *Defence* and H.M.S. *Warrior,* two British heavy cruisers, and the German light cruiser *Wiesbaden.* The first two were a wash. Nothing resembling shipwrecks were found within five miles of where they were supposed to be. A large anomaly was hit over the approximate position of *Wiesbaden,* but we couldn't get close enough for a more detailed view, due to fishing nets floating all around the area. The practice is called gill fishing. The Danish fishermen, in particular, found that fish tend to gather around shipwrecks and geological rises on the seabed. So they drop nets attached to floats around the protrusions, leave them for a few days, and then pull them in, hopefully filled with fish.

After Colin's belly-filling dinner, which always included boiled potatoes, Jimmy and I usually poured scotch while Bill played movies over the video monitor. One has to be the most boring movie ever made, a Kipling story titled *Kim,* with Peter O'Toole. Some old Indian Hindu beggar wanders around India for fifty years looking for a river. Rivers are a dime a dozen in India. We could only believe that he was overly picky.

The British still have great affection for their lost empire in India. Bill and I fell asleep, but the Scots thought it was marvelously entertaining. On the other hand, our favorite flick for the North Sea crossing was Stephen King's

Creepshow. They thought it disgusting. Different cultures, different taste in films.

We no sooner docked in Thyborøn than the sea turned nasty. Other than complain, there was little choice but to wait for calmer weather. Bill and I walked into the town bank and converted a few traveler's checks to Danish kroner. While we were standing at the counter, the whole bank felt as though it were rocking back and forth. Too many days at sea does that to you. Your equilibrium takes a while to adjust to a floor that doesn't roll.

I often wondered why anyone would want to live in Thyborøn. The town is pretty and clean and picturesque, the people are courteous and friendly, but the wind blows so hard eleven months out of the year that all trees within five miles of the coast grow horizontally. Though it was June and the sun shone bright, the wind chill factor reminded me of a Telluride, Colorado, ski slope in January.

While waiting for the sea to calm, Bill and I conferred with the local fishermen and drank beer with the town officials. Sitting on the beach and gawking at all the gorgeous blonde Scandinavian girls sunning in the sand, wearing only bikini bottoms and no bras, quickly became our favorite pastime. You'd have thought they were in Acapulco the way they lay there without a single goose bump, while we big chicken foreigners were bundled in heavy coats and sweaters.

One afternoon, I took a walk along the quay and was observing the fishermen unloading their catch after returning to port. Out of the corner of my eye, I happened to catch Bill on the opposite dock from me, panning the harbor with his video camera. The instant his lens was aimed in my direction I began jumping up and down and doing all sorts of crazy gyrations. I was too far away to be recognized, and he didn't notice me through his viewfinder.

Later, during dinner, he began running the tape on the monitor. As the camera panned the opposite dock, I pointed to the wildly dancing figure and said, "What's that guy doing?"

Bill stared. "I didn't catch that before. He looks like he's in a spastic fit."

Jimmy, John, and Colin gazed quizzically at the crazy image on the monitor. "No fisherman I know would act like that," said John matter-of-factly.

"How odd," I said, fighting off laughter. "Maybe he's one of those dock entertainers who dance for money."

Colin swallowed the bait. "I never seen any dock dancers."

I strung the joke for another five minutes before Bill wised up. "If I didn't know better, I'd say that looks like Clive."

So there I am, recorded for all time, making an absolute ass out of myself.

Generally, the time ashore proved productive. I met with Danish diver-archaeologist Gert Normann Andersen, who had spent a great deal of effort searching for lost ships along the Jutland Coast. His wreck projects operated on even a smaller shoestring than mine. His only piece of detection gear was a grappling hook, which he and his partner dragged up and down the shoreline. A deal was struck between the quiet Dane and the demented American. If we helped him look for several wrecks he had yet to discover, he'd use his findings to put us in the ballpark of *U-20*. As it turned out, it was a profitable arrangement for both sides.

The weather was still rotten, but with Andersen and his diving partner on board, we headed south to the site where *U-20* grounded sixty-eight years before. The seas rolled with six-foot waves that *Arvor* brushed aside as if she were on a Sunday cruise up the Thames. Thanks to her stabilizers, violent pitch and roll were kept to a minimum. Poor Bill Shea went ashen and retired to his stateroom less than a mile out of Thyborøn, and we didn't see him again until we docked that evening.

Two hundred thousand years from now, it's doubtful whether Denmark as we know it today will exist. The sea is eroding the coastline at an incredible rate. Concrete bunkers and gun emplacements the Germans built during World War

II to repel invasion are already sitting in ten feet of water a hundred yards from shore. This erosion is a boon to marine archaeologists and wreck hunters. Hundreds of ships that ran aground up and down Jutland and were buried under the beach for the past five hundred years now lie exposed out in the water.

We anchored near Vielby Beach. The site was not difficult to pinpoint because older residents remembered seeing *U-20*'s conning tower rising above the water some distance from the beach. Several told of how they stood and watched as she was blown up. A few sweeps with the side scan sonar and we had a target. The Danish divers went over the side and soon returned. They had found the wreck, but rough seas were kicking up sand on the bottom and visibility was reduced to only one or two feet. About 1 P.M., the wind died and the sea calmed and cleared enough to see five feet. Everyone dove and surveyed the wreck. Andersen produced an excellent sketch showing her final disposition.

U-20 now lies nearly four hundred yards from shore in seventeen feet of water. When the sea isn't restless, she is an easy dive. The lower section of her hull lies exposed. The conning tower and various pieces of debris are scattered around in the sand. The diesel engines still sit in their mounts, and the Danish divers found a propeller shaft coupling with an engraved brass plaque, giving the manufacturer and date it was installed in *U-20*. There it was, signed, sealed, and delivered. A certified identification.

I would have liked to dive on the wreck and recover artifacts for display at maritime museums in the United States, but archaeologist Andersen and the Danish government did not approve. So I came away with only side scan recordings and a drawing by the divers.

The broken corpse of *U-20* has far more significance for Germany, England, and the U.S. than Denmark. I'm sure that if someone took the time and made the effort to apply for a permit for a survey and artifact-retrieval project, the Danes would grant it.

I also hope the country acknowledges the tremendous

contribution Gert Normann Andersen and his associates have made on behalf of Danish marine archaeology. Without his fortitude, *U-20* would still lie undiscovered. In my book, he gets all the credit while I felt privileged just to work with him.

It was now my turn to repay the favor.

Sweeping the coast between *U-20* and Thyborøn, we located several wrecks the Danes later surveyed and identified. Two of them were historically significant: the Royal Swedish steamship *Odin,* run aground in 1836, and the *Alexander Nevski,* a Russian steam frigate that was stranded while carrying the crown prince in 1874. According to the records, everyone was saved from both ships, including the Russian crown prince.

We returned to Thyborøn and bade goodbye to the Danes after several rounds of good Danish beer. The next morning we found a large sailboat tied to the *Arvor.* Since every space was taken along the dock, yachting courtesy dictated that the owner of the sailboat ask permission of *Arvor*'s skipper to moor his sailboat to the outside of our boat and walk across our deck to and from the dock. Permission as a rule was always granted.

The problem? There was no request.

Jimmy Flett, a kind gentleman, said nothing and graciously allowed the yachtsmen passage over his deck. The sailboat's crew consisted of two married couples, German to the core. They'd stare at our motley crew and babble in their guttural language, which grates on the ears. My dad tried to teach me German but it would have been easier to build a nuclear bomb in the bathroom. He never spoke the language after coming to America. The only words that stuck in my brain were nasty, and of little use for tuning into their conversations.

They played some crazy Kraut rock and roll during all hours of the night and day with the volume set somewhere between Thunderclap and Nuclear Detonation. The women wore your average, garden-variety brief bathing suits. But the men advertised their pubic hair in string bikinis. Our crew of good conservative Scotsmen were not entertained. They were wishing for the sound of bagpipes.

I saw it as my duty to prevent another Battle of Jutland by engaging in sadistic foreplay. The Cussler with a song in his heart had a fiendish plan. When the Germans began blasting their rock and roll across the harbor, I counterattacked with my Dixieland jazz tapes. It was no contest. Bill Shea heads up the video department of Brandeis University. He hooked up enough speakers with enough decibels to blow the three little pigs' brick house down. At dawn the German sailboat retreated to the other side of the harbor. Life became good.

From the standpoint of sea-search technology, World War I shipwrecks are not that difficult to find. I'm the first to admit that we accomplished little of archaeological significance. But our efforts were greatly appreciated by fishermen from four countries. We turned over copies of all our documents, giving precise locations to their government fisheries offices. Having more accurate wreck positions made it easier for many of them to sail directly to the wrecks and drop their gill nets. This magnanimous and benevolent good deed resulted in the most harrowing experience of the trip.

Danish fishermen are a fascinating breed. They live in rather plain red brick homes with simple peaked roofs, kept immaculately clean at all hours by gorgeous blonde wives, infiltrated by incredibly well-behaved blond children. They also own huge, modern fishing boats equipped with enough instrumentation to impress the crew of a space shuttle. Their investment must be staggering. I saw no boat that cost less than a million American dollars.

Fisherman Poul Svenstrop kindly offered to drive Jimmy Flett and me to the port of Ringkøbing, where he docked his boat, containing his sonar fish-detection records. Our purpose was to compare his wreck-site positions with ours. The forty-five-mile drive to Ringkøbing from Thyborøn was leisurely. Svenstrop, who spoke excellent English, swapped sea tales with Jimmy and questioned me about publishing books. I found that every self-respecting Dane writes stories and poems. During the dead of winter, it seems to be a national pastime.

After stepping aboard his boat, a floating factory as compared to the smaller trawlers I was familiar with along the East and West coasts of the United States, we studied our collective wreck positions. I pointed out two sites that he and his fellow fishermen had been unable to find and gave him confirmed positions, while he showed me three that I had missed. I was especially interested in the North Sea's midchannel between Ringkøbing and Hull, England. I showed him my estimated position of *U-21*. Svenstrop knew of two wrecks in the general area, but had no knowledge of their size or construction. He did say neither seemed very large.

Like most fishermen, Svenstrop was not interested in maritime history. He could point out the position of a shipwreck that he'd recorded on his exotic-fish-detecting gear, but he couldn't tell you its name, construction, or date of its sinking. He flat didn't care.

The ordeal began on the return trip to Thyborøn. No more congenial conversation during a leisurely journey. Svenstrop envisioned himself as a race-car driver who should have had a lifetime seat at a Grand Prix pit area. He flattened the accelerator of his Volvo station wagon until it almost touched the radiator. No matter that a cloudburst dropped a curtain of water that cut visibility to about a hundred feet.

Though never having owned a Volvo, I am quite aware of their outstanding roadholding abilities. But traveling at eighty-five miles an hour over a paved cowpath with no dividing line, barely wide enough for one car and even less for one coming from the other direction, and dodging a minefield of potholes while plunging through a downpour, goes far beyond mere reckless adventure.

Jimmy Flett, having faced the worst the sea and Germans could throw at him, sat in the front seat as rigid as a bronze sculpture. I lay in the back petrified, one hand clutching the door handle, praying my life insurance was paid up and my estate in the hands of a good attorney.

There were no fences along the road and local cows acted

as if they had the right-of-way. Svenstrop must have kept score. I saw notches on his steering wheel. I could have sworn the cows turned to vapor as we seemingly passed through them. Svenstrop laid on the horn and never deviated one inch as a Holstein loomed up in the windshield. I'd heard of playing chicken but never cow. When we finally pulled into Thyborøn, my hair had turned white. Jimmy headed straight to the galley for his favorite bottle of scotch.

I'll bet Jutland farmers found many a gallon of sour milk in their buckets that day.

The weather improved a bit and we headed out into the North Sea in search of the warships sunk during the great naval engagement off Jutland between the Royal British Navy and the German Imperial Navy in 1916. Our first target was the British battle cruiser H.M.S. *Invincible*. As mentioned earlier, we swept over the position marked on Admiralty charts and found her huge remains slightly over a mile from where she was supposed to be. Next came two German destroyers and H.M.S. *Defence,* a British battle cruiser that suffered a direct hit, which penetrated her powder magazine and blew out her bottom. Almost all of her crew of a thousand died with her. It took thirty-six hours before we found her massive, partially silted-over hulk. Except for jagged pieces of her wreckage protruding from the muck, she reads on the side scan as a huge mound.

The next phase of the project was to cross the North Sea to the fishing port of Bridlington on the Yorkshire coast, where we planned to meet up with NUMA president Wayne Gronquist. I then wanted to make a brief, third attempt to find John Paul Jones's *Bonhomme Richard*. During the crossing, we had only to make a short detour to the approximate position where Otto Hersing scuttled his beloved *U-21*. I laid out a nine-square-mile search grid and converted it to Jimmy's Loran charts.

At last, the time came to bid a fond farewell to the hospitality of our Danish friends and the thriving metropolis of Thyborøn and sail off into the sunset. With the Royal Yacht

Club ensign flying at the stern jack staff and the NUMA flag flapping at the mast, we tooted our air horn to the people of the town and headed out through the harbor jetties.

I might mention that NUMA does indeed have its own banner. Nothing jazzy, just an old sailing ship on a red-, white-, and blue-striped background with the word EUREKA. The flag has been flown on almost all our expeditions since 1978 and is beginning to look a bit faded and frayed.

Two hours out of Thyborøn, we ran into a violent Force 8 gale that beat the sea into a foaming cauldron, with waves ten to twelve feet high. I couldn't recall many roller-coaster rides that were worse than this one. Furniture, table settings, and assorted debris were soon strewn all over the main saloon. Below, my cabin looked as though a bomb had gone off. Nobody bothered to tidy up the boat.

There is no experience that can match standing in the wheelhouse of a sixty-four-foot boat as the bow dips into a trough, while you stare up at the crest of the next oncoming wave fifteen feet above you, then watch the wall of water surge over the boat in a frenzy of green water and white spray.

It looked odd to see the windshield wipers beating back and forth while submerged. What made the situation especially unsettling was the MAYDAY calls from some of the smaller fishing boats far out in the North Sea. Jimmy offered over the radio to turn the *Arvor* toward the stricken boats, but sea-rescue fleets from both Britain and Denmark, no strangers to the vicious whims of the North Sea, declined his assistance and replied that they had rescue ships on the way.

The automatic pilot went on strike along with the stabilizers that reduced the boat's roll. Poor Bill Shea took to his bunk for the next forty-eight hours, and never made an appearance until we docked. He was so sick that Colin and I struggled down the passageway every hour to his stateroom and checked to see if he was still among the living. We also made certain the sideboards were up on his berth to keep him from being pitched out onto the deck.

It seemed strange to hear a wind howl like banshees and see a rampaging sea under serene blue skies free of clouds. The sight was ugly and beautiful at the same time. Jimmy, John, and Colin spelled each other at the wheel during the night, while I sat on the bench in the wheelhouse behind the helmsman and gazed at the little red digital numbers on the Loran that blinked off the distance we had yet to travel before reaching Bridlington.

I felt little fear of whatever the North Sea forced on us. Knowing that my steadfast crew of Scotsmen had come through much worse weather, and the *Arvor III* was built like a concrete privy, I felt as secure as a toad under a waterfall. I even refrained from complaining about all the bruises I had received from being constantly thrown into objects much harder than my body.

Strange as it seems, I found it all exhilarating. Jane Pauley once asked me on the *Today Show* if I might have been a sea captain in a prior life. I answered, "I'd like to think so." Perhaps the genes were passed along by my ancestor Roger Hunnewell, a fisherman who was lost at sea in the middle 1600s off New York.

Colin, unable to cook, offered me a roast-beef sandwich, which I gratefully accepted. Then I tied myself to a chair mounted on the deck and promptly dozed off.

Though it doesn't seem logical, being pitched about during a storm at sea acts like a narcotic. You become incredibly drowsy and actually fall into a deep sleep while your head flops from side to side like a hand puppet with palsy. I was lucky in never becoming seasick. My practice is to take a couple of Dramamine pills the first day I step on a boat. After a day at sea my body adjusts and I never have to bother with medication again. I came very close to getting sick this trip, but it was more from the diesel fumes drifting through the cabins with the portholes closed than from the action of the waves.

By the time we reached *U-21*'s last reported position, the winds and seas had decreased by half. Hardly ideal conditions for a grid search, but I had come too far not to make the effort. Bill was still on his back, but Jimmy Flett was game. So we threw over the side scan sensor and began running search lanes in a rotten sea that showed no consideration.

For six hours we rolled and pitched before we found a wreck that produced a perfect likeness of a small freighter, but no submarine. I found a cassette tape in *Arvor*'s library of Franz Liszt and listened to the rousing strains of his *Second Hungarian Rhapsody* while the boat tumbled along at a breathtaking five knots.

The chair I used in front of the side scan recorder was not bolted to the deck. Jimmy turned to tell me that we had reached the end of one lane and he was coming around to start another. At that moment, we were hit broadside with a monstrous swell. My chair went over and I did a backflip, disappearing from Jimmy's view around a bulkhead. He sent John back to see how badly I was mangled.

Clutching a handrail for support, John stared down at me lying on the deck. "Did you strike your head?" he asked.

"No," I replied. "My eyes always cross like this when I'm under stress." After two minutes of massaging another four or five bruises and black-and-blue marks, I was back in business.

Settling behind the recorder, I saw that *U-21* had appeared as a tiny stain far off on our starboard side while I was flat on my back. Jimmy struggled to run four more passes right over the wreck. It was useless to lower the camera in a rotten, uncooperating sea. Dimensions on the sonar recording indicated an approximate match and the outline of a submarine.

Our navigation instruments put her at 54 14 30 by 04 02 50.

We found the only two ships in the area that Svenstrop positioned on his personal charts. There are no other wrecks on any chart within a radius of twenty miles. The U-boat lies slightly less than a mile east of the Admiralty, German, and Danish records. She was a nice little discovery. As far as historic firsts went, we now knew the grave sites of *Housatonic, Hunley,* H.M.S. *Pathfinder,* and *U-21,* and could go back to them at any time with little effort.

Much had been accomplished in less than a month, and we still had almost three weeks to go. Now it was on to the port of Cherbourg, France, to search for the famous Confederate raider *Alabama* and Belgian troop transport *Léopoldville*.

9
Part

The Troop Transport *Léopoldville*

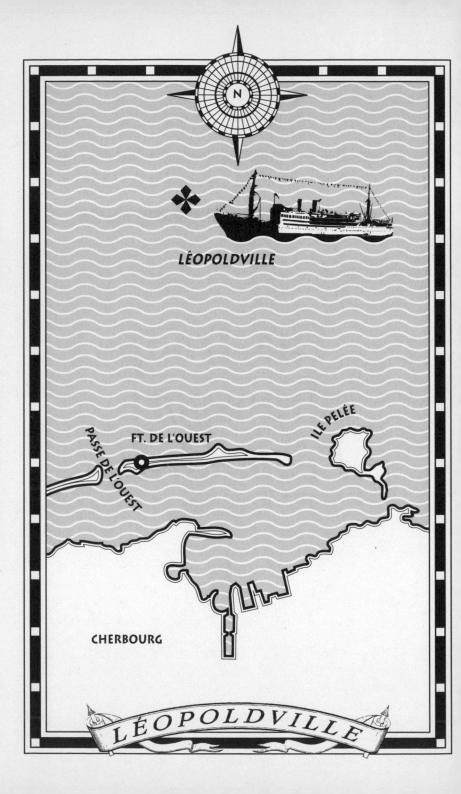

I

Silent Night, Deadly Night

Christmas Eve, 1944

A CHILL WIND AND A LIGHT SNOW BLEW ACROSS THE HAR-
bor in Southampton, England, December 23. Pier 38 seemed
as busy as a baseball stadium before the start of the World
Series. Shuffling slowly forward, more than two thousand
GIs of the United States Army's 66th Infantry Division,
known as the Black Panthers, milled about the pier, waiting
to board the troopship *Léopoldville*. Like a lethargic dis-
ease, a general lack of enthusiasm had infected the men.
World War II was six months past D-Day and winding down
to a conclusion, or so everyone thought.

The troops waiting to board believed the dirty job of
mopping up pockets of German resistance would be their
only legacy. In a war that had seen many great heroes, these
troops feared they would never have the chance to show
their courage.

Word spread about the German Army's launching a coun-
terattack referred to as the Battle of the Bulge, but few took
any stock in the rumor. Details were sketchy and vague. It
was a weak German thrust broken by Patton, some said. The
Krauts were already crushed, came a report from nowhere.

Merely a last gasp by the Germans, who were on the verge of surrender. They couldn't have been more wrong. The soldiers beginning to march up the gangways would have been astounded if they had known they were going into battle against a massive German assault that had shattered American forces in the Ardennes Forest.

Adding fuel to the malaise among the troops was their unexpected movement. The 66th Division had recently been billeted at a staging area near Dorchester. With no orders and little to do, they all looked forward to an enjoyable Christmas in their warm barracks. Presents were purchased in the nearby city to be passed around or sent home as gifts. Company cooks had carefully planned a feast with turkey and all the trimmings to be washed down with gallons of beer and an ancient British concoction called mead. A number of local girls were persuaded to attend. But promises of good cheer were dashed when they received orders to move out and take trains to Southampton. There they were to board a foreign troop transport, chartered by the British Navy.

Torn from their cozy billets so close to Christmas, the men of the 66th were now standing in the freezing air while hasty decisions were made about their future movements: 2,235 were about to board *Léopoldville,* while the rest of the division were loaded aboard the H.M.T. *Cheshire,* a British transport newer and in better shape than the Belgian liner. The division's trucks and heavy equipment were loaded onto LSTs for the trip across the English Channel to Cherbourg.

Earlier in the afternoon, two thousand paratroopers had been loaded aboard *Léopoldville,* and then told to disembark because they were on the wrong ship. No reason was offered for the mix-up. Knowing the army, most simply shrugged and never bothered to ask. It was an ominous sign none knew how to read.

The paratroopers did not know until later how lucky they were to celebrate Christmas Day.

The men of the 66th were finally cleared to board two hours after midnight of the 24th and didn't finish until eight in the morning. With the snarling black panther patches worn proudly on the sleeves of their olive-drab winter coats, the men trooped aboard *Léopoldville*. Disorganization was the order of the day. Because of the prior foul-up with the paratroopers, no berthing assignments were made for the men of the 66th in advance. They were hurriedly assigned compartments as they stepped onto the main deck. Units were broken up, dividing friends, splitting squads from their companies.

The confusion was a further omen of the tragedy to come.

Platoon Sergeant Robert Hesse of Heavy Weapons Platoon, Company D, 264th Regiment, dutifully followed instructions directing him and his buddies through an open hatch and down a steep wooden stairway into cargo holds that had been converted into cramped quarters for transporting troops. Seven crudely constructed wooden decks with low ceilings and bunks stacked four high now filled the cargo holds. The men were crammed together in dimly lit steel caverns like passengers on a New York subway during peak rush hour. Ventilation was far from adequate. The air soon became warm and stale, the smell of perspiration adding to the stuffy atmosphere.

Twenty-year-old Hesse from Roselle, New York, thankfully dropped his pack, duffel bag, and rifle onto the crowded deck and removed his helmet. "So this is home for Christmas," he muttered to no one in particular.

Captain Charles Limbor stared through the wheelhouse window at the mass of humanity climbing his ship's gangway in the bitter cold and observed the disorder silently. Shifting legs that were beset with poor circulation and at times most painful, he tried to find a comfortable position. Born and raised in Belgium, he had been employed by the Belgian Lines for nearly twenty-five years. Limbor stood slightly under six feet tall. His skin was naturally tanned, unusual for someone Flemish. Genes, he often mused, from some forgotten ancestor in the Belgian Congo in Africa. His hair was gray, silver at the temples, and his eyes brown. At age forty-six, he was withdrawn and quiet and kept to himself. Those officers who had sailed with him on numerous voyages found him difficult to approach, but they all considered him a competent seaman.

His actions twelve hours later would be completely out of character.

He studied a message from his radio operator and turned to his Chief Officer, Robert de Pierpont. "We'll be accompanied by the British troopship *Cheshire* and a small fleet of American landing craft."

"And our escorts?" asked de Pierpont.

"One French and three British destroyers."

"I hope they notified the Germans there will be no trespassing."

"No sign of the Luftwaffe since D-Day," Limbor said, sighing. "And the German E-type torpedo boats only make hit-and-run strikes two hundred miles north of here."

"There still could be U-boats lurking about," said de Pierpont.

Limbor shrugged indifferently. "Not with so many Allied warships guarding the Channel and the skies filled with subhunting aircraft. Most of the U-boats are out in the Atlantic chasing convoys. I doubt if any are operating in this area."

Although she had undergone a complete refitting only eight months before, to the American troops boarding *Léopoldville* she looked tired, old, rundown, and dirty. Built in Hoboken, New Jersey, in 1929 by John Cockerill & Sons, she went into service for the Royal Belgian Lloyd Lines, transporting cargo and passengers from the Belgian Congo and other ports in Africa to her home harbor of Antwerp, Belgium. After the war broke out, she was refitted in Liverpool from passenger liner to troop transport. During the next four years, she carried mostly British troops to and from the Mediterranean. After the invasion of France, she made twenty-four crossings from England to the beaches of Normandy, landing over 53,000 men. Until her final voyage,

Léopoldville transported 124,240 soldiers safely through dangerous waters to their destinations.

Léopoldville was rated at 11,500 tons, with a length of 479 feet and a 62-foot beam. Her engines could push her through the water at a maximum speed of 17 knots. She carried 14 lifeboats, with a capacity of 797 persons; 4 large rafts; 156 Carley floats; and 3,250 life preservers. She was armed with 10 Bofors guns, one 3-inch bow gun, a 4-inch stern gun, and one 3-pounder antiaircraft gun. The crew numbered 120 Belgians, 93 Congolese, and a British contingent of 34 officers and men, who manned the guns and supervised the troop loading and landing.

Because of the Christmas holiday, many of the British crew were on leave and didn't make it back to the ship in time for the boarding. As a consequence, no one checked off the units of the 66th Panthers as they trudged on board.

Twin lines of soldiers curled around the docks to the gangways of both *Léopoldville* and *Cheshire,* like tentacles from beasts that lived within the ships' hulls. During the disorganized loading procedure, several infantry companies of the 66th were mistakenly sent aboard *Cheshire.* Medical detachments assigned to *Léopoldville* found their bandages and medicines loaded onto the wrong ship. Company clerks were frustrated in keeping track of the men who were on one ship while their records went on the other. By a lucky stroke, one company of foot soldiers, lingering at the coffee and doughnut tables, missed their call to board *Léopoldville.* By the time they regrouped, they were ordered onto *Cheshire.*

Amid the chaos and foul-ups, the morning broke on Christmas Eve.

By 9 A.M., the transports were finally loaded and ready for the short voyage across the Channel. The troops nestled down in their packed compartments. Most tried to sleep, stomachs grumbling as the soldiers thought wistfully of a breakfast that was never served.

Slipping the pier, *Léopoldville* steamed from Southampton Harbor. In her wake, *Cheshire* followed like an obedient hound. Both ships were fully loaded. All told, nearly 4,500 troops set out that day for the nine-hour Channel crossing.

Just past the breakwater, the harbor pilot was taken off the lead ship. Passing over the antisubmarine nets, the troop transports entered the Channel. Steaming through the watery expanse separating the mainland and the Isle of Wight, *Léopoldville* and her convoy met the destroyer escorts. H.M.S. *Brilliant, Anthony,* and *Hotham,* along with the Free French frigate *Croix de Lorraine,* took up defensive stations around the troopships. It was business as usual.

At 2 P.M. the order was radioed from *Brilliant* for the transports to commence a zigzag course. Oddly, with so many Channel crossings under her hull, this was the first time *Léopoldville* had been ordered to perform the maneuver. The British gunners were poised at their stations. The officers made a brief inspection of the ship as it was under way. Everything appeared secure. Nothing was overlooked, nothing that is except a lifeboat drill. Each unit was verbally assigned to an assembly area on deck, but few knew exactly where to go. Life belts were scattered in stowage compartments and none were issued.

The first submarine alert came at half past two. The ASDIC system aboard *Brilliant* detected an underwater object. Raising a black flag to signal the troopships, the destroyers set off to drop depth charges. Fifteen minutes later, the drill was over. It was written off as a false alarm. But there was to be no relief. A short time later, another contact was made. Once again the destroyers sprinted ahead of the convoy and dropped depth charges. Whether they found a U-boat or not was never determined.

By the time the second submarine alert had ended, the sea was becoming nasty. Waves were running eight to nine feet from crest to trough and the men inside the ships began to suffer. Many became seasick and rushed for the heads. Others vomited where they were at the time. They cringed at seeing rats scurry about that looked as big as cats. The Belgian crew made an attempt to feed the uncomfortable troops, but those who were not sick found the food inedible.

Some ate from the boxes of C-rations they had brought with them in their packs.

The air inside *Léopoldville* rapidly became foul, tainted by sickness and bad food. Diesel fuel reeked everywhere, adding an unwelcome contaminant to the air. The throbbing of the engines and thumping of the propellers could easily be felt by those leaning against the cold steel of the hull. Most men sat on their duffel bags or tried to get some rest in the hammocks. They pulled blankets over their overcoats to keep warm. Only a few engaged in conversation or played cards. None jokingly griped as they did on most crossings.

Spray whipped across the bridge wings of *Léopoldville* as the next watch filtered up and took their stations. Along with the navigator, helmsman, and the rest of the wheelhouse crew, the captain was due to be relieved. Instead, Limbor remained on the bridge, as he usually had during Channel crossings since D-Day.

Seven hours into the voyage, the wind and sea around the convoy grew to Force 6. The 2,235 men on *Léopoldville* were now only twenty-five miles north and slightly east of Cherbourg.

Over one-third of them had less than two hours to live.

Although Germany was still building U-boats fast and furiously in the winter of 1944–45, the Allies were sinking them as fast as they left the dock. Oberleutnant Gerhard Meyer did not doubt that his days were numbered. Commander Meyer's *U-486* was one of very few submarines lurking in and around the English Channel. Dropping to the bottom by day and rising only at night, *U-486* was constantly harried by hordes of destroyers and subhunting aircraft.

Completed nine months before *Léopoldville* began her fateful voyage, *U-486* was the latest in German underwater design. The Type VII C-class submarine was equipped with a folding snorkel to allow the boat to remain under the surface for extended periods. No longer did the submarine have to show herself to charge batteries. The snorkel vented the diesel engines and she could now cruise at forty-eight feet, her periscope depth, for days on end.

Having made the long trip from his base in Norway, Meyer would have preferred to be anywhere but in the cold waters off the coast of Normandy this Christmas Eve as he peered through his periscope. The time was 5:45 in the evening. It was dark with a lingering light reflecting on the clouds to the west. The sea was choppy, goaded by a brisk gale.

Folding down the etched steel hand controls, Meyer rested his forehead against the eyepiece and stared into the lenses of the periscope. The sky was a gray tempest. Tufts of clouds, their shapes constantly changing, reflected the dying light of the sun. Curtains of sleet, riding the winds of the coming storm, raced over the water, then changed direction as if on a whim. The tempestuous sea rolled over the exposed tip of the periscope.

Rotating the shaft, Meyer looked toward shore, five miles away. Inside the protected harbor of Cherbourg, the lights of the town flickered in the gathering night. He swung the viewer back to the open sea, peering through the gloom toward England. And then he saw something.

He made out the outlines of two large ships and a pair of destroyers. There were also several other vessels, smaller ones he took for the American LST landing craft. The shot had to be quick and neat, no chance for a second attempt. Meyer had a healthy respect for the destroyers, which he knew would be all over the *U-486* within a minute after the torpedo launch.

"Ready tubes one and two," he ordered quietly.

At 5:56 P.M., Meyer ranged on the largest ship in the convoy. The bow of the submarine moved almost imperceptibly as Meyer lined up the shot. Then he gave the order to fire. "Down periscope and dive!" he shouted. "Quickly, quickly! Full speed toward the coast to throw off the dogs!"

Meyer did not wait around to observe the destruction of lives caused by his torpedoes. All he knew for certain was that one had missed, but he was pleased when he heard the muffled explosion of the one that struck home.

"We hit her," he announced to his crew, who burst out in cheers.

A member of the British contingent on board *Léopoldville* was acting as a lookout in the crow's nest on the aft mast. At six o'clock on the nose, he shouted down to the crew manning the four-inch stern gun. "Hey, mates, I just saw the bubbles from a torpedo!"

"Are you sure?" yelled back a young lieutenant.

"I saw the bubbles."

"Keep a sharp eye—"

"Another one, another one!" the lookout cut him off. "Torpedo to starboard!"

Deep in the bowels of the ship, most of the soldiers were asleep when the torpedo slammed into number-four hold starboard aft. Rivets burst and flew like rifle bullets. Hundreds died without knowing what struck them. Observers on deck swore they saw parts of bodies hurled high in the air.

Nearly all the men assigned to compartments G-4 and F-4 were never seen again.

Compartment G-4 was occupied by 185 troops. Immediately above in compartment F-4, 170 soldiers were sleeping in their hammocks. The steel girders supporting the bulkheads buckled. Deck F collapsed into Deck G, taking the stairways with them and preventing escape. Cries of pain and panic were quickly snuffed out by the tremendous surge of water into the hull. Hundreds were engulfed by the sea and sudden darkness. Estimates placed those who died instantly at 315. Fewer than twenty men made it to the decks above. One, a nonswimmer, was swept out through the hole made by the torpedo and was pulled back aboard from an outside deck by men who spotted him.

Walter Blunt of L Company heard the screams and muffled cries only after his head broke from the water. The swirling debris reeked of oil and gunpowder. He found himself wedged in a hole in the deck above. His head and shoulders protruded into the upper compartment, but he was wedged tight and couldn't struggle free. Waves washed over him as the ship began to sink beneath him, the dirty water rising higher and higher and causing him to hold his breath until he nearly passed out. He was thinking, This is a hell of a way to die, when a light beamed on his face, and his company commander, Captain Orr, leaned over him.

"Give me your hand, son. You'll be all right."

Blunt was pulled free and helped to the outside deck, where he was placed in the only lifeboat carrying wounded GIs who had survived the explosion. Out of Blunt's 181-man unit, 74 were killed and 61 injured.

Walter Brown of Company F owed his life to being sea-sick. Feeling the effects of the rough seas, he left his compartment and climbed to a head near the outer deck, where he planned to throw up. He had no sooner walked up to a sink than the torpedo hit. Knocked unconscious, he awoke to find water spraying on him from broken overhead pipes. He saved himself by leaping onto the deck of a small ship that came alongside as *Léopoldville* began her slide to the bottom. He was the last man to escape the ship without jumping into the water.

Only Brown and five others survived from Company F. One hundred fifty-three went down with the ship.

Staff Sergeant Jerry Crean, Company B, was playing cards when he felt the impact and the ship suddenly slow to a stop. Receiving no instructions, Crean gathered the twelve men of his platoon and led them up to the open decks. He made sure they stuck together while he returned with enough life jackets to outfit them all. At seven o'clock, an hour after the *U-486* sent her torpedo into *Léopoldville,* Crean was told help was on the way. Rescue vessels and tugs were reported to be coming from the nearby harbor to tow them in. But as the ship rolled on a ten-degree list, he realized for the first time that "this damn thing is going to sink."

Finally, when the "Abandon ship" order was announced, if it was announced, it came in either Flemish or French and went untranslated. If the American officers in command had known earlier on the ship was sinking, many more lives could have been saved.

Several of *Léopoldville*'s officers worked hard to save the ship and maintain order, but the sudden and unexpected disaster overwhelmed them. The Congolese crew wasted little time in collecting their personal effects and heading for the lifeboats. The ship's physician, Dr. Nestor Herrent, offered his services to the ship's British physician, Major Mumby, and doctors of the 66th Division. His two nurses had already abandoned him, departing in the first lifeboats to leave. The medical men all worked together to care for the growing tide of wounded men brought to the infirmary.

On the bridge, Captain Charles Limbor appeared overly calm. Some described him as being in a state of shock. He did not seem to have comprehended the enormity of the situation. Slowly, he struggled to regain a sense of control as it became apparent the ship was in danger of sinking. He never quite made it.

Informed that water was rapidly rising in the engine room, he ordered the engines shut down. Believing that tugs were on their way to tow *Léopoldville* to shore, he ordered the anchor dropped to keep the ship from drifting with the tide. It was an error in judgment that was compounded by a thousand other mistakes that fateful night.

Confusion was mixed with calmness as uninjured soldiers of the Panther Division either stood in formation on the open deck waiting for orders or simply milled around, puzzled about what to do. All they were told was to wait or make way for the crew.

They watched in amusement that soon turned to outright rage as the Congolese crew struggled to lower the lifeboats. There was some cheering as the troops thought the boats were being prepared for them. But then it became apparent the crew were abandoning the ship on their own. One or more boats tipped and spilled the crew into the sea. None of the Congolese made any attempt to rescue their passengers. They soon rowed off, carrying luggage, radios, personal belongings, even a parrot in a cage, leaving no one on the ship who knew how to lower the remaining lifeboats and rafts. The soldiers also swore that officers wearing coats with gold braid rowed away with the crew. It was generally agreed that the crew took several boats when one would have been sufficient for their small number.

Several soldiers were killed or injured in trying to free the boats from their mountings and davits. Many attempted to cut away the ropes holding the many rafts, but did not have knives. The soldiers actually managed to launch a boat, but it was quickly filled by the *Léopoldville*'s crew while the Americans stood by in disbelief.

Throughout the debacle, Captain Limbor did or said nothing. Normally a strict disciplinarian, he stood mute without making the slightest attempt to display command. Fifty years later, survivors still curse Limbor and his Belgian and Congolese crew.

Sergeant Gino Berarducci of Company I was ordered into a lifeboat by a British officer. He believes it was the only boat that left *Léopoldville* with uninjured American soldiers on board.

A report fifteen years later by the U.S. Inspector General stated, "There was little doubt that the crew of *Léopoldville* was negligent in performance of their duties. They were not at their posts instructing passengers, reporting condition of the ship, and launching lifeboats. They seemed interested only in themselves."

Bewilderment seemed to strike the minds of the other ship captains. While the British destroyers rushed about dropping depth charges, the troopship *Cheshire* stood by for nearly an hour less than two hundred yards away from *Léopoldville*. The men on board *Cheshire* thought they heard a muffled explosion in the distance, and then it appeared to them that the other troopship was beginning to list. Their ship's officers did not comprehend the horrendous debacle that was taking place before their eyes. They did not have a clue to the growing crisis. They could only stand and stare through the darkness at the stricken ship until *Cheshire* finally turned away and headed into Cherbourg. Soon *Léopoldville* was lost in the darkness, and their attention turned to the lights of the harbor.

* * *

Only five miles from land, *Léopoldville* still had a chance of being beached if the tow ships arrived soon. But word was not getting through. Everyone was celebrating Christmas Eve, and very few personnel were on duty. All potential rescue boats sat idle, their crews on leave. The town bars and restaurants were filled with revelers. Flickering lights and festive decorations framed the shop windows as both the military and civilian residents celebrated the last Christmas of the great war. They had no way of knowing a life-and-death struggle was taking place just off shore.

Thirty minutes passed before Convoy Commander John Pringle, captain of H.M.S. *Brilliant,* signaled Cherbourg, *"Taking off survivors. Need assistance."*

By waiting too long to give the order to abandon ship, Limbor had sentenced the ship to become a war tomb.

The officers at the harbor-entrance control post were startled at the unexpected request. *"Survivors of what?"* they inquired.

"Léopoldville hit. Need assistance."

No message came from *Léopoldville* at all.

On shore, military bureaucracy reigned supreme. Messages were sent, received, and passed on. Orders were given but not relayed. High-ranking officers enjoying Yule parties could not be bothered. Finally, men of decision began to take responsibility for the rescue operation—men like Lieutenant Colonel Tom McConnell at Fort L'Ouest at the harbor entrance.

McConnell was a successful Indiana businessman before the war and minced no words in describing the situation to his superiors. He turned the phone lines blue with descriptive language, demanding, pleading, castigating sergeants and generals alike in an attempt to get a rescue operation under way. In no uncertain terms, he notified the general in command of the port that he was taking it on his own authority to send out rescue vessels. By the time McConnell's efforts had sent army rescue tugs on their way to the sinking ship, fifty minutes had passed.

Ensign Natt Divoll, the navy duty officer at Fort L'Ouest, wasn't having much better luck until he connected with

Lieutenant Commander Richard Davis. When Divoll's call came from the fort, Davis didn't merely cut through red tape, he shredded it. Less than five minutes after being notified of *Léopoldville*'s situation, Davis had two PT-boats racing toward the stricken ship. Two minutes later, a third left port. He then sent officers into town to pull sailors and soldiers from the bars. Shortly after 7 P.M., Davis had Cherbourg started toward mobilization.

Minutes later, the first lifeboats carrying Congolese crewmen arrived at the docks and were questioned. Hospitals were notified, food and beds arranged. The rescue was at last being coordinated.

The people on shore began to realize a disaster was in the making, but the soldiers on board *Léopoldville* still hadn't been warned that the ship was slipping away beneath their feet.

In a precise display of skilled seamanship, Commander Pringle took the bull by the horns and brought his destroyer alongside *Léopoldville*. Only thirty-nine years old, Pringle had spent twenty-two of them at sea. As his ship approached, Pringle's crew threw out mooring lines. With no Belgian crew to catch them, the British destroyer was finally secured alongside by soldiers, the ship's British gunners, and sailors from *Brilliant,* who leaped aboard *Léopoldville*.

The high seas pounded the much smaller hull against the larger one. Steel plates buckled and groaned in protest as they scraped together. The sounds were ominous, and Pringle realized he could not remain tethered to the troopship for very long. Still, the look of apprehension in the soldiers' faces was enough to repel any thoughts he might have of backing away quickly.

He would keep the two ships together for as long as possible before *Brilliant* was battered to scrap. Soon shouts came from his men to the soldiers.

"Jump, Yank, jump!"

The evacuation was without focus. No officers were directing the movement, and the job of organizing fell to the sergeants and NCOs. As the ship continued its list, the troops realized that the chance of *Léopoldville*'s remaining afloat was diminishing with every minute. Those still below-decks were directed topside. They huddled on the open decks, exposed to the frigid wind, overcoats tightly buttoned. Most still carried rifles, packs, and helmets.

The cold, dark night, the violent sea, the waves plunging and thrusting the little destroyer up and down like a toy boat, made the leap a terrifying undertaking for the young men crowded on the decks of the troopship. It was made all the more appalling by the men who mistimed their jump and missed the destroyer, falling into the water between the two ships before being crushed to death as the surge drove steel plates against steel plates.

By 7:20 H.M.S. *Brilliant* had managed to take aboard almost seven hundred soldiers of the 66th. The other destroyers of the convoy, *Hotham, Anthony,* and *Croix de Lorraine* had given up the hunt for the U-boat and headed for port. With no damage reports coming from *Léopoldville,* they were still unaware the troopship was in danger of sinking.

Pringle was growing more concerned for his ship. The constant impact caused by the turbulent sea had loosened the steel plates of *Brilliant*'s hull. From belowdecks, his engineering officer reported the pumps were keeping up with the sudden flood of water but the flow was increasing. His radioman reported that he picked up signals from PT-boats and rescue tugs that were rushing to the scene.

"Sever the lines holding us to *Léo!*" Pringle shouted to the officer directing the evacuation below on the open deck.

Bob Hesse, the platoon sergeant from New York, along with a handful of his men, edged across the forward part of the ship until they reached the anchor chain on the forecastle. Someone from the British destroyer yelled at them.

"We're cutting off, Yanks! You'd better jump now! It will be your last chance!"

To Hesse it looked as if two-thirds of *Léopoldville* was already underwater. The bow had risen until they thought they were in the clouds. Hesse looked at his men, including Alex Yarmosh, Ed Riley, and Dick Dutka, and said, "Let's go. Every man for himself."

They all stood on the railing, waiting for *Brilliant* to rise within jumping distance for what was perhaps the last time. As the smaller ship lifted on the next wave, they jumped together, all six of them. Every man landed safely. To Hesse, it seemed like he was leaping off the Empire State Building.

British sailors, armed with axes, cut away the lines and *Brilliant* backed away from *Léopoldville*. Commander Pringle planned to head for Cherbourg and disembark the survivors he had saved before returning for another evacuation. He did not believe that *Léopoldville* would be on the bottom of the English Channel before he could leave the dock.

The big rescue tug *ATR-3* arrived and pulled along the opposite side of the doomed troopship. Skipper Stanley Lewandowski was cussing up a storm at the waves already closing over the stern of *Léopoldville*. He was damned mad.

Twice he had attempted to maneuver alongside before the ship sank, but was stopped by the davits of the lifeboats that hung out and down. Had the Belgian crew remained a few minutes more and loaded the lifeboats properly, the davits would have been retracted and Lewandowski could have pulled his boat abreast of the railing.

His radioman, Seaman First Class Hugh Jones, tried to contact the *Léopoldville,* but received no reply. Lewandowski had been equally frustrated by a group of two hundred men standing at attention on the bow. Entreaties for them to jump aboard went ignored. Later, as he pulled them from the water, he was told an officer wouldn't allow them to jump. Now the Belgian ship was disappearing before his eyes.

"Pull them poor kids aboard!" he shouted to his crew as he clutched the spokes of the helm and threaded his massive tug into the sea of heads floating in the wreckage. Three of his crew jumped overboard to help heave exhausted and freezing soldiers onto the deck of the tug.

There were many heroes that night who gave their lives saving others. One was Colonel Ira Rumburg, whose widow did not know how her husband died until Staff Sergeant Jerry Crean told her fifty years later.

Rumburg, a huge man at six feet eight inches, who weighed in at 250 pounds, had fastened himself to a rope. For over an hour as the ship slowly sank, he was lowered into the hold again and again, coming up with one man under each arm every time. Crean believed the colonel made over ten trips before *Léopoldville* slipped stern first to the bottom, taking Rumburg with her.

Captain Hal Crain died as a legend. Struggling through the oily water in the darkness deep within the demolished holds, Crain saved man after man, diving into flooded compartments, pulling out the half-drowned and the injured. Dozens of men gave credit to the officer for rescuing them. Hal Crain did not live to be thanked by those he saved. His posthumous Soldier's Medal was awarded to his widow and baby son.

Crean was also awarded a Soldier's Medal for his work in saving lives that night. Leading a dozen of his men down a rope ladder, he struggled for two hours, swimming around keeping everyone together. He found duffel bags and debris in the water and made his men hold on to anything that could float. He has never forgotten the few who simply gave up and drifted away into the darkness.

PFC Steve Lester of K Company sacrificed his own life to save four others who were trapped around him in the glass-enclosed area on the deck as the ship sank. He smashed the windows with his hands and lifted his buddies through the shattered openings. The last to go, he didn't make it. The Soldier's Medal was awarded posthumously to his wife and three small children.

British Gun Layer Bill Dowling helped pull men trapped below through a hatchway. Those who were injured were carried to the infirmary by Dowling and his mates.

Sergeant Albert Montagna had the distinction of helping both Rumburg and Crain bring a score of men out of the hell below before he found himself floating in the icy water beside the ship.

In the infirmary, the doctors and medics remained working over the injured. Stretcher cases were carried out and laid on the deck. A few were lowered onto the *Brilliant.* Many were literally thrown onto the decks of tugs and a Coast Guard corvette. A few stretcher cases were washed off the deck as the ship began her plunge to the bottom. They sank like stones, with their occupants helplessly strapped aboard.

The heroism of those who went down into the stricken hold to pull up the wounded, the stories of those who leaped into the water and were rescued by the efforts of men on the rescue vessels can never be forgotten by soldiers of the 66th who still live.

Except for their heroic efforts in saving the injured and those trapped below, none of the officers made a command decision. They were untrained for such a disaster and were as lost and helpless as their men. And yet the conduct of the troops on board *Léopoldville* for the two hours prior to its sinking went down in military annals as one of the finest examples of discipline ever observed. All stood in blind obedience awaiting orders that never came.

A deep rumbling sound came from within the hull of *Léopoldville* as the cold water reached and burst her boilers. Creaking and groaning, the bow lifted in the air and began a downward spiral as the ship began her final journey to the seabed. Bodies were seen to fall like leaves from her open decks. At 8:30 P.M., with a mighty hiss of escaping steam, the troopship vanished under the black water stern first and was seen no more.

It was estimated that over a thousand men were left floating in water with temperatures as low as 48 degrees F. Many were sucked down with the *Léopoldville,* including Captain Limbor, whose body was never found. Only now did panic set in as the men struggled to stay alive in the frigid water. Men who couldn't swim seized those who could and dragged them under.

It was as if a crowd at a football game gave out a great roar. Hundreds of men were shouting, crying, begging for help from God. Many pleaded for their mothers. Some cursed anyone and everyone responsible for their plight. A great number simply gave up and died by drowning or from exposure. Those who survived the horrible ordeal relived it for many years through their nightmares.

Vince Codianni of Company K was one of several men who were trapped under a glass passengers' shelter as the ship lurched to port and began her plunge. Codianni was pulled under when his clothing caught on part of the glass shelter. A strong swimmer, he struggled free and gained the surface, but not without injury. His front teeth had been knocked out, his tongue slit in two, and his neck and arms badly gashed by shattered glass.

Incredibly, Codianni survived two hours in the frigid water, his clothes frozen to his body, listening to cries of help before they finally faded into the night. He was found and pulled from the sea more dead than alive by a French tug.

Private Edwin Phillips, Headquarters Company, was pulled from the water and laid on the deck of a navy minesweeper. Thinking he was dead, a crewman gave him a nudge with his foot. "You can't be alive," he said.

"I am too," Ed murmured softly.

"That's good," said the crewman. "We're not supposed to pick up dead bodies."

Phillips went on to live a long and healthy life.

The crews of the tugboats, Coast Guard corvettes, and French fishing boats worked like madmen to pick up the mass of men fighting cold and waves and death. Hypothermia came quickly to those who didn't drown. Cold and exhaustion sapped their strength along with the heavy waterlogged overcoats and boots most of them had failed to cast off. Tired and numb to the point of unconsciousness, few had the strength to climb aboard the rescue craft on their own. Almost all were saved by sailors and fishermen who hoisted the half-dead soldiers over their boats' sides or jumped in the water to help them.

Lewandowski kept his tug on station. His men took on seventy survivors before the cries in the night faded and he reluctantly turned his boat back to the harbor. The first boats to arrive in Cherbourg with survivors carried a few of the dead. The boats that returned later carried many more. As time went on, fewer and fewer of those picked out of the water were still alive, while the number of dead grew in staggering numbers.

On reaching the docks, a great number of the 66th's survivors were left to fend for themselves. Some were placed in tent cities or any barracks or building that offered shelter from the cold night. Hundreds, suffering from exposure and shock, were taken to hospitals. The dead were laid in rows along the dock. Medics went from body to body, checking to see if any were still among the living. They were accompanied by a priest who checked the dead's dogtags and gave last rites to the Catholics amid the dead.

Of *Léopoldville*'s crew, Captain Limbor was the only officer to lose his life. The ship's carpenter and three Congolese also died. Because the Admiralty still refuses to divulge information on the sinking, any loss among the ship's British contingent is unknown. The 66th Panther Division was decimated. Over 1,400 men were rescued. Approximately 300 died in the blast from the torpedo, while 500 died later in the water. The official death toll stands at 802.

It was a tragedy compounded by fate, miscalculation, blunders, and ignorance. If the evacuation of the ship had been carried out properly, hundreds of families would not have received telegrams notifying them of the loss of their loved ones.

The official investigations were varied but limited. Those back home were told only that their sons or husbands had died or were missing in action. Few ever became aware of the real truth behind their loss. *Léopoldville* was swept under the carpet and the sinking buried in official files.

Except for those brought back for interment in the United States, the men whose bodies were recovered lie buried in the Omaha Beach Cemetery in Normandy. Inside the cemetery you will find a ceremonial colonnade called the Garden of the Missing which honors 1,557 American GIs whose bodies were never recovered. At the rear, engraved on the wall, you will find the names of the missing men who still lie at the bottom of the English Channel with the *Léopoldville*.

There are two endings to the tragedy the survivors of the *Léopoldville* would like to see before they join the hallowed ranks of their buddies, who passed on ahead. One is a monument at Arlington National Cemetery, honoring the 800 who died with the ship. The second is a postage stamp dedicated to their memory.

Is it asking too much for our government to acknowledge their sacrifice?

The submarine that set the stage for the terrible tragedy, the *U-486*, was herself sunk by the British submarine *Tapir* four months later. Oberleutnant Gerhard Meyer and his entire crew perished.

Only the battleship *Arizona*, sunk during the Japanese attack on Pearl Harbor, lost more men than *Léopoldville*. The troop transport was closely followed by the ill-starred cruiser *Indianapolis*, whose death toll came to 783.

II

Curses, Foiled Again

July 1984

SOMETIMES IT IS HARD TO SEPARATE REALITY FROM COMIC relief. Despite the best-laid plans of mice and Cussler, the second phase of the '84 North Sea Expedition developed and ended like a comic opera produced and staged by inmates from a mental institution. If I'd known the fiasco the NUMA crew of *Arvor III* was about to encounter in Cherbourg, I'd have ordered Jimmy Flett to keep right on going and steer a course for the harbor at Monte Carlo.

After finding and surveying *U-21*, we reached Bridlington, England, on a level sea under a bright blue sky—one of the few times I'd seen Bridlington without a cloud in sight. On my earlier visits during the *Bonhomme Richard* search projects, it rained incessantly. A working-class resort town, filled with gaudy casinos and amusement centers, Bridlington is clean, the people friendly. The homes along the side streets in the old section of town exude a rustic Edwardian charm.

I've seen entire families strolling along the beach promenade through a torrential downpour, with matching rain slickers on mum and dad as well as the children, including babies in strollers and the family dog. They were going to enjoy their vacation, by God, come rain, sleet, or fog. Considering England's too frequently dismal weather, I've always been amazed by the humorous disposition of the Brits. Unlike residents of Seattle, who sit under bright lights during ninety straight days of gray skies to keep from falling into fits of depression, the English, Scots, and Welsh endure with a grin and remain incredibly cheery.

Arvor III probed her bow into the small man-made harbor at Bridlington and settled her wide beam against the south quay. Bill Shea, several pounds lighter, rose from the dead and stared through the door at the serene harbor and fishing boats moored to the docks.

"I knew it, I knew it," he said, shading his eyes from the sun. "I've died and been sentenced to spend eternity in Bridlington for my sins."

"At least it isn't raining," I replied.

"Give it another five minutes." Bill looked at me with a *you poor fool* look. "Don't you know that at the instant of death you always pass through a tunnel into a bright light?"

What could I say? Bill's theory was flushed down the drain after we experienced clear skies for the next four days.

We took advantage of the good weather and calm seas by spending a couple of days searching a grid area marked by a pair of psychics for the remains of the *Bonhomme Richard.* The record of our magic department remained unbroken. Five straight strikeouts. Nothing of interest was seen. The seabed was as clean as a toilet bowl at grandmother's house.

Bill and I welcomed an invitation by Manny and Margaret Thompson of Bridlington, our good friends and supporters during the *Bonney Dick* search projects. Splendid people with a pair of broad-shouldered sons, Manny and Margaret own and operate amusement centers that are popular in Britain. After three weeks aboard *Arvor III,* we thought their lovely home looked to us like a five-star hotel, solidly planted in the ground with no inclination to pitch and roll. We had to clutch our bed headboards the first night while our internal workings acclimated to a stable position.

I called home and wished my wife, Barbara, a happy

birthday. I do believe it was the only time in forty-one years I missed being with her for the occasion.

Margaret Thompson is one of the loveliest women in the whole of Yorkshire. She stands out among the other ladies of the coastal towns, and Manny is as generous and helpful as a saint. Well, maybe he's not quite ready to be canonized, but he's still one hell of a great guy. During the earlier *Bonhomme Richard* expeditions, our crew made jokes about the local girls, especially those over the age of twenty-five, who they swore took ugly pills. In all fairness, the women married early, usually fishermen, and went downhill. They were attractive in their teens but seemed to lose any interest in appearance once they bore children. The running joke was that Yorkshire held a beauty contest and nobody came. The crew then held their own contest. A bottle of fine scotch to the man who found and had his picture taken with the prettiest lady in all the Yorkshire counties over the age of twenty-five. Margaret was eliminated because she was born and raised outside the area before Manny married her.

I won the contest. While returning to *Arvor III* one morning after buying a nautical chart of the coast, I was stopped on the pier by a photographer who was taking photos of people passing by with girls dressed up like Miss Piggy. I promptly paid him for the privilege, and as soon as the pictures were developed, I claimed the scotch. Surprisingly, none of the other guys protested.

A friend of the Thompsons gave Bill and me a tour through a Russian automobile distributorship. The cars were basically Fiats, manufactured just outside Moscow. I built better soapbox derby racers when I was a kid. Next to these heaps, Yugos looked like Bentleys. None of the paint matched on the doors, the upholstery was patched together like a quilt, and the engine looked like a power unit out of a scrapped snowblower. I do believe Ronald Reagan studied one of these cars and came up with his scheme to break the Soviet Union by bluffing them into a technology race.

On the day we were to depart for Cherbourg and begin the search for *Alabama* and *Léopoldville,* Wayne Gronquist, who was supposed to arrive from Austin, Texas, failed to show up at the dock. We waited nearly an hour and still no Wayne. The tide, which rose and fell as much as ten feet and often left *Arvor III* lying in the mud, was dropping rapidly. Jimmy informed me that if we didn't leave within the next few minutes we would become a fixture at the quay for the next twelve hours.

Demonstrating my talent for command decisions, I said to Jimmy, "You're the skipper. When you say we go, we go."

Jimmy clanged the engine-room bell and started the diesels as Colin and Bill cast off the mooring lines. Just as in the movies, here comes Wayne running madly across the quay. Jimmy shifted the engines into drive and never looked back. Bill and I were cheering and urging Wayne to run faster. He made amazingly good time considering he was carrying a huge tote bag.

I do believe Wayne set some sort of broad-jump record that day. He sprang off the quay, tote bag and all, barely landing on the deck of *Arvor III* in the arms of Bill and me. "Why in hell were you late?" I demanded. "You knew we had to beat the tide or lose another day."

"Sorry," Wayne answered like a chastened collie. "I was buying a camera."

"You could have done that before you left Texas."

"I thought I could buy one cheaper here."

Bill stared at the camera slung around Wayne's shoulder. "You figured you could buy a Japanese camera cheaper in England than in Texas?"

"Don't they sell for less out of the country?" asked Wayne innocently.

"Nothing sells for less in England," Bill explained, "especially in Bridlington."

"Gosh, I thought I got a pretty good deal."

You could plumb the depths of Wayne's mind, but you'll never fathom his powers of reason. He shot almost fifty rolls of film in the next three weeks. After a while he became wise and never left his camera sitting around by itself. At first he wondered why he only took five pictures, set the camera down to do something or other, and when he returned the roll was finished. Only when he developed the film after going home to Austin, Texas, did he find twenty shots of his breakfast eggs, twenty shots of his sneakers, twenty shots of a dead fish prone on the dock, etc.

As we left the North Sea and passed through the Straits of Dover into the English Channel, Bill was in seventh heaven. The sea was a pond. No waves rocked *Arvor III*. The trip was smooth and delightful. Jimmy watched in detached amusement as Wayne performed his yoga on the foredeck. Thereafter, the Scots called Wayne Yogi Bear.

The cliffs above Cherbourg came into view and we slipped into the harbor past the breakwater, the old fort, and monstrous oil rigs on their way to the North Sea. Jimmy had radioed ahead for a berth in the yacht basin and we tied up not far from a nice hotel with a gourmet dining room. During innocent conversation with the dockmaster, we mentioned that we had come to Cherbourg to search for the Confederate raider *Alabama*. Inquiring as to when we were to launch the search, he was told the next day.

When the time came to make the effort, we never left the dock. Six uniformed customs agents, red pillbox hats perched on their greasy heads, came aboard first thing in the morning and proceeded to tear the boat apart while asking a multitude of foolish questions. We all bit our tongues, dug our nails into our palms, and cooperated, wondering why we were singled out for such nasty treatment. Was this any way to welcome foreign visitors?

They pried open every cabinet, probed every suitcase, every box and container, large and small. They went through the engine room with dental mirrors, searching behind every pipe and manifold. The heads, the galley, the staterooms, nothing went unprobed. I half expected a demand for a strip search. They questioned the purpose of the side scan sonar, the magnetometer and video equipment, wanting to know every detail of their operation.

Finally, after they were satisfied we were not carrying a nuclear bomb, the head honcho, who looked like a cross between Inspector Clouseau and Ace Ventura with a mustache, asked me the purpose of our visit to France. With nothing to hide, I guilelessly told him we were hunting for the wreck of the Confederate raider *Alabama.*

I was then informed in no uncertain terms that we could not search in French waters without permission. Permission from whom, I asked. The commander of the local French naval district, Clouseau answered as if he were conversing with a fungus.

My blood ran cold, my nerve endings turned to ice. Oh, dear God, not the French Navy. I hate dealing with the navy, any navy. For them to grant permission to a civilian for anything more than a petition to go to the bathroom is nearly impossible. Subordinates who universally enjoy saying *no* before passing the request up the chain of command to some nebulous officer in the throne room are as common as bacteria.

Deploying our forces, we counterattacked. Wayne Gronquist donned his cowboy boots and custom-made cowboy hat, settled his watch and chain in the pockets of his vest, and assaulted the offices of the admiral commanding the Cherbourg naval district. You have to see and know Wayne to know that he is the kind of guy who won't take no for an answer. He is soft-spoken, with limpid blue eyes, a great prospector's beard, and a body thoroughly established by yoga. He looks amazingly like old photographs of Jeb Stuart, the famous Confederate cavalryman.

The first order of the day was to hire a translator, since our combined vocabulary consisted of such phrases as "Where is the bank?" and "Can I honk your horn?" While standing on the dock, a fellow came up to me and launched a conversation in French. I raised my eyebrows, puckered my lips, and replied, "No parlez vous français." I thought I was saying, "I don't understand French." What I really said was, *"You* don't speak French." No wonder he looked at me like all the nuts had spun off my screws.

After sizing up Gronquist in his Texas attorney attire, the French admiral politely suggested that the Texan and his friends take the next stagecoach out of Cherbourg. Instead, Wayne boarded a train for Paris and camped out at the

United States Embassy. Acting like Ben Franklin during the Revolutionary War, he cut quite a swath in diplomatic circles. In the meantime, I was swept up in an orgy of dramatic grandeur by holding press conferences and calling every bigwig I knew in Washington.

Unless they've finally decided to join the rest of the world, at that time you could not make a long-distance phone call in France with a credit card on a public phone. They refused to accept my AT&T card. In England, it often takes a while to get an operator, but the call goes through without problem. In Denmark, I simply put a silver krone in the slot, dialed the two-digit number for the international code, and gave the operator, who always replied in English, my card number and the number I was calling. Presto, I was talking to my wife as if she were in the booth beside me. Not France. You either have to use a private-residence phone or check into a hotel and call from your room. And since no Frenchman was about to allow a crazy American in his house to make overseas calls on his private phone, I was forced to check into the local inn and be hosed by the management.

Now the harassment began on all flanks. Odd as it sounds, we rather enjoyed it.

While *Arvor III* was moored to the dock in the yacht basin, helicopters flew over the boat while cameramen leaned out and shot overhead pictures of us sunbathing on the deck. We also took great delight in sneaking up on the people sitting in cars or crouching behind seawalls observing the boat and crew through binoculars. An American yachtsman and his wife, whose ketch was tied up across the dock from *Arvor III,* told us two Frenchmen in army uniforms came aboard one evening when we were all having dinner at a nearby dockside restaurant. He said it appeared to him as if they'd bugged our boat. I asked how he could know that. He replied that he was a retired investigator from the Chicago Police Department and knew about such things.

We tried to find any listening devices but failed. So we all began talking in bizarre accents and unintelligible languages and discussing economic doctrines as related to Antarctica. Back into the stereo player went my Dixieland jazz tapes. Jimmy and the Scots made comments about the Froggies, as they called them, never having won a war, which I'm sure did not win us any points with their navy.

One evening after dinner, Jimmy Flett and I were sitting on the deck enjoying brandy and cigars when he noticed bubbles in the water illuminated by the lights along the quay. Walking inside the cabin, we alerted Bill, who turned on the video equipment. We then carefully lowered the underwater video camera over the side. In great anticipation the entire crew stared at the video monitor as Bill popped on the lights attached to the camera. Suddenly, the startled faces of two French navy frogmen, their eyes bugging through the lenses of their underwater face masks, burst on the screen. An instant later they stroked into blackness and were gone.

What in hell was going on? we all wondered. Why were we being treated like spies?

In Washington, NUMA's chief director, Admiral Bill Thompson, former Naval Chief of Public Information, hit on every officer he knew in the French Navy, rallied the Pentagon, and pestered the White House. Things became so confused that the French Embassy sent a message to our State Department saying, "We apologize for this incident."

The State Department, in total ignorance of our predicament, replied, "We apologize too."

According to my literary agent in Paris, I became the darling of the French press with my ranting and raving. I was especially irritated because Jacques Cousteau was flitting all over the waters of Chesapeake Bay as if he owned it without an American official mentioning anything so mundane as a permit. French naval officials were particularly embarrassed. They thought they were dealing with a scurvy crew of treasure hunters, and had no idea their nemesis was a high muckety-muck author, who made the bestseller lists in France. The firestorm of publicity was hardly what they expected.

Some pretty high officials in the French government regretted our situation, but said there was nothing they could do. Who was this local-yokel admiral? I inquired. And why did he carry so much weight? I thought sure that if he realized that our presence represented nothing more than an innocent search expedition without artifacts being snatched, he would allow us to begin the hunt. How could the crew of *Arvor III* threaten French national security?

During this cockamamie absurdity, our crew took time to do some sightseeing. My son, Dirk, joined the expedition. He took time off from his job at Motorola in Phoenix, Arizona, flew to Paris, and arrived by train at Cherbourg. Together, we all walked the famed beaches of Normandy, Omaha and Utah, and the British invasion sites at Gold, Juno, and Sword. The sandy shores of Normandy, though deadly to those who landed in June of 1944, are the most spectacular beaches in the world. Their vast golden sand stretches for miles. But for the lack of tropical weather and temperate water, they would put anything the Caribbean or the Pacific has to offer to shame.

We strolled through the immaculately kept American cemetery on the bluffs above Omaha beach and read the names inscribed behind the columns of the great amphitheater, noting several of those who had died and gone missing on the *Léopoldville.*

On the light side, Bill made a lasting impression on the good citizens of Cherbourg. He walked to the town laundromat, piled his clothes into a machine, and inserted French coins. So far so good. Then he poured in half a box of concentrated laundry detergent. Rather than sit around and wait, he met up with Dirk and me for lunch at a nice little bistro.

Forty-five minutes later as we walked back to the laundromat together, we rounded the street corner and walked into a giant wall of soap bubbles. We all stared dumbstruck like the first guy in a science-fiction movie to see the alien creature. The overabundance of concentrated detergent created the greatest display of soapsuds the city of Cherbourg had seen since the fat-rendering factory blew up in 1903.

Bill dashed into the advancing blob of bubbles and disappeared. Somehow groping his way inside the laundromat, he snatched his clothes from the machine and beat a hasty retreat back to the boat. He spent the next day and a half rinsing thickened goo out of clothes with a hose and nozzle beside the dock.

Wayne added to the gaiety after Dirk came back from a toy store in town and produced a pirate costume. Wayne waved the Jolly Roger flag, donned a pirate hat, eyepatch, and a hook. Then he would sneak up on the French security people spying on us, threaten them with his plastic hook, and shout, "Haarrrh!"

I would have given my left foot to read the reports that were written by French security on our activities.

After two weeks of futile combat, I struck our flag. I felt there was nothing more to be accomplished. The French admiral refused to capitulate. He played his cards with great anal retentiveness. I still don't recall his name. I turned over my records, charts, and projections to the French school-teacher who acted as our translator rather than carry them back to Colorado with me on the airplane. He agreed to keep them safe until my return. I was sure we would get the mess ironed out during the coming months and come back with a permit in hand the following summer.

Short of mooning the customs officials as we departed Cherbourg Harbor, I could not stop myself from firing the last shot. Since a side scan search for *Alabama* involved a fairly extensive grid, I could not risk that attempt, knowing the French Navy would be all over us before lunch. But I figured that finding a ship the size of *Léopoldville* within a short time was far from impossible. Paying our dock fees and casting off, we set sail for her grave early one morning before the sun came up. Playing cat and mouse with government officials in a foreign country is not a game for amateurs, and I was about as green as a farm boy staring up at tall buildings in Fargo, North Dakota. The trick was to find *Léopoldville,* identify it, then beat it out of French waters to Britain. Though no helicopters flew over the dock, and we did not spot any binoculars aimed in our direction, I still assumed we were being observed every inch of the way. If *Arvor III* was followed, then all bets were off, and we would continue over the horizon for Britain.

Our one advantage was that Wayne and I had requested permission to search only for *Alabama.* We never mentioned *Léopoldville.* Since *Arvor III* was heading away from the Confederate raider's final resting place, with our course set west toward Weymouth, England, I hoped it appeared to the French officials that we had given up and were leaving Cherbourg for good.

Strangely, *Léopoldville* is mismarked on nautical charts of the Cherbourg area. There is a large wreck marked about a mile to the north, but its position is not where we found the ill-fated troopship. I decided to take the Admiralty position as gospel and work from there.

I was leery of dropping the side scan over the side. Should we spot a helicopter or fast boat heading in our direction, it would take us too long to pull in the sensor and shut down the equipment before they saw what we were up to. We would literally be caught in the act.

Because we were hunting for an object nearly 500 feet in length and 62 feet wide, I gambled on using only our boat's built-in echo sounder. This meant we had to go almost directly over *Léopoldville* in order to record its hulk. Again, I deviated from my normal routine of mowing the lawn within either a square or rectangular search grid. I asked Jimmy to throw out a small buoy over the Admiralty's position and then circle around it, working outward and widening each spiral circumference. The seabed was flat with a depth of 160 feet.

An hour and twenty minutes into the chase, the echo sounder recorded an anomaly rising 60 feet off the bottom. It was a lucky hit. Two more passes confirmed a huge, long object pointed toward Cherbourg, but on a slight angle, no doubt caused by currents swinging *Léopoldville* on her anchor before she sank. She lies just 300 meters northwest of the recorded position. Our navigation readings put her at 49 44 40 by 01 36 40.

I regretted that we had no wreath to drop over the side,

or a ceremony prepared. Though the sun was shining brightly, it didn't take great imagination to picture that night of horror. We slowly circled the wreck, watching its mass rise from the bottom on the echo sounder. It was a heartrending moment, but we knew the French Navy would not allow us to hang around. We all kept one eye aimed on the entrance to Cherbourg Harbor.

"Throw out the side scan," demanded Dirk.

"Be nice to see more of her," said Jimmy.

"No peeky, no findy," added Bill.

I'm easy. Over went the sensor, on went the power to the side scan. Clickety-clack, went the recorder. "Will the boat five miles north of Cherbourg please return to port immediately," came a voice in perfect English over the radio.

"My God!" I muttered. "How did the French catch on so quickly?"

"We're in their submarine testing ground," said Jimmy. "They probably have sensors stationed on the bottom that pick up sonar signals."

"Now you tell me." I groaned and turned to Bill. "Did we get a reading on our first and only pass?"

"Not the best. She casts an immense shadow on the recorder. Looks intact and fairly well preserved. She's not spread around the bottom like some we've found. I'd guess that she's lying on her starboard side."

"Will the boat five miles north of Cherbourg please return to port immediately," came the disembodied voice again.

"I wonder if he does children's parties," Bill mused to no one in particular.

"At least he said 'please,' " Dirk reminded me.

I looked at Jimmy. "How far to British waters?"

"About eighteen miles."

"What do you think, skipper?"

Before he could answer, our party pooper was back. "Will the boat—"

Jimmy Flett is a man among men. He smiled slyly, reached up, and turned off the radio.

I nodded. "All right, that concludes the entertainment part of the program. Let's get the hell out of here."

With Jimmy grimly gripping the spokes of the wheel, his eyes set toward England, the rest of us stood on the stern and watched for French patrol boats or helicopters to come chasing after us. With our trusty boat pounding along at all of nine knots, it was like robbing a bank and then making our getaway in a bulldozer.

I was certainly in no position to endanger lives on board *Arvor III* by putting up any resistance. Except for a grappling hook and a couple of Swiss Army knives, our only other arsenal of weapons was Colin's incredible bounty of small boiling potatoes. Not exactly a morale builder, but a well-aimed volley might stop a patrol boat for all of about ten seconds.

Down deep, I didn't think even the French Navy would attack a British boat flying the Royal Yacht Club ensign with four virtuous Americans on board. We had caused enough problems in the news media to make them wary about inciting an international incident. Besides, such an affair would only enhance the sale of my books, a noble endeavor to which they had no wish to contribute.

There comes a time in the affairs of men when fortune shines down through the clouds. Trumpets can be heard along with a drum roll and the lilting sound of harps. Vengeance is mine, quoth Mickey Spillane. The time came for the meek to inherit the sea. As *Arvor III* was entering the harbor of Weymouth, we passed a French Navy missile frigate coming out that was participating in NATO exercises.

"How close can you shave him, Jimmy?" I asked.

"Thirty feet be okay?"

"Thirty feet will do just fine."

To the French sailors roaming the decks of the missile frigate, *Arvor III* simply looked like another fishing boat coming into port. They hardly gave a second look as Bill, Dirk, Wayne, and I lined up on the stern deck. The stunned expression on their faces was like a narcotic to me as our barrage of boiling potatoes struck, burst, and sprayed over men and ship alike. They never knew what hit them. They didn't know why. And I guess they never will.

We were in friendly waters now and all they could do was shake their fists and shout awful things at us in French.

Revenge is sweet indeed.

Jimmy and John escorted us to the train station for the journey to London. I found it hard to say goodbye to our Scots crew. We had all gone through wild times together in the past six weeks and become quite close. Bill was especially touched at the parting, treasuring a photo he took of Jimmy and John waving as the train pulled from the station.

As shipwreck expeditions go, this one possessed the fondest memories. Much had been accomplished. Our only failure was not being allowed to hunt for *Alabama*. It was never my intention to set off a wave of controversy. But we scored well overall and had a boatload of fun while we were at it.

I laid over in New York and held a news conference on board the aircraft carrier *Intrepid* to announce our finds. I especially wanted to tell the tragic story of the *Léopoldville* and its sinking on Christmas Eve of 1944. It seemed strange that so few people were aware of the disaster and staggering loss of life. Every government that was remotely involved ignored the tragedy and treated it like an insignificant event not worth dwelling on. The United States Army and Navy acted as though it never happened. The British Admiralty scarcely gave it mention, while the Belgians played down the cowardly actions of the crew.

We gave it our best shot and put *Léopoldville* on the six o'clock TV news shows and in every major newspaper in the country. Suddenly, families who had simply received telegrams soon after the sinking saying only that their loved ones were killed in action, now began to ask questions. It warmed our hearts to be instrumental in steering a number of wives, brothers, sisters, and survivors to the Panther Veteran Organization, made up of men who had served with the 66th Division.

Bob Hesse, president and one of the founders of the Panther Veteran Organization, showed up at the news conference, and I introduced him as a survivor. He was accompanied by Alex Yarmosh, Ed Riley, and Dick Dutka, three of the men who had jumped onto the deck of the H.M.S. *Brilliant* that terrible night. There wasn't a dry eye in the house. Never dreaming that any *Léopoldville* survivors would surface, I was deeply touched. Over the years, Bob and I, along with many of the Panther Vets, became good friends. I spoke at one of their reunions and was privileged to be named as an honorary member.

In a book I wrote entitled *Cyclops,* I made the following dedication.

> To the eight hundred American men who were lost
> with the *Léopoldville,* Christmas Eve, 1944, near
> Cherbourg, France.
> Forgotten by many, remembered by few.

The final act of the Cherbourg incident, however, was far from over. The French were full of surprises, however inappropriate.

Shortly after I returned to my home in Colorado, I read of the dastardly slap in the face given me by the French Navy. One of their salvage ships had launched a search two weeks after we made our great escape from Cherbourg. And guess what? They found *Alabama.* They claimed to have searched for twenty years, discovering the wreck site only after new research material was brought to their attention.

Mine!

I was surprised at the timing. Then a member of the U.S. Embassy in Paris wrote and informed me that the captain of the salvage vessel was given documents showing the general location. Coincidentally, the cousin of the salvage-ship commander happened to be the schoolteacher with whom I left all my research material and my estimated position for *Alabama.* The schmoes. Not only were they proud of it, they were smug about it.

I underwent a total personality change and was suddenly taken sober. I looked and felt like a basset hound who forgot where he buried his bone. I was sorely tempted to walk into a fancy French restaurant and ask for their hot cereal of the day. It sprang into my head like a Hallmark pop-up greeting card. The French Navy held a grudge against NUMA for pelting its missile cruiser with potatoes? Could discovering the remains of *Alabama* have been their way of getting even?

The French went one step farther when American archaeologists began creating proposals for survey and artifact recovery. In a letter to the U.S. State Department, the French Ministry of Foreign Affairs stated in no uncertain terms that since the wreck lies within their territorial waters it belongs to France. It did not matter whether or not our government considered *Alabama* to be the property of the United States. Their Minister of Culture and the Higher Council on Archaeological Research lost no time in funding and putting together an extensive recovery project, with the choice artifacts going to a new conservation facility and museum in Cherbourg.

Sometime later, Kevin Foster, who is with the National Park Service, was invited to dive on the *Alabama* site with French archaeologists. Acting as though their archives were a national treasure, they reluctantly allowed him to study their documentation on the shipwreck. While going through nautical charts, he discovered a chart with my name on it.

I later asked Kevin, "Did you see my estimated position of the wreck site?"

"Yes," he answered. "It was marked with a little Maltese cross."

"How far was I off target?"

"Less than half a mile."

Half a mile. With our trusty side scan sonar, the crew on board *Arvor III* could have easily found the wreck in one day's search.

In the final analysis, I'd have to say we'd been had.

My involvement with the French Navy and the *Alabama* died hard. Several months later, I received a telephone call from a gentleman claiming to be a deputy director of the Central Intelligence Agency. What could the CIA possibly want with me? I wondered. Dirk Pitt occasionally walked the hallowed halls of Langley, but I'd never laid eyes on the place.

"What is this call about?" I asked, firm in my belief that I was as pristine and white as the driven snow.

"Your glittering performance in Cherbourg last summer," he came back.

"All right, so I got a little carried away with the potato war."

"The potato war?"

"Isn't this call about my assault on a French missile cruiser?" I asked naïvely.

"I haven't heard about that one," he replied.

"Forget I mentioned it."

"My boss, who is a big fan of your books, suggested I call and brief you on the mess you caused in Cherbourg."

Now I was *really* intrigued. "If that rotten French admiral had given me permission to look for the *Alabama,* there would have been *no* mess."

"Believe me, the admiral wasn't too happy about your clandestine find of the *Léopoldville.* A good thing you took off for England. If you had returned to Cherbourg, French security forces, waiting on the dock, would have confiscated your boat and locked you and your crew up in the local slammer."

Good old Jimmy Flett, I thought. I owed him big time.

"No big deal," I said. "Hardly cause for an international incident."

"Did you know that the waters around Cherbourg are submarine-testing grounds?" he inquired.

"Yes, I was aware of the areas. They're well marked on the navigation charts."

"What you could not have known, Mr. Cussler, is that the French had just completed their newest nuclear submarine and planned to test it ten days before your arrival."

"If I had known, I couldn't have cared less," I said, becoming more audacious.

"What you also were not aware of was the fact that every intelligence office and agency in a dozen different nations, the CIA, the KGB, British MI-5, the Israeli Mossad, to name a few, spent great sums of money and long hours in setting up their individual covers to covertly observe the French nuclear submarine's test program."

I began to identify with the guy who wakes up in a motel room after a night of heavy drinking, reaches behind him, and touches a warm female body. Then his eyes fall on a set of false teeth in a glass beside the bed.

"A few days before the trials are to take place," he continued, "who should sail into Cherbourg Harbor but Clive Cussler, his merry band of pirates, and a boatload of underwater detection equipment."

It all became clear. Now I felt a kinship to a woolly mammoth that sank in the La Brea tar pits.

"Not knowing what to make of your theatrical appearance, the French Navy got cold feet and postponed the tests of their new submarine for six months. All the foreign intelligence undercover operations were then blown away. There was no way for any of us to sit it out for another half year, so we all packed up and went home."

"I failed my country," I murmured lamely.

"Not your fault," he consoled me. "But the agency would like you to do us a big favor."

Off in the distance I heard a band playing "The Stars and Stripes Forever." Redemption was about to smile. "You have but to name it."

"The next time you and your NUMA crew plan a shipwreck expedition, would you please notify our offices at Langley of where you're going so we can operate on the other side of the world?"

I was too numb with shock to reply. I had no idea representatives of the Central Intelligence Agency did stand-up comedy.

Finally, I muttered, "I'll drop you a postcard."

Then he politely said, "Thank you, goodbye," and hung up.

And so ends the great NUMA follies of 1984. We didn't discover *Titanic*. That was Bob Ballard's great accomplishment. Nor a Spanish galleon like *Atocha*, with gold and silver treasure spilling out of her timbers. Mel Fisher deserves the honors of that achievement. But we did find and survey several ships of historic significance. I suffered no mutinies, no injuries, and no shipboard damage. All things considered, we were extremely lucky from Aberdeen to Cherbourg to Weymouth.

I'm not sure whether that sounds like a song title or a double-play combination for a baseball team.

Part

10

They Can't Be Found if You Don't Look

Postscript

THERE AREN'T MANY THRILLS THAT PARALLEL THAT OF swimming through a shipwreck. I've always compared it to walking through a cemetery. You can sense and sometimes visualize the ghosts of the crew who lived on board and died without anyone to record their passing. The currents, the gloomy visibility, the silence broken only by the hiss of your air regulator, all add to the eeriness.

Thanks to recent advances in deep-sea technology, a very few tantalizing secrets in the deep have finally been unlocked and recorded on film and videotape. We have mapped and photographed almost every square inch of the moon, but we have viewed less than one percent of what is covered by water. To find the bones of ships and aircraft that have lain untouched in the depths is an experience known to a very few. Those who seek and occasionally find go under a variety of titles. Adventurers, oceanographers, marine archaeologists, treasure hunters, all in one form or other search for historic vessels that have disappeared into the unknown. Sometimes they're successful. More often they fail. The odds are stacked against them. But as long as they are driven by insatiable curiosity, new discoveries will continue to surface.

The lure of shipwrecks is a siren's song. There are literally millions of sunken ships. I've often wondered how many ancient wrecks lie beneath the silt of the Nile River in Egypt. The Mediterranean is strewn with them. The Great Lakes alone have nearly 50,000 recorded shipwrecks, beginning with famed explorer Sieur de La Salle's ship *Griffin,* launched and vanished during 1679 somewhere in Lake Michigan, and going up to the *Edmund Fitzgerald,* lost with all hands on Lake Superior in 1975. The seabed between Maine and Florida contains huge fleets of sunken vessels. Well over a thousand steamships rest under the banks and levees of the Mississippi River.

They all have stories to tell.

I actually walked the decks of one ship that vanished into the unknown.

During the spring of 1964, I took a few weeks' vacation before I was to start as creative director in charge of television production for a large advertising agency. After painting the house, I had ten days left to do nothing. My wife worked and our three children were in school. A friend persuaded me to work as a crew member on a beautiful yacht called the *Emerald Sea,* which was docked behind a spacious mansion at Newport Beach, California.

It was pleasant work maintaining miles of varnished wood and wiping the engines. I remember being surprised after a trip to Catalina Island off California. I was given a uniform and ordered to look after the passengers while the skipper manned the helm. The guests of the yacht owner never suspected that they were served their drinks and hors d'oeuvres by an advertising executive instead of a common deckhand. And I didn't mind at all when they tipped me fifty-dollar bills as they stepped onto the dock. I must admit it wasn't easy trading the teak decks of the *Emerald Sea* and the saltwater smell for a sterile office on Sunset Boulevard.

The yacht that was tied up next to *Emerald Sea* was a large two-deck vessel, built in the 1920s. I could look across the dock onto its spacious awning-covered rear deck and visualize a crowd of men in tuxedos doing the Charleston with flappers in fringed dresses and bobbed hair. There were times I could have sworn I heard the strains of a jazz band. I believe she was called *Rosewood*. She was an elegant lady and oozed style whenever her elderly owner, a wealthy widow, took her out and partied on the bay.

I became friendly with one of her deckhands, Gus Muncher, who swore he doubled in the movies once for Errol Flynn, but looked more like Peter Lorre. Gus would give me a tour of his boat, then we'd sit on the dock and eat lunch, swilling bottles of beer and swapping stories about the different boats and their owners moored about the harbor. The scandals were often juicy.

Gus claimed he was only working on the yacht to save enough money to get him to Tahiti, where he dreamed of operating a small ferryboat between the islands.

I lost track of Gus after I put on my Brooks Brothers suit and went back to work creating hard-sell drivel urging the masses to buy various and sundry products they could live without. Two years later, I ran into my old skipper from the *Emerald Sea* at a restaurant. I asked him if he'd seen Gus.

"Gus," he said sadly, "is dead."

"No," I muttered. "How?"

"He went down with the *Rosewood*."

"I had no idea it sank."

The skipper nodded. "The old lady who owned her died and the estate sold it to a car dealer in New Jersey. After passing through the canal, the *Rosewood* vanished with all hands in deep water west of Bermuda. Gus was one of a crew of three on board."

"Poor old Gus," I murmured. "He never saw Tahiti."

My memory of Gus faded over the next fifteen years. After I bade a happy farewell to the advertising agency and could finally make a living as a writer, my wife, Barbara, and I stopped over in Tahiti for a vacation after completing a book tour in Australia. While Barbara was doing some gift shopping in a village on the island of Bora Bora, I walked into a little bar overlooking the island's famed turquoise lagoon. Out of the corner of my eye I noticed a fellow wearing a wide-brimmed straw hat, a flowered shirt, and a pair of ragged shorts. He was sitting next to a striking Tahitian lady with flowing black hair and a smile sparkled by gold fillings. A thick red beard covered half his face, but I recognized him in an instant.

I stepped to his table and stared him in the eye. "Is that really you, or am I seeing a ghost?"

"Just to show you I'm alive, I'll buy you a beer," Gus Muncher said, laughing. "Just forget you ever saw me." He then introduced me to his wife, Tani.

"So you made it to Tahiti after all," I said, fighting a desire to pinch his arm and see if he yelled.

"Got me a fifty-foot catamaran, and make a good living carrying goods and passengers around the islands."

"Your dream come true."

"You remembered," he said with a grin showing under his beard.

"I heard you went down on *Rosewood.*"

"In a manner of speaking, I did."

"I'd like to hear about it."

"Not much to tell. We opened all the sea cocks and she went down like a stone in a thousand fathoms."

I stared at Gus incredulously. "Doesn't make any sense to sail a perfectly good yacht nearly five thousand miles and then scuttle her."

Gus's eyes beamed like a lighthouse. "Can you think of a better place to sink a boat for the insurance than the Bermuda Triangle?"

I should have voiced an argument about morals and legality, but sitting there in a bar overlooking spectacular scenery with an old friend who I thought had died, it just didn't seem appropriate. After two beers, Barbara found and collected me, and I bade Gus and his lady goodbye.

Ten years later, I met a French official from the Society Islands and asked if he knew Gus Muncher. He nodded and sadly informed me that Gus, his wife, his catamaran, two paying passengers, and a cargo of eighty chickens went missing in a storm off Mooréa. A search turned up no trace.

I've always wondered if Gus slipped off the earth again

or was truly on the bottom of the sea. I suppose a clue might be found if one investigated insurance-company records to see who received the settlement for the loss of Gus and his boat. I was curious, but not knowing the name of his catamaran and which marine casualty company settled any claims and to whom, I turned my back and went on to other projects. I kept his memory but let the mystery die with him.

For some odd reason, I've never been big on doing documentaries on NUMA's expeditions. I almost never take pictures during a search. My publicity lady once insisted on giving me two little automatic Kodak cameras, thinking that by making it easy I'd finally shoot a record of events. My son, Dirk, shot about three frames, which I have yet to develop after four years.

I probably don't receive all the hoopla I should because I don't solicit the big photo publications and television programs. I once called the *National Geographic* to see if there was any interest in my forthcoming expedition to search for the *Bonhomme Richard*. During a conversation with a lady who said she was in charge of editorial assignments, I was told in no uncertain terms, "We're not giving out any funds."

"I don't need funding," I replied. "I'm paying for the search out of my book royalties."

"Don't expect us to pay for anything," she announced acidly.

"Won't cost you a cent."

"Then why did you call?"

"Just to alert you that a search expedition was being launched to find John Paul Jones's famous ship. I thought perhaps you might be interested."

"We don't fund shipwreck hunts."

"We've been through that," I said, exasperated.

"Call us if you find it."

"Then what?"

"We'll assign a writer and a photographer to do the story."

"I'm a writer."

"We prefer a professional," she said matter-of-factly. End of conversation.

A few years later, I was in Washington, D.C., for my walk-on role in the awful movie based on my book *Raise the Titanic!* On the way to the hotel where they were shooting a press-conference scene with Jason Robards, I stopped off at the editorial offices of the *National Geographic.* I walked up to the receptionist and asked to speak to any editor who could spare me a few minutes.

She was gracious enough to call four different editors and say I was in the lobby. After the last call, she looked at me sheepishly and said, "I'm sorry, Mr. Cussler. None of them wish to talk to you."

Scorned by the *National Geographic.*

"If someone should ask," the receptionist murmured sweetly, "what should I tell them you wished to see them about?"

"Just tell them I ran in here to get away from a mugger and didn't know when I was well off."

Shattered and distraught, I went back to my room at the Jefferson Hotel, and except for the two hours I spent repairing a nonoperating grandfather clock in the sitting room, I cried in my pillow the rest of the night.

Not content with putting demoralizing and hilarious concerns behind me, I then alienated the *Smithsonian* magazine.

Nicholas Dean, a truly fine photographer from Edgecomb, Maine, was assigned by the *Smithsonian* magazine to shoot a photo story on NUMA's discovery of *Cumberland* and *Florida.* He shot rolls of film on the divers and the artifacts recovered from the wrecks. Then, for some reason, the editors of *Smithsonian* killed the story. Nick received a small kill fee, but not nearly enough to cover his expenses after flying round trip from Maine and spending five days on the expedition.

Several years later, I was called by the secretary of one of *Smithsonian* magazine's senior editors and asked if I would check out a story on a shipwreck for any inaccuracies. Since it was a ship I was familiar with, I agreed. The story arrived in the mail, I read it, made a couple of suggestions, and sent it back.

The secretary then notified me by phone that the fee for my editorial expertise was $200. Overwhelmed, but keeping my emotions in check, I told her not to send the check to me, but rather make it out to the editor.

"I don't understand," she said, confused.

"I insist my compensation go to him," I reaffirmed.

Unenlightened, she muttered, "It makes no sense for a writer's fee to go to an editor."

"It does in this case."

"May I ask why you're doing this?"

"Yes. Tell your boss that the two hundred bucks is a bribe. I'm paying him never to mention my name in the *Smithsonian* magazine."

The secretary came unglued. "You don't want your name in our publication. This is unheard of."

"There's always a first."

I have no idea what they ever did with the check. I know I never got it.

NUMA has been fortunate in achieving so much with so little. Nearly sixty sunken wrecks in lakes, rivers, and seas have been found and surveyed. I've covered only a handful in this book. A few were discovered by luck, most only after long hours of investigation and hard work. Cost is, of course, always a factor with any expedition. But if the hunt is not overly complicated and can be conducted with simplicity, the price remains low.

Despite stories by fiction writers like me, the search for historic treasure is seldom dangerous and all too often is downright tedious, but it is still an adventure that can be enjoyed by dedicated people or families out for a weekend of fun. Discoveries can be made anywhere and may take place within walking distance of your backyard. You'd be amazed at how many famous historical sites remain lost because nobody ever bothered to look for them.

I suppose it would be more practical to sink my book royalties into municipal bonds and real estate, something that would yield a financial return. Lord knows my accountant and broker think I belong under restraint in an institution. But my philosophy has always been that when my time comes, and I'm lying in a hospital bed two breaths away from the great beyond, I'd like my bedside phone to ring. A big, blonde, buxom nurse, taking my pulse for ebbing vital signs, leans over my face, picks up the phone, and holds the receiver to my ear.

The last words I hear before I drift off are those of my banker telling me my account is ten dollars overdrawn.

The bottom line is that when the final curtain drops the only things we truly regret are the things we didn't do.

Or, as an old grizzled treasure hunter put it to me over a beer in a waterfront saloon late one evening, "If it ain't fun, it ain't worth doin'."

To those of you who seek lost objects of history, I wish you the best of luck. They're out there, and they're whispering.

Current List of National Underwater & Marine Agency Shipwreck Surveys and Discoveries

C.S.S. *Hunley*

First submarine in history to sink a warship. After torpedoing the U.S.S. *Housatonic* off Charleston, South Carolina, in February 1864, the *Hunley* and her nine-man crew vanished.

U.S.S. *Housatonic*

Union Navy sloop-of-war. First warship in history to be sunk by a submarine, the Confederate torpedo boat *Hunley*, outside of Charleston, South Carolina, 1864. All but five of her crew were rescued.

U.S.S. *Cumberland*

Union Navy frigate. First warship in history to be defeated and sunk by an armored vessel. Rammed by the Confederate ironclad *Merrimack*, Newport News, Virginia, 1862. Over 120 of her crew were killed.

C.S.S. *Florida*

Famous Confederate sea raider that captured and sank nearly fifty United States merchant ships during the Civil War. Captured at Bahia, Brazil, and scuttled near Newport News, Virginia, 1864.

Sultana

Side-paddle-wheel steamboat whose boiler exploded and turned the boat into a holocaust, 1865. Worst North American ship disaster. Two thousand died, mostly Union soldiers. Fatalities exceeded those of the *Titanic* 47 years later.

Invincible

Armed schooner, first flagship of the Republic of Texas Navy. Captured arms and supplies from Mexican merchant ships that were turned over to General Sam Houston. Sunk in battle off Galveston, Texas, 1837.

Zavala

Passenger steamboat converted to armed warship by the Republic of Texas Navy in 1838. Probably the earliest armed steamship in North America. Grounded in Galveston Bay, Texas, 1842.

Lexington

Extremely fast side-paddle steamboat. Constructed by Cornelius Vanderbilt in 1835. Burned and sank in Long Island Sound, New York, in 1840. One hundred fifty-one men, women, and children were lost.

U.S.S. *Akron*

United States Navy rigid airship (dirigible) capable of docking and hangaring nine aircraft while in flight. Crashed off Beach Haven, New Jersey, in 1933. Seventy-three crewmen were lost.

U.S.S. *Carondelet*

Venerable Union Navy ironclad. Fought in more battles than any other warship in the Civil War. Built by inventive genius James Eads. Sank in the Ohio River long after the war, in 1873.

U.S.S. *Weehawken*

Only Union Navy monitor to have defeated and captured a Confederate ironclad in battle. She also led the first attack on Fort Sumter. Sank in a storm outside of Charleston, South Carolina, 1864.

U.S.S. *Patapsco*

Union Navy monitor of the *Passaic* class. Fought throughout the siege of Charleston. Struck a Confederate mine and sank in the channel off Fort Moultrie in 1865. Sixty-two of her crew were lost.

U.S.S. *Keokuk*

One-of-a-kind Union ironclad with two nonrevolving gun towers. Generally referred to as a citadel ironclad. Struck over ninety times by Confederate guns at Charleston in 1863. Sank soon after the battle.

C.S.S. *Arkansas*

Tough Confederate ironclad that single-handedly battled the entire Mississippi River fleet under Admiral Farragut and won. Burned by her crew above Baton Rouge, Louisiana, to prevent capture in 1862.

C.S.S. *Manassas*

First armored ship built in the United States, and the first ironclad to see battle. Designed primarily as a ram. Burned and sank in the Mississippi River during the battle for New Orleans in 1862.

C.S.S. *Virginia II*

Strong Confederate ironclad that helped to keep General Grant's army from crossing the James River to take Richmond. Burned by her crew at Drewry's Bluff by order of Admiral Semmes of *Alabama* fame, 1865.

C.S.S. *Fredericksburg*

Confederate ironclad of the James River fleet under command of Admiral Raphael Semmes. Actively engaged until end of war. Blown up by her crew at Drewry's Bluff, 1865.

C.S.S. *Richmond*

Confederate ironclad that guarded the reaches of the James River for nearly three years. When Richmond fell, she was destroyed by her crew near Chaffin's Bluff in 1865.

Northampton

Fast side-wheel Chesapeake Bay steamer used by the Confederates as a supply ship. Sunk as an obstruction below Drewry's Bluff in James River, 1862.

Jamestown

Large passenger steamer, seized by Confederates. Fought gallantly in Hampton Roads, Virginia, with the *Merrimack*. Sunk as obstruction at Drewry's Bluff in 1862.

C.S.S. *Louisiana*

Mammoth Confederate ironclad that carried sixteen guns. Unfinished and able to fight only while moored along shore during the battle for New Orleans, she was blown up by her crew to prevent capture, 1862.

U.S.S. *Varuna*

Union Navy gunboat. Rammed three times by Confederate vessels during the battle for New Orleans. She was credited with sinking six enemy ships before being forced ashore and burned, 1862.

U.S.S. *Commodore Jones*

Union Navy side-wheel gunboat, formerly a New York ferryboat. Destroyed by a very sophisticated Confederate two-thousand-pound electrical mine in the James River, 1864.

U.S.S. *Phillipe*

Union Navy gunboat that was shelled by the Confederate guns at Fort Morgan, set afire and sank in the entrance to Mobile Bay during Admiral Farragut's attack on the city, 1864.

C.S.S. *Governor Moore*

Confederate Navy gunboat, converted from a passenger steamer. Put up tough battle against Union fleet during battle for New Orleans. Sixty-four of her crew died. Run aground and burned, Mississippi River, 1862.

C.S.S. *Colonel Lovell*

Confederate cotton-clad ram. Saw much action on the Mississippi River near Tennessee. Fought valiantly before being rammed and sunk during the battle for Memphis, 1862.

C.S.S. *General Beauregard*

Confederate side-wheel ram. Attacked Union flotilla during the battle for Memphis, and was heavily damaged before sinking along the west bank of the Mississippi River, 1862.

C.S.S. *General Thompson*

Confederate side-wheel ram. Fought up and down the Mississippi River along Tennessee before being burned and run aground during the battle for Memphis, 1862.

Platt Valley

Side-wheel steamer, snagged on wreck of *General Beauregard* and sank below Memphis, 1867.

Saint Patrick

Four-hundred-ton side-wheel steamer, burned and sank above Memphis in 1868.

C.S.S. *Drewry*

Confederate gunboat. Fought on James River for three years before being badly shot up and sunk by Union Army artillery fire in the middle of Trent's Reach, 1865.

C.S.S. *Gaines*

Confederate gunboat that fought a losing battle with Admiral Farragut's fleet during the battle of Mobile Bay. The *Gaines* was run aground behind Fort Morgan and burned, 1865.

Stonewall Jackson

Confederate blockade runner, formerly the British packet side-wheel steamer *Leopard*. Run aground on Isle of Palms, South Carolina, 1864.

Rattlesnake

Confederate blockade runner. Caught by Union blockading fleet while trying to enter Charleston Harbor off Breach Inlet with cargo of arms, and burned, 1863.

Raccoon

Confederate blockade runner. Burned and sunk by Union gunboat outside Charleston Harbor while running out to sea with cargo of cotton, 1863.

Ruby

Confederate blockade runner that had many successful runs. Finally chased ashore at Folly Island, Charleston, and destroyed, 1864.

Norseman

Confederate blockade runner, small British screw steamer, run ashore off Isle of Palms, Charleston, 1865.

Ivanhoe

Confederate blockade runner. Caught by Union gunboats and destroyed near Fort Morgan at the entrance to Mobile Bay, Alabama, 1863.

Foreign Ships Discovered
and Surveyed

Waratah

Blue Anchor passenger liner that disappeared off the east coast of South Africa in 1911. Over two hundred passengers and crew were lost. One of the great mysteries of the sea.

H.M.S. *Pathfinder*

British scout cruiser. Second warship to be sunk by a submarine and the first by a German U-boat. Torpedoed in the North Sea by the *U-21* in August of 1914.

U-21

First German U-boat in history to sink an enemy ship. Also sank two battleships near Turkey in World War I. Foundered while under tow in North Sea, 1919.

U-20

German World War I submarine that sank the Cunard liner *Lusitania.* Stranded on Jutland shore, Denmark, in 1916. Later blown up by the Danes in 1926.

H.M.S. *Acteon*

British fifty-gun frigate, stranded and burned during battle off Fort Moultrie, South Carolina, during the Revolutionary War, 1776.

H.M.S. *Invincible*

British battle cruiser. Blown up and sunk by German naval gunfire during the Battle of Jutland in the North Sea, May of 1916. Admiral Hood and 1,026 of his crew went down with the ship.

H.M.S. *Indefatigable*

British battle cruiser. Blown up by German naval gunfire and sunk during the battle of Jutland in the North Sea, 1916. Over one thousand men went to the bottom with her.

H.M.S. *Defence*

British heavy cruiser. Blown up and sunk with all hands during the Battle of Jutland, 1916.

H.M.S. *Shark*

British destroyer. Sunk by the German Imperial fleet during the Battle of Jutland, 1916.

H.M.S. *Hawke*

British cruiser sunk by the German submarine *U-9*, sixty miles off Scotland, October 1915; 348 of her crew were lost.

Wiesbaden

German heavy cruiser burned and sank during the Battle of Jutland off the Denmark coast, 1916.

V-48

German destroyer, sank during the Battle of Jutland, 1916.

S-35

German destroyer, sank during the Battle of Jutland, 1916.

Blücher

German heavy cruiser, which was destroyed and sank during the Battle of Dogger Bank in the North Sea, 1916.

U-12

German submarine, sank after being rammed by the British cruiser *Ariel,* off Scotland in 1915.

UB-74

German submarine, sank off Weymouth, England, after being depth-charged by a British gunboat, 1916.

Glückauf

Prototype of the modern oil tanker. First to use all bulkheads to store oil. First to place engines in stern. Stranded on Fire Island, New York, 1893.

Vicksburg

British steam freighter stranded on the shore of Fire Island, New York, near Blue Point, during a storm in 1875.

Alexander Nevski

Russian steam frigate that ran aground on the east coast of Denmark near Thyborøn, 1868. The Russian crown prince was on board. All were saved.

Arctic

British steamship stranded on the coast of Jutland, Denmark, 1868.

Kirkwall

British steamship that ran aground on the shore of Jutland, Denmark, 1874.

Odin

Very early Royal Swedish steamship, much copied in models, built in 1836. Ran ashore near Thyborøn, Denmark, in 1836.

Commonwealth

British freighter sunk by German U-boat during World War I in the North Sea off Flamborough Head, 1915.

Charing Cross

British freighter torpedoed by German U-boat off Flamborough Head during World War I in 1916.

Chicago

Very large ten-thousand-ton British freighter sunk by German U-boat off Flamborough Head in 1918.

Léopoldville

Belgian liner converted into troop transport during World War II. Torpedoed by German U-boat on Christmas Eve, 1944, off Cherbourg, France. Over eight hundred American GIs died in the tragedy.

Additional Sites Surveyed

Merrimack

Many magnetometer contacts around site where famous Confederate ironclad was blown up and destroyed off Craney Island, Portsmouth, Virginia, in 1862.

Great Stone Fleet

Large number of subbottom profile and magnetometer contacts where sixteen old New England whalers were scuttled to block channel leading into Charleston Harbor, 1861.

Galveston Graveyard of Ships

Ten to twelve ships that ran aground on old shoal outside of Galveston Bay between 1680 and 1880 and now lie buried in sand.

Swamp Angel

Remains of parapet where famous eight-inch Parrott gun lobbed 150-pound projectiles into the city of Charleston nineteen hundred yards away, during 1863.

Torpedo Raft

The remains of Union Navy antitorpedo raft used by monitor *Weehawken* during battle for Charleston, 1863, lies in a marsh at the north end of Morris Island, South Carolina.

Lost Locomotive of Kiowa Creek

Site where Kansas Pacific freight train was swept away by flood in 1876. It turned out the train was secretly recovered, repaired, and placed back in service under new number. What we discovered was a 120-year-old insurance scam.

Index

Page numbers in *italics* refer to maps.

THE SEA HUNTERS II

More True Adventures with Famous Shipwrecks

by

Clive Cussler

and

Craig Dirgo

For twenty-three years, Clive Cussler's NUMA®—the National Underwater and Marine Agency—has scoured the rivers and seas in search of lost ships of historic significance. His teams have been inundated by tidal waves and beset by the vagaries of man and nature, but the results—and the stories behind them—have often been dramatic.

Here are more true tales of sea—and land—adventures, as Cussler and his crews set out to track down history.

"A first-rate adventure book sure to please any student of history and the odd Pitt fan who takes the plunge." —*Publishers Weekly*